Body Impossible

OXFORD STUDIES IN DANCE THEORY
Mark Franko, Series Editor

French Moves: The Cultural Politics of le hip hop
Felicia McCarren

Watching Weimar Dance
Kate Elswit

Poetics of Dance: Body, Image, and Space in the Historical Avant-Gardes
Gabriele Brandstetter

Dance as Text: Ideologies of the Baroque Body, Second Edition
Mark Franko

Choreographies of 21st Century Wars
Edited by Gay Morris and Jens Richard Giersdorf

Ungoverning Dance: Contemporary European Theatre Dance and the Commons
Ramsay Burt

Unworking Choreography: The Notion of the Work in Dance
Frédéric Pouillaude

Making Ballet American: Modernism Before and Beyond Balanchine
Andrea Harris

Choreomania: Dance and Disorder
Kélina Gotman

Gestural Imaginaries: Dance and Cultural Theory in the Early Twentieth Century
Lucia Ruprecht

Dancing the World Smaller: Staging Globalism in Mid-Century America
Rebekah J. Kowal

Moving Modernism: The Urge to Abstraction in Painting, Dance, Cinema
Nell Andrew

Choreography Invisible: The Disappearing Work of Dance
Anna Pakes

The Fascist Turn in the Dance of Serge Lifar:
Interwar French Ballet and the German Occupation
Mark Franko

One Dead at the Paris Opera Ballet: La Source 1866–2014
Felicia McCarren

When Words Are Inadequate: Modern Dance and Transnationalism in China
Nan Ma

Body Impossible: Desmond Richardson and the Politics of Virtuosity
Ariel Osterweis

Body Impossible

*Desmond Richardson and
the Politics of Virtuosity*

ARIEL OSTERWEIS

OXFORD
UNIVERSITY PRESS

Oxford University Press is a department of the University of Oxford. It furthers the University's objective of excellence in research, scholarship, and education by publishing worldwide. Oxford is a registered trade mark of Oxford University Press in the UK and certain other countries.

Published in the United States of America by Oxford University Press
198 Madison Avenue, New York, NY 10016, United States of America.

© Oxford University Press 2024

All rights reserved. No part of this publication may be reproduced, stored in a retrieval system, or transmitted, in any form or by any means, without the prior permission in writing of Oxford University Press, or as expressly permitted by law, by license, or under terms agreed with the appropriate reproduction rights organization. Inquiries concerning reproduction outside the scope of the above should be sent to the Rights Department, Oxford University Press, at the address above.

You must not circulate this work in any other form
and you must impose this same condition on any acquirer.

Library of Congress Cataloging-in-Publication Data
Names: Osterweis, Ariel, author.
Title: Body impossible : Desmond Richardson and the politics of virtuosity / by Ariel Osterweis.
Description: New York : Oxford University Press, [2024] |
Series: Oxford Studies in Dance Theory / Mark Franko, series editor |
Includes bibliographical references and index.
Identifiers: LCCN 2023057249 (print) | LCCN 2023057250 (ebook) |
ISBN 9780190645823 (paperback) | ISBN 9780190645816 (hardback) |
ISBN 9780190645847 (epub) | ISBN 9780190645830 (updf) |
ISBN 9780190645854 (ebook other)
Subjects: LCSH: Richardson, Desmond. | Male dancers—United States—South Carolina—Biography. | Fiorello H. LaGuardia High School of Music & Art and Performing Arts (New York, N.Y.) | Complexions (Dance company)—History.
Classification: LCC GV1785.R483 O78 2024 (print) | LCC GV1785.R483 (ebook) |
DDC 792.8092 [B]—dc23/eng/20231215
LC record available at https://lccn.loc.gov/2023057249
LC ebook record available at https://lccn.loc.gov/2023057250

DOI: 10.1093/oso/9780190645816.001.0001

Paperback printed by Marquis Book Printing, Canada
Hardback printed by Bridgeport National Bindery, Inc., United States of America

*I dedicate this book to my children, my truest teachers –
Dashiell, Zane, and Soleil*

Contents

Series Editor Foreword   ix
Acknowledgments   xi

Introduction: Virtuosity: I Know It When I See It   1

1. *Fame* Nation: Queer Black Masculinities and a US Presidential Scholar in the Arts   24

2. Choreography's Photographic Skin: Sweat, Labor, and Flesh in Alvin Ailey American Dance Theater   56

3. The Muse of Virtuosity: Complexions Contemporary Ballet and Choreographic Falsetto   78

4. Difficult Fun: The Racial Politics of Improvisation in William Forsythe's Ballett Frankfurt   109

5. Otherwise in Blackface: American Ballet Theatre and San Francisco Ballet's *Othello*   145

6. Bad: Freakery, Iconicity, and Michael Jackson's Ghost   175

Conclusion: Desmond Richardson on Tour: Virtuosity's Futures   201

Bibliography   207
Index   213

Series Editor Foreword

Ariel Osterweis's *Body Impossible: Desmond Richardson and the Politics of Virtuosity* tracks the astonishing career of the African American dance artist from his early days in preprofessional training at New York City's Fiorello H. LaGuardia High School of Music & Art and Performing Arts to his performances of the choreography of many prominent choreographers of the late twentieth and early twenty-first centuries. Throughout this book Osterweis holds our attention on Richardson's body as simultaneously virtuosic, queer, and racialized even as she scrutinizes the continuities and frictions that emerge between these categories as they are set in motion in distinctly different choreographic contexts. This account of Richardson's career overlaps with multiple neighboring fields: visual studies, gender and sexuality studies, photographic studies, black studies, and performance theory. It is politically alert to the troubling racial and sexual double binds to which the black dancing body is subject on the US dance concert stage.

In some ways similar to a biography, it is in fact a nonbiography, being instead an emergent genre in dance scholarship that might be thought of as the biography of the dancer's work. The chronological presentation opens out onto a kaleidoscopic set of contexts concerning photography, masculine identity, queer of color theory, the cultural history of the US, critical race theory, and dance theory (most notably: classicism, improvisation, and the black radical tradition). These contexts are captured by and refracted in the phenomenon of virtuosity itself as the author engages with the meaning of virtuosity as speed and energetic excess in Richardson's performances themselves. Another innovative aspect of this study is the focus on the dancer's work over and above that of the choreographer as well as the continuous resistance to the predominantly "white" postmodern perspective of downtown versus uptown as the focus of innovative dance activity. As a dance scholar, Osterweis practices a particular form of analytic speed and excess of her own by drawing us into the analysis from multiple and constantly shifting perspectives, engaging with a kind of theoretical virtuosity.

Mark Franko

Acknowledgments

Sometimes your work knows you before you know yourself. What I mean to say is that, even though my research and scholarship dating back to college and graduate school were preoccupied with queer of color analysis and issues of sexuality, gender, and race, it was not until writing this book that I fully came into my own identity as a queer, mixed-race, nonbinary lesbian. And before that, choreographers who hired me as a dancer in New York City did so due to my "alien" appearance and unconventional ways. Indeed, Dwight Rhoden endearingly referred to me as a "misfit," and Mia Michaels called me a "bird" and a "creature." And anyone who is mixed-race can attest to the fact that one is met with questions like, "What *are* you?" and experiences a range of treatment, from fetishization to applause. Having trained at the San Francisco Ballet School from age four to sixteen, where I always felt a bit out of place, I was relieved to find solace in the intensity of the contractions at the Martha Graham School of Contemporary Dance in New York: I could finally make movement expression my own. I experienced nothing short of a pelvic awakening while training in Graham technique. Then, upon the advice of my Graham teacher Carol Fried, I auditioned for the Scholarship Program at the Alvin Ailey American Dance Center. That moment coincided with the first time I saw Desmond Richardson perform. Once I experienced Richardson in Ullyses Dove's *Episodes* and landed a full scholarship to train at Ailey, my goals became clear: I wanted to dance like Desmond Richardson and become a professional contemporary dancer. After reading José Esteban Muñoz's *Disidentifications: Queers of Color and the Performance of Politics* and Wayne Kostenbaum's *The Queen's Throat: Opera, Homosexuality, and the Mystery of Desire*, I realized that my emulation of Richardson, my desire to move the way he moved (and the gender and racial complexity therein), was not so much what Judith Butler might refer to as the performance of gender passing or what Anne Anlin Cheng might call racial melancholia, but a disidentification—a queer identification with an unlikely figure. Richardson was flexible yet strong, vulnerable yet in command; he possessed that *je ne sais quoi* that I would come to find was . . . virtuosity.

Curiosity can create a life. As a teen, I was asked by a high school teacher to teach my peers a segment on dance history, and I had to do some digging to find out more about modern dance; at the time, there wasn't much modern dance training in San Francisco, and after reading about Martha Graham, I was convinced I needed to move across the country to study at the Martha Graham School in New York. Later, in graduate school, I was searching for scholarly books to read on virtuosity in dance and performance and didn't find many publications on the topic; that led me to write *Body Impossible*. Beyond my deep intellectual training in Anthropology at Columbia University and in Performance Studies at the University of California, Berkeley (where I earned my BA and PhD, respectively), most central to my research (no matter how retrospectively considered) was my empirical, embodied experiences training at The Ailey School for two years and dancing professionally with Complexions Contemporary Ballet for two years under the mentorship of Richardson himself. In 1994, the rhetoric of "fun" was central to Richardson's experimental forays: one day after taking his (and Complexions co-founder and choreographer Dwight Rhoden's) class at Steps on Broadway in New York, Richardson approached me and asked if I would be interested in "having fun and messing around" with him and Rhoden in the studio—that is, if I would want to join Complexions. At the time, play, fun, and experimentation seemed more urgent than pointe shoes, 501C3 nonprofit status, or health insurance. Such embodied memories inform my dance research; even experiences from the past without intended scholarly use become important sites of knowledge for the dance scholar. Having entered such dance environments before ever versing myself in dance and performance theory (let alone anthropology, studies of race, and cultural theory), I admittedly experienced conflicting thoughts and sentiments when returning to these events in my mind years later. Nevertheless, a distanced and reflective relationship to the embodied aspect of this excavation allows for complex readings that can account for self-contradictory impulses. In other words, to engage in embodied research as a knowing scholar seeking a certain research outcome can limit one's experience to the cautious or the homogeneous. Yet, to gaze backward and ask, "Why *was* I being asked to move in that way with that person, with wet hair, in an androgynous leotard?" is to confront the range between ecstasy and discomfort of one's own racialized and gendered subjectivity from a distanced temporal space. Such a practice inherently questions the myth of the objectivity of the researcher. Instead, the distance of time can provide a necessary gap only ever feigned by the

ACKNOWLEDGMENTS xiii

objectivity of the otherwise emotionally distant scholar. The embodied sensitivity needed for dance research demands not objectivity but intimacy. Any intimate dance experience is, however, incomplete, haunted by the alienating breaks and limits inherent to the passing of time and the integration of cultures.

In addition to mining my embodied memory of dancing professionally with Richardson and Complexions, training at The Ailey School, performing with companies and artists such as Mia Michaels RAW, Heidi Latsky Dance, Homer Avila, Jennie Livingston, and Fred Ho on stages and in galleries and studios, trying my hand at choreography, and going out to clubs in New York, Dakar, Paris, Seoul, Amsterdam, and London throughout the 1990s and the aughts, I employed a varied research methodology that included ethnography, dance and performance analysis, theoretical investigation, discursive analysis, and archival research. My ethnographic research consisted of rehearsal observations, performance viewings, and numerous interviews with Richardson himself. Most of my research was conducted in New York City, where Richardson is based and Complexions Contemporary Ballet is located. The company rehearsed in various studios in the New York City area and performed on stages at Lincoln Center, the Joyce Theater, and more. Additionally, I conducted interviews with company co-director Rhoden, choreographers William Forsythe and Lar Lubovitch, teacher Penny Frank, and dancers from the Alvin Ailey American Dance Theater, Ballett Frankfurt, and Complexions, including Stephen Galloway, Francesca Harper, Christina Johnson, and Jodie Gates. Dance and performance analysis included observing live, recorded, and televised performances. Finally, archival research was conducted at the Alvin Ailey American Dance Theater, Complexions, and the New York Public Library for the Performing Arts. These archives gave me access to historical and contemporary performance videos, critical reviews, performance texts, photographs, and promotional posters. For access and rights to photography, I am thankful to Gene Schiavone, Alvin Ailey American Dance Theater archivist Dominique Singer, Complexions Contemporary Ballet, Michael Van Horne at the Robert Mapplethorpe Foundation, the National YoungArts Foundation, Sharen Bradford, Dominik Mentzos, Tobias Round at the Roy Round archives, the National Museum of African American History & Culture at the Smithsonian, Mark Andrew, Rachel Neville, Nikolai Krusser, and Desmond Richardson. Needless to say, reading academic scholarship, poetry, and literature fed me throughout the writing process, and I will never stop moving my body or attending performances. I delight in witnessing my students grapple with creative ideas and academic concepts as they set out to make their own works of dance, performance, writing, and scholarship. Those of us working in dance and performance are always positioning and repositioning ourselves in relation to virtuosity, with all its complexities—what Forsythe might call "*The Vertiginous Thrill of Exactitude*," Fred Moten might call "improvisatory exteriority," Dionne Brand might call "*being* in the Diaspora," and Desmond Richardson might call "fun."

Virtuosity takes time, it takes effort, and it takes patience. Writing about virtuosity, it would seem, also takes time, effort, and patience. It also takes patience for those supporting someone writing about virtuosity from backstage. To that end, I have so many fierce friends, family members (chosen and otherwise), mentors, colleagues, dance world homies, and beloved artists to acknowledge and thank! As internal and solitary as writing can feel at times, sitting down at a desk is only one part of writing, which is, ultimately, a documentation of having existed with others—having sweat together on the dance floor, having whispered seedlings of ideas into each other's ears over snacks and drinks, having texted about segments of sentences at 2 a.m., and having recognized yourself in the gesture of a lover. While virtuosity loves speed, there's nothing slower than academic time—except, that is, academic time suspended by the spunky gift of kids or the attenuated sense of urgency or productivity brought on by a global pandemic. How, in words, can I thank my people? Each and every acknowledgment that follows comes with a squeeze.

I have so much tenderness and love for my Chookies—my dazzling kids—Dashiell, Zane, and Soleil. We are on a beautiful journey together, and every moment with my fam fam is just . . . everything! I cannot thank Desmond Richardson enough for his artistry, trust, generosity, kindness, and years of thoughtful conversations. From my Ailey School and Complexions years, I am so grateful to Rhoden, Denise Jefferson (who directed The Ailey School with aplomb and granted me scholarships to train with the best), and teachers Milton Myers, Kazuko Hirabayashi, Finis Jhung, and Ana Marie Forsythe. As an Ailey student, I had the tremendous opportunity to dance in choreography by Bill T. Jones, Andre Tyson, and Ray Tadio, and also got the chance to perform with the company in *Memoria*, choreographed by Ailey himself. In addition to Richardson and Rhoden, I so admired Ailey dancers Elizabeth Roxas, Dana Hash, and Sarita Allen and choreographer Donald Byrd. During the 1990s and aughts, I befriended

ACKNOWLEDGMENTS XV

Isabelle Lumpkin, Alexandra Damiani, Morley Kamen, Nathan Trice, Christina Sanchez, Catherine Meredith, Hope Boykin, Olivia Bowman-Jackson, Kevin Boseman, Tao Fei, Candice McKoy, Ioana Alfonso, Brooke Wendle, Ron Todorowski, Jenn Perry, Zainab Jah, and Claire Missingham, some of whom I went on to collaborate with choreographically, dramaturgically, or academically. Choreographer John Jasperse later brought me into another dramaturgical project (*Within between*)—what poetic rigor filling his studio. While it could be difficult to imagine a pairing of classicism and the avant-garde, my childhood years at the San Francisco Ballet School, where I fell in love with performing, actually awakened my appreciation for abstraction—abstraction that lived well with virtuosity, as I had the opportunity to observe William Forsythe and dancer Tracy-Kai Meier rehearsing *New Sleep* with San Francisco Ballet. I'll never forget San Francisco Ballet ballet master Robert Gladstein and teacher Irina Jacobson, and Alonzo King around the corner at Lines Ballet. My mother, Suno, brought me to all the performances she could throughout my 1980s San Francisco upbringing (I would perform at the War Memorial Opera House one night and see a show at Project Artaud the next); I carry with me her sense of adventure and idiosyncratic Korean-punk spirit—I learned from her about the proximity of fabulousness and pain. I thank my father, John, for being the epitome of the meeting point of work ethic and a (Jewish) sense of humor. My brother, Max, and Uncle Moko Fall; my aunts Marian and Laurie Osterweis; cousins Sarah Rivkin, the Bunims, and the Lawrences; along with the memory of my Imo Hayok, Halmeoni and Harabeoji Chung Hyang, and In Ju Kay, and grandparents Harriet and Steven Osterweis give me comfort.

At ballet school, I met my oldest friends, affectionately called the "Joy Luck Club" since we were all Asian Claras in San Francisco Ballet's *Nutcracker* (Le-Lan Jorgensen, Margarita Arguelles, and Shanti Crawford). Later on, a very special Bay Area-born but New York-residing crew became the "Clumps": Eisa Davis, Damani Baker, Ron E. Miles, Jennifer Newman, Camille Lowry, and Rozz Nash are friends for life. Then came Columbia Anthropology, where I had the great pleasure of studying with Michael Taussig and Elaine Combs-Schilling (my thesis chairs), Rosalind Morris, Robin D. G. Kelley, Marilyn Ivy, John Pemberton, and Kate Ramsey. Dean Peter Awn was also a great support. My sense of dance ethnography and predilection for sociocultural theory was nurtured at Columbia, and I continued my studies at UC Berkeley, where I pursued my PhD in Performance Studies. I couldn't have asked for a more discerning and dedicated dissertation committee, which included Shannon Jackson (my stellar dissertation chair), Linda Williams, Brandi Catanese, and Thomas DeFrantz, all of whom continued to provide valuable feedback on my writing over the years. The Berkeley years were also made special by Kaja Silverman, who taught close readings of art and text; Trinh T. Minh-ha, who told me I shouldn't fear a thing; Stefania Pandolfo, who encouraged me to publish my first academic article on Faustin Linyekula and necropolitics; Lisa Wymore, who performed with me in a duet I choreographed when we were both seven months pregnant; and Sue Schweik, Petra Kuppers, and Neil Marcus, who introduced me to disability studies and performance. Poet Robert Grenier was a good sport when I choreographed a piece based on his *Drawing Poems*. I also learned so much about international performance programming from Angela Mattox during my internship at the Yerba Buena Center for the Arts and later as a guest scholar at the Portland Institute of Contemporary Art. Throughout the years writing about performance, I have enjoyed the epistolary friendship and mentorship of Barbara Browning, Ralph Lemon, Rebecca Schneider, Susan Manning, André Lepecki, Janice Ross, and Susan Leigh Foster. And I'm so indebted to Brenda Dixon-Gottschild for her groundbreaking dance scholarship. Roderick Ferguson's development of queer of color critique; Kobena Mercer, Robert Reid-Pharr, and Mark Anthony Neal's writing on queer black masculinities; Daphne Brooks's theory of Afro-alienation; Sianne Ngai's concept of ugly feelings; Louis Chude-Sokei's writing on Bert Williams; Francesca Royster's research on post-soul music; Anya Peterson Royce's earlier exploration of virtuosity; Hortense Spillers's theories of the body and flesh; the Kulturen des Performativen working group on virtuosity; the poetry and prose of Essex Hemphill, Nathaniel Mackey, Theresa Hak Kyung Cha, and Fred Moten; the filmmaking of Marlon Riggs and Isaac Julien; and Anne Anlin Cheng's research on race and mutability have been indispensable to my writing.

As a professional dancer and then while studying at Columbia as a returning, nontraditional student, before dashing up to Harlem on the subway each day, I would take Horton classes with Milton Myers and progressive ballet classes with Zvi Gotheiner and Christine Wright, whose dance philosophies became my life philosophies. Believe it or not, I first learned of the field of dance studies itself from a sweaty post-ballet class dressing room chat at 890 Broadway with Juliet Neidish, who introduced me to Mark Franko. Franko has been a caring mentor and rigorous, demanding editor of mine ever since. During Franko's editorship, I served as book reviews editor at *Dance Research Journal*, where I learned a great deal about the evolution of critical dance studies. In addition to my undergraduate and graduate training, I am lucky to have engaged in the Mellon Dance Studies in/ and the Humanities gatherings and, as an exchange scholar at Columbia University's Institute for Research on Women and Gender, to have studied with Saidiya Hartman and Tina Campt in the Columbia-Duke course, "Haunted Visualities," where we were visited by Krista Thompson and Anne Anlin Cheng, whose work has been influential. So much of the work of *Body Impossible* was first presented at conferences gathered by the Dance Studies Association, Performance Studies International, the American Studies Association, and the American Society for Theatre Research.

Before Franko brought this book into his Studies in Dance Theory series at Oxford University Press, Oxford Senior Editor Norm Hirschy took an interest in the project and has been patiently dedicated for years. Just prior to our time as graduate students together at Berkeley, Emily Wilcox and I shared a fascination with virtuosity; we met at a UC Riverside conference, where I first met Jacqueline Shea Murphy and Anthea Kraut, both of whom have deepened the field. I've so enjoyed conversations over the years with dance scholar friends Aimee Cox, Katherine Profeta, Melissa Blanco Borelli, Rebecca Rossen, Freya Vass, Sarah Wilbur, Clare Croft, Kate Elswit, Paul Scolieri, Joanna Dee Das, Ajani Brannum, Meiver De la Cruz, Jill Nunes Jensen, Kathrina Farrugia-Kriel, Julian Carter, and VK Preston; choreographers and dancers Trajal Harrell, Miguel Gutierrez, Wayne McGregor, and Antoine Vereecken; artists Julie Mehretu and Yve Laris Cohen; and performance scholars Deb Levine, Tavia Nyong'o, Patrick Anderson, Christina Knight, Kate Duffly, Matthew Morrison, madison moore, Eddy Francisco Alvarez Jr., and Renu Cappelli. I have no idea what I'd do without the friendship of Damon Young, whom I met in Linda Williams's final Porn Studies seminar at Berkeley; Damon has been a generous reader and interlocutor for years. Thank you to Églantine Colon for her draft reading and feedback. Rebecca Walker keeps it real as a reader, mentor, and friend. My mentees have been wonderful: Maya Stovall, Alexsa Durrans, Gwenmarie White, Aye Eckerson, C. Bain, Marissa Osato, Shoji Yamasaki, A. C. Smith, Clara Lee, Jobel Medina, Madison Hicks, Chenhui Mao, Kayla Aguila, and more. My colleagues at Wayne State University in Detroit (my first tenure-track job) were incredible: Meg Paul, Biba Bell, Doug Risner, Eva Powers, and Jeff Rebudal. Working at Skidmore, I met the illustrious Bina Gogineni. Christine Kim, Edgar Arceneaux, Ron Athey, Hayv Kahraman, Rachel and

xviii ACKNOWLEDGMENTS

Greg Kurstin, Ken Foster and Nayan Shah, Sam Paige, Ed Patuto, Jana Carter, Chris and Roberta Hanley, Ikechukwu Onyewuenyi, Rowena Arguelles and Nina Lederman, Nguyen Edwards, Patty Vargas, Kaye Kramer, Cindy Banks Morrow, Leanna Creel and Rinat Greenberg, Judy Choi, Rosanna Llorens, Julie Anderson, Ted Collins, Suk-Young Kim, and the faculty and parents of the Debbie Allen Dance Academy: you welcomed me so warmly to Los Angeles. Faculty friends I work (or worked) with at CalArts are stuck with me; we are the weirdest family and I love you all: Sharon Lockhart, Juan Pablo Gonzalez, Mads Falcone, Gabrielle Civil, Nina Menkes, Tisa Bryant, Dimitri Chamblas, sam wentz, Julie Bour, Jimmy "Cricket" Colter, Eyvind Kang, Yusha-Marie Sorzano, Rosanna Tavarez, Ernest Baker, Francesca Penzani, Roman Jaster, Salar Mameni, Julie Tolentino (who brought me back into performance without "performing"), and the REDCAT staff. There are always more people to thank and acknowledge, and I promise to make it up to anyone I've forgotten! To all my students, past and present: thank you for your inspired creativity; I do this for you.

Figure I.1a, b, c Desmond Richardson at the barre (See color plates).
© 2022 Mark Andrew Images.

Introduction

Virtuosity: I Know It When I See It

Flung out and dispersed in the Diaspora, one has a sense of being touched by or glimpsed from this door. As if walking down the street someone touches you on the shoulder but when you look around there is no one, yet the air is oddly warm with some live presence. That touch is full of ambivalence; it is partly comforting but mostly discomforting, tortured, burning with angered, unknowable remembrance. More disturbing, it does not confine itself to remembrance; you look around you and present embraces are equally discomforting, present glimpses are equally hostile. Art, perhaps music, perhaps poetry, perhaps stories, perhaps aching constant movement—dance and speed—are the only comforts. Being in the Diaspora braces itself in virtuosity or despair.

—Dionne Brand[1]

A virtuoso for the ages, Desmond Richardson (b. 1968) is a dancer renowned for delivering commanding performances over decades in contexts ranging from the stages of Alvin Ailey American Dance Theater (AAADT) and Ballett Frankfurt to featured appearances with Michael Jackson and Prince. He was born in Sumter, South Carolina, to a Caribbean mother from Barbados and an African American father and was raised by his mother in Queens, New York, where he would dance at house parties with his family of artists. Richardson set his dance practice in motion as a B-boy, popping and locking in Queens before attending Fiorello H. LaGuardia High School of Music & Art and Performing Arts (the "*Fame*" school) in Manhattan and earning a contract with Alvin Ailey in the 1980s. In 1994, he co-founded

---

[1] Dionne Brand, *A Map to the Door of No Return* (Toronto: Vintage Canada), 26.

Body Impossible. Ariel Osterweis, Oxford University Press. © Oxford University Press 2024.
DOI: 10.1093/oso/9780190645816.003.0001

Complexions Contemporary Ballet with choreographer Dwight Rhoden. Richardson is one of the most visible and admired African American dance artists and played a significant role in inaugurating what I call in this book the "virtuosic turn" of 1990s and 2000s concert dance in the US. He modeled his career after acclaimed Black dancers Alvin Ailey, Carmen de Lavallade, Arthur Mitchell, and Judith Jamison, continuing a tradition of soloism and individual artistry, and the height of his fame just preceded the popularity of ballerina Misty Copeland.[2] It is unusual, if not unheard of, for a dancer to possess the breadth of technical expertise necessary to dance with companies as rooted in classical ballet as are American Ballet Theatre (ABT) and San Francisco Ballet (SFB) and to also have the chops to breakdance, pop and lock, and star on Broadway in *Fosse* numbers with equal aplomb.[3] The *New York Times* refers to Richardson as "one of the great virtuoso dancers of his generation."[4] In addition, he has appeared as a guest artist on the television show *So You Think You Can Dance*, reaching audiences who would not otherwise have access to concert dance. Richardson's personal style epitomizes the idea of virtuosity as—and of—versatility, allowing him to define and exceed the vast expanse that lies between the popular and the avant-garde. Especially before the ubiquity of social media, concert dancers who focused their time on proscenium stages (and not film and television) rarely attained star status. As indicated by the freedom and mobility to freelance and guest star with multiple major dance companies, he shares such status with a select

---

[2] Ailey, de Lavallade, and Jamison were all important mentors throughout Richardson's career.
[3] Richardson was nominated for a 1999 Tony Award for Outstanding Featured Actor for *Fosse*.
[4] Jennifer Dunning, "DANCE REVIEW: The Many Aspects of Complexions," *New York Times*, August 1, 1995.
 "Sheathed only in tights and a vest, his remarkably muscular body looks sculpted." "Gyrates." "'He's totally different from any performer I've even seen. Besides his amazing musicality, he moves like a panther.' In fact, Fosse's moves felt natural to Mr. Richardson. 'Jazz is in my body,' he said. 'I was a street dancer before I was anything else.'" "'Instinctively, Desmond conveys poetry in movement,' said Mr. Lubovitch, who choreographed the lead in Ballet Theater's 'Othello' for him. 'Then there's his superb technique. As a dance linguist, he speaks eloquently in all styles. Nothing he performs is flat or uninflected.' Mr. Faison went further: 'He is the most magnificent dancer America has produced in years.'" "Alvin taught me the importance of versatility. He said: 'If you can sing, you have to sing; if you can act, act. You'll bring all that to the stage, and it's so very relevant.'" "So far, no one company has given Mr. Richardson a chance to exhibit the full extent of his abilities." "'Billy [Forsythe] made me see how I make decisions [. . .] and how and where movements originate in my body and mind.' In Europe, he also discovered that artists use their skills quiet [sic] differently from the way they do in the US. 'There, a performance is all about the work,' he said. 'It's not about the performers. The dancers invite you into what they're doing; it's not in your face. Unfortunately, here everything has to be pow! Right now!'" "'Technique should only be an accoutrement. [. . .] A dancer must breathe life into every gesture. Then his spirit and individuality color it. It's what I work for.'" Valerie Gladstone, "DANCE: From Street Dance to Classical Ballet to Broadway," *New York Times*, December 27, 1998, section 2, p. 33.

group that includes the likes of Rudolf Nureyev, Mikhail Baryshnikov, and Sylvie Guillem in the 1980s and 1990s, and Copeland in the 2010s.[5] As his repertoire expanded, Richardson gained more control over his career, seamlessly traveling between commercial and concert dance settings. For aspiring dancers training in a variety of institutions, from nonprofit conservatories to for-profit studios, Richardson's dancing has become the prototypical example of a predominant contemporary strand of the stylistic mode that is virtuosity.

Body Impossible: Desmond Richardson and the Politics of Virtuosity responds to the need for rigorous theoretical investigation of *virtuosity* in dance and performance studies. To that end, this book is not a biography and is, instead, a project focused on cultures and theories of performance, with Richardson's artistry at the center of its inquiry.[6] Focusing on the decades approaching the millennium, this book brings dance into conversation with paradigms of race, gender, sexuality, and class to generate a socioculturally attentive understanding of virtuosity. Virtuosity obscures the border between popular and high art, and Richardson's versatility epitomizes the demands on the contemporary virtuosic dance artist. I argue that discourses of virtuosity are linked to connotations of excess, and that an examination of the formal and sociocultural aspects of virtuosic performance reveals underrecognized heterogeneity in which we detect vernacular influences on high art. In doing so, I account for the constitutive relationship between disciplin*ed* perceptions of virtuosity's excess and the disciplin*ing* of the racialized body in national and transnational contexts. In a media-driven culture devoid of systematic dance education, let alone dance education that focuses on racial and ethnic breadth and understanding, concert[7] dance audiences in the US tend to value Eurocentric aesthetics, and African American influences on ballet and contemporary dance either go undetected or are received as excessive. The paradox of audience reception is that perceptions are actively disciplined through a passive omission

---

[5] Today one thinks also of Maria Kochetkova (b. 1984). All dancers mentioned here are principal ballet dancers, and the ability to earn "guest artist" status is most often bestowed upon virtuosic ballet (as opposed to modern/contemporary) dancers, largely due to the relative financial stability of major ballet companies and ensuing opportunities. Richardson's excellence in ballet affords him increased mobility and notability.

[6] A biography, after all, would concern itself more with the poetics and psychology of the vicissitudes of life choices and the joys and anguish of everyday stops along an amply populated and narrativized journey.

[7] My statement here focuses on *concert* dance audiences; a different kind of argument could be made for/about, for example, social media's dance audiences (and participants). For example, TikTok presents a different set of issues, wherein audiences and participants may be exposed to many black popular dances, but without much knowledge of their cultural foundations.

of non-Europeanist styles and influences by journalism and the educational system (thus critics and audiences themselves). Virtuosic modes often insist on speed, complexity, and seemingly unending climax. Virtuosic performance exposes a great deal about cultural taste: audiences are skeptical of inexhaustible movement while simultaneously expecting it of Black dancers. This ambivalence characterizes responses to virtuosity in dance emerging during the mid-twentieth century. Because virtuosity is as derogatory a designation in certain contexts as it is celebratory in others, it is important to examine the foundation and evolution of the concept's instability.

I have selected six distinct performance contexts between the 1980s and the present through which to analyze Richardson's contributions to dance and virtuosity. Keeping questions of identity in the foreground, I interrogate the racialized and gendered politics of dance, and the role of versatility in Richardson's career. This book concerns itself with both the discourse of virtuosity and the mechanics of its production as a mode or quality. Richardson's virtuosity is especially distinct in its mobilizing of multiple dance styles and techniques. Despite his overall signature style, one that privileges hybridity over singularity, Richardson knowingly emphasizes certain techniques in certain settings to respond to the call of the work in question. I place a great deal of focus on Richardson's concert dance career, specifically on his work with the companies of AAADT, Complexions Contemporary Dance, ABT, SFB, and Ballett Frankfurt, and also look into his time at LaGuardia High School and his work with Michael Jackson. In doing so, I trace a dialogic relationship between ballet and modern dance techniques and black street dance styles such as popping and voguing. Such a study provides an opportunity to extend the scope of critical dance studies, performance studies, black studies, and gender and sexuality studies to include thorough investigations of virtuosity, race, and sexuality at the intersection of concert and popular dance cultures. After house and hip-hop dancer Jimmy "Cricket" Colter, I will adopt throughout this book the understanding that the larger category of "street dance" includes the following subcategories: club forms (house dance, punking/waacking, vogue), breaking (the first dance of hip-hop), freestyle hip-hop/hip-hop dance, funk styles (popping, locking), and dance hall. "Hip-hop" has become the umbrella term; so has "popping." There are many forms that fall under popping (strutting, bopping, robot, waves, etc.).[8]

[8] "Black vernacular dance or vernacular dance are terms coming from academia; I use them if I need to, but I mainly stick to the language of the culture. That's how I learned it, so that's how I relate it." Jimmy "Cricket" Colter, conversation with the author, October 2022.

While not inaccurate to refer to street dance as "black vernacular dance," I will be culturally and stylistically specific when relevant. Transcending boundaries of style, Richardson has attained a status of exception and experiences wide acceptance in the face of the exclusion of other dancers of color. We thus detect racialized cultural practices of consumption in which virtuosity cannot stand alone as such; audiences often expect of Black male dancers the fulfillment of athletic ability, charisma, and muscularity that reads as heteronormative virility. What emerges from my research is a close study of the relationship between aesthetics and politics as pertaining to queer black masculinities in dance. At the crux of this book's exploration is the idea of the repetitive yet transmuting *embodiment* of the cultural: virtuosity is at once contained by and in excess of culture's hold. Movement in its many iterations—of the body, through space, and across cultures—is central to *Body Impossible*.

From Africanist Aesthetics to Black Radical Performance

At no point in its analysis of its sites does *Body Impossible* lose hold of the urgency of the fact that Black men in America continue to be the object of exploitation, appropriation, and violence, and that black masculine bodies come to stand in ontologically for black masculine *being*. Throughout *Body Impossible*, Richardson portrays, agitates, and reflects on the politics and violence of Reaganism and the New Jim Crow alongside the development of his idiosyncratic yet inclusive style of queer black virtuosity. While virtuosity in certain heteronormative contexts can be an extension of respectability politics' insistence on black excellence, in its queer excess, virtuosity can function as a mode of escape and agency, as the virtuoso transgressively generates pleasure and queer joy for themselves and attuned audiences alike. At the book's core is a mining of the performative potential of virtuosic black queer corporeal performance through and beyond that of Desmond Richardson. Richardson's uniquely embodied but ever-mutable technique challenges assumptions that the hyperkinetic black body submits to a capitalist imperative to move, on the one hand, and is essentially diasporic, on the other.

Throughout the book I return to Brenda Dixon Gottschild's concept of Africanist aesthetics in American dance to chart the ways Richardson encapsulates Africanism in certain contexts and exceeds the hold of such aesthetics in others. I find Gottschild's discussions of the Africanist embrace of "soul" and constant motion especially relevant to Complexions' choreographic aesthetic, one that refigures black spirituality and kineticism. Gottschild argues that Africanist aesthetics embrace the idea that "the universe is in a dynamic process-in-motion, not a static entity."[9] Calling for a choreography that works against capitalism's speed and motion, André Lepecki writes, "Modernity creates its kinetic being based on a primary 'accumulation of subjectivity'.... The intrusion of the still in choreography (the still-act) initiates a direct ontopolitical critique of modernity's relentless *kinetic interpellation* of the subject."[10] Lepecki's influential argument, however, does not account for modernity's simultaneous limiting of movement of those whose agency is most compromised. If we adhere to the perspective that American capitalism is founded on slavery and extends into the prison industrial complex, then the assumption that restlessness and kineticism signal an accumulation of subjectivity associated with capitalistic drive is far from universal. For American dancers working in the African diaspora, highly kinetic choreography draws from traditions resistant to stasis, to capture. Thus, not only stillness but also motion can question "being," staging what Lepecki calls an "ontopolitical critique." Gottschild's formal interrogation of choreography reveals that particular movement styles informed by Africanist aesthetics embrace constant motion and speed, and that such movement is not necessarily demonstrative of a procapitalist project. As opposed to the Protestant ethic of efficiency put forth by Max Weber, Africanist aesthetics embrace forms of movement that may not contribute to maximum capitalist productivity. After all, as cited in this introduction's epigraph, Dionne Brand writes, "Art, perhaps music, perhaps poetry, perhaps stories, perhaps aching constant movement—dance and speed—are the only comforts. *Being* in the Diaspora braces itself in virtuosity or despair."

In my engagement with Gottschild, I implicitly invoke Sianne Ngai's observation that African American identity is often equated with "animated" performance and that such affective "zeal" has become naturalized in the American imagination through "bodily signs."[11] Ngai suggests that these signs are taken for "natural" or "authentic" qualities of African American existence. To some extent, Gottschild celebrates animatedness without

---

[9] Brenda Dixon Gottschild, *Digging the Africanist Presence in American Performance: Dance and Other Contexts* (Westport, CT: Praeger Publishers, 1996), 11.
[10] Lepecki, *Exhausting Dance: Performance and the Politics of Movement* (New York: Routledge, 2006), 58.
[11] Sianne Ngai, *Ugly Feelings*, "Animatedness" (Cambridge: Harvard University Press, 2007).

acknowledging its potential to perpetuate stereotype. The danger in continually redeploying images of blackness *as* overcoming—moreover, as overcoming via physical-kinetic means such as dance—is that it allows for the perpetuation of what Ngai refers to as "race as a truth located . . . in the . . . highly visible body."[12] Ngai writes,

> It is the cultural representation of the African-American that most visibly harnesses the affective qualities of liveliness, effusiveness, spontaneity, and zeal to a disturbing racial epistemology, and makes these variants of "animatedness" function as bodily (hence self-evident) signs of the raced subject's naturalness or authenticity.[13]

Nowhere is the racial epistemological logic of truth-as-bodily-animatedness more accentuated than in the particular dance contexts of the Ailey company; my exploration of Richardson's training in that world launches my chronicle of the racial politics of highly kinetic American choreography. Later, Richardson's work with Complexions begins to refigure movement aesthetics of animatedness by exaggerating the elements that Gottschild identifies as Africanist. For example, movement is sped up and performed in abundance, black dance forms are inserted into ballet, and the work is executed with a "cool" façade. The superhuman quality of Complexions' dancing (of—and after—Richardson) complicates racial epistemological assumptions of "naturalness" or "authenticity" by introducing a futuristic movement aesthetic that can only be performed by a very select few. With Ballett Frankfurt, Richardson furthers his foray into experimental movement, as he is asked to improvise in very complex ways and to draw on a movement vocabulary informed by ballet, hip-hop, and contact improvisation, traditions influenced by European and African diasporic traditions. Thus, animatedness is rendered in hyperkinetic form, exaggerated to the point of distortion and disorientation, for both dancer and viewer. As such, Richardson's career traces a shift in the visual performance of bodily racial epistemology from stereotypical animatedness to its excessive overemphasis and deconstruction, ultimately working in and through the illegible space of the "break."

---

[12] Ibid., 95.
[13] Ibid.

"The break," according to poet and scholar Fred Moten, defines the space of black performance and, like Moten's writing, embraces opacity and resists analysis. In other words, the break is not a gap that is devoid of content; instead, Moten has described it as a disruption or invagination. For Moten the "rich nonfullness" of blackness's "articulation" takes place "by and through an infinitesimal and unbridgeable break."[14] Richardson's improvisation style (expanded upon when working with Dwight Rhoden in Complexions and William Forsythe in Ballett Frankfurt) epitomizes black radical performance practices that foreclose any possibility of a "breakdown," rendering a parsing out and analysis of movement components impossible.

Through a prolonged investment in both classical and vernacular dance forms, Richardson arrives at such an engagement with the break. While he practiced hip-hop and breaking in conjunction with ballet and modern dance during his youth, it was not until dancing with Complexions and Ballett Frankfurt that he brought together improvisational methods from black street dance and experimental postmodern dance, weaving both into classical ballet. Thus, Chapters 3 and 4 on Complexions and Forsythe allude to W. E. B. DuBois's belief that African American artists should have equal access to Western civilization, and that such access comes together with black vernacular culture to produce "double consciousness." Paul Gilroy, after DuBois, theorizes the relationship between mastery and minoritarian culture. In his discussion of Du Bois in Germany, Gilroy interrogates the role of the vernacular in black culture, writing that

> *The Souls of Black Folk*... sensitized blacks to the significance of the vernacular cultures that arose to mediate the enduring effects of terror. [Du Bois used] black music as a cipher for the ineffable, sublime, pre-discursive and anti-discursive elements in black expressive culture.[15]

Gilroy also brings attention to

> Du Bois's desire to demonstrate the internal situation of blacks, firmly locked inside the modern world that their coerced labour had made possible. To this end, he carefully displayed a complete familiarity with the

---

[14] Fred Moten, *In the Break: The Aesthetics of the Black Radical Tradition* (Minneapolis: University of Minnesota Press, 2003), 255, n.1.
[15] Paul Gilroy, *Black Atlantic: Modernity and Double Consciousness* (Cambridge: Harvard University Press, 1993), 119–20.

cultural legacy of western civilisation. He claimed access to it as a right for the race as a whole, and produced a text that demonstrated how he regarded this legacy as his own personal property.[16]

Gilroy rearticulates how DuBois is part of a strategy within African American intellectual history in which this kind of display of complete familiarity is part of an overall formation of a "doubly conscious" racial subject. In mastering ballet technique while maintaining the "cipher" of hip-hop dance styles, Richardson too participates in a cultural strategy of double consciousness. Thus, Richardson's mastery of classical ballet technique correlates with DuBois's mastery of Western literary forms. Such mastery allows for mobility within—and expansion of—arts of the dominant class. Richardson's innovation lies in his ability to lend ballet and contemporary dance a break-informed impulse, to reconfigure its connective tissue from within. Hence, virtuosity emerges not only as mastery but also as the supplementation of that mastery with a barely legible excess. In this case, that excess comes in the form of a dialogic coexistence of dominant and vernacular forms.

Virtuosity

Virtuosity provides the principal theoretical thread of this book. It falls prey to the phrase "I know it when I see it." While the claim "I know it when I see it" circulates in everyday lingo in regard to various phenomena, it was uttered most memorably in reference to obscenity in the 1964 Supreme Court case *Jacobellis v. Ohio*. At the time, Justice Potter Stewart said, "I know it when I see it" to try to describe "hard-core pornography," which he decided should be excluded from protection as free speech. Perhaps it is no accident that, like pornography, virtuosity has been labeled by some as "obscene" and is often met with the assured ambiguity of "I know it when I see it." Alternatively, to claim "I know it when I see it" is, in celebratory contexts, to claim the ability to recognize "genius," "talent," and exceptionalism. Both pornography and virtuosity indulge in extremes, and such excess is often difficult to define, due either to a sense of overwhelm in its presence or to a commitment to explicitness, from visual (or written) depictions of sexual penetration to musical or danced executions of uncompromising technical

---

[16] Ibid., 121.

brilliance. "Extreme," "excess," "explicit," "exceptional," and "execution" all share the root "ex-," which means "out." "Out" indicates an externalizing or an exceeding of a boundary. We will find that it is virtuosity's insistence on visibility that likens its reception to that of pornography, which film scholar Linda Williams describes as the "frenzy of the visible."[17] After all, a virtuoso has no trouble showing off and showing out. What will viewers do, however, with all that visual abundance?

Is virtuosity only recognized as such by an audience familiar with the cultural specificities of an artistic form? Certain cultural contexts produce unique gauges of ability, from the competent to the virtuosic. Or is virtuosity perceived as such because it seems to transcend—or exceed—a familiar cultural framework? Led by Gabriele Brandstetter at the Free University of Berlin, the Kulturen des Performativen working group defines *virtuosity* "as the potentially excessive enhancement of artistic practice" and the *virtuoso* "as a new artist type who, since the seventeenth century, has influenced not only artistic concepts but also the very notion of performance in various cultural, social, and political domains."[18] Brandstetter and her colleagues Bettina Brandl-Risi and Lucia Ruprecht, among others, focus on the concept in terms of theatrical and embodied performance. Musicologist Susan Bernstein suggests:

> In the modern European languages, the terms *virtuoso* and *virtuosity* date from the Italian cinquecento. At that time, the terms stressed the sense of "possessing virtue" (from the Latin *virtus*)—force and valor—in art, science, or skill, including war. The second sense of "efficacy in producing particular effects," though itself not value laden, tends toward the disparaging tone of "mere" skill that is less than art. . . . The virtuoso is a sociohistorical figure that merges within the confines of a specific history of music, of the economics and politics of entertainment and spectacle, and of journalism.[19]

Bernstein remarks that the terms "virtuoso" and "virtuosity" can be by turns celebratory and pejorative depending on the context. The fluctuating

---

[17] After "French film theorist and filmmaker Jean-Louis Comolli who had written an influential essay, 'Machines of the visible.'" Linda Williams, "Motion and E-motion: Lust and the 'Frenzy of the Visible,'" *Journal of Visual Culture* 18, no. 1 (April 2019): 97–129.

[18] http://www.sfb-performativ.de/seiten/b12_vorhaben_engl.html.

[19] Susan Bernstein, *Virtuosity of the Nineteenth Century: Performing Music and Language in Heine, Liszt, and Baudelaire* (Stanford, CA: Stanford University Press, 1998), 11–12.

"Historical change in the dual evaluation of virtuosity, turning from cheerful mastery to deceptive mockery, can be seen in the short interval between Mozart (1756–91), the virtuoso universally

connotations of virtuosity historically reflect the ways different systems of value and evaluation can be applied to it in varying cultural contexts, and how terminological and ideological friction tends to be caused where art and entertainment intersect. Richardson's performances are received with a parallel range of connotations that have been associated with virtuosity historically. Moreover, when performing with Complexions, he is seen as favorably virtuosic, with the capacity to redeem the company's overall aesthetic, one repeatedly charged with being flamboyant. As Bernstein observes, such designations are circulated most often in newspapers, and virtuosity would not have become such a historical possibility without journalism. Much dance journalism (whether printed or online) addresses the art form through limited terms of success or failure, tropes that confer and complicate virtuosity.

Part of the discernment of excess in the work of Complexions is its incessant velocity, its aesthetic of speed. Bernstein points to the technical instrument of the musical virtuoso, which becomes complicated by the dancing virtuoso, whose instrument is her body, not an external supplemental device. Choreographic speed and velocity find themselves in unexpected proximity to the concept of acceleration in journalism. As Bernstein explains:

> [The] escalation of print means an increase in the number of information sources as well as a generalized information *acceleration*.... This acceleration characterizes both journalistic production and its consumption. The overwhelming quality of this acceleration is ... one of the most prominent characteristics of the virtuoso, whose technique often aims more at speed than at quality, mistaking speed for skill, difficulty for expression.[20]

Journalism both creates the conditions necessary for the possibility of virtuosity's cult and mirrors those characteristics that typify the virtuoso's performance, namely, speed and difficulty. Such acceleration comes with

---

hailed as genius and prodigy, and Paganini (1782–1840), the first really professional virtuoso, a technician made popular in part by rumors of possession by the devil evident in his uncanny mastery of his instrument." Ibid., 12. "Virtuosity both produces and exposes the mundane and material conditions of production—need, greed, egotism, and calculation—common to both the journalistic page and the virtuoso's face. The figure of the journalist evokes an entire set of familiar nineteenth century concerns: political disillusionment, lack of commitment, pleasure and profit seeking, the alienation and isolation of the individual." Ibid., 14.

[20] Susan Bernstein, *Virtuosity of the Nineteenth Century: Performing Music and Language in Heine, Liszt, and Baudelaire* (Stanford: Stanford University Press, 1998), 15.

casualties; Bernstein warns that virtuosity's fetishization of acceleration can jeopardize artistry.[21] I depart somewhat from Bernstein's suggestion that speed negatively affects the quality of a virtuoso's performance, and difficulty impinges on expression; at least as it pertains to Richardson, speed and difficulty lend themselves to the quality and expression of virtuosic performance. I do believe, however, that artistry can be compromised during a futile pursuit of virtuosity's flourishes. While there are numerous colloquial and scholarly meanings of virtuosity, in my study I make a distinction between ability, skill, and virtuosity. I suggest that ability is latent, skill is developed, and virtuosity is an extension of skill such that the virtuoso has developed impeccable technique, and that excellence converges with charisma and a curious excess. Virtuosity deserves to be, at minimum, examined over the entirety of a piece, and ideally studied over the course of a performer's career. Central to the concept of virtuosity is the question of balance, literally and metaphorically: precisely upending the terms through which excellence is thought to be achieved and sustained, virtuosity always indicates a degree of excess, and that excess can be technical, cultural, or gendered. Richardson seems to find a balance between danger and acceptability in his performances, transgressing the norm without entering a state of vulgarity or cultural rejection.

Fame, Nation, and Photographic Skin

Chapter 1, "*Fame* Nation: Queer Black Masculinities and a US Presidential Scholar in the Arts," examines how queer and closeted black masculinities are depicted in 1980s American dance and its translations into film and photography. Focused on Richardson's high school years at LaGuardia, during which time he earned the Presidential Scholar in the Arts award, this chapter takes place against the backdrop of Reaganism, the culture wars, and the New Jim Crow. The year of the award, 1986, was a politically charged time of conservativism that negatively impacted Black Americans. It was the same year that Ronald Reagan signed the Anti-Drug Abuse Act and photographer Robert Mapplethorpe published his book of photographed Black male nudes, *Black Book*. Reagan actively defunded many of the programs that Lyndon Johnson had established. The year 1986 marked six years since Reagan's 1980

---

[21] This particular line of thought is similar to Anya Peterson Royce's distinction between artistry and virtuosity in the performing arts.

attempt to abolish the National Endowment for the Arts (NEA) and three years before the 1989 NEA scandal involving Mapplethorpe and Andres Serrano, among others. Mapplethorpe's images were implicated in the culture wars, inciting numerous national debates on "obscenity," fetishism, classicism, sexuality, religion, and blackness. In 1992, Patrick Buchanan (in)famously declared at the Republican National Convention, "There is a religious war going on in this country. It is a cultural war, as critical to the kind of nation we shall be as the Cold War itself, for this war is for the soul of America."[22] The culture wars and what Michelle Alexander elaborates on as the "New Jim Crow" (including a continuation of Nixon's War on Drugs through channels such as the school-to-prison pipeline)[23] coalesced against the backdrop of Reagan's defunding of the arts and calculated disregard for the AIDS crisis.

Do you remember Leroy from *Fame* ... and Irene Cara's aspirational lyrics, "I'm gonna live forever?" In *Looking for Leroy: Illegible Black Masculinities*, African American studies scholar Mark Anthony Neal laments culturally habituated readings of black male bodies as criminal (and therefore only legible as criminal) and suggests that Leroy's masculinity (which he labels "queer") is illegible. I respond to this text by claiming that I have *found* Leroy, as *Fame*'s central character is a Black teenager without formal dance training who rises to the top of his class, excelling as a hugely talented dancer. Richardson's story parallels that of Leroy, and *Body Impossible* makes legible the nuances of queer black masculinity that Neal laments as illegible. Only about a decade older than Richardson, the actor who played Leroy (Gene Anthony Ray) was HIV positive and died in 2003. This chapter comments

---

[22] Patrick Joseph Buchanan, "Culture War Speech: Address to the Republican National Convention," August 17, 1992.

[23] "President Ronald Reagan officially announced the current drug war in 1982, before crack became an issue in the media or a crisis in poor black neighborhoods. A few years after the drug war was declared, crack began to spread rapidly in the poor black neighborhoods of Los Angeles and later emerged in cities across the country. The Reagan administration hired staff to publicize the emergence of crack cocaine in 1985 as part of a strategic effort to build public and legislative support for the war. The media campaign was an extraordinary success. Almost overnight, the media was saturated with images of black 'crack whores,' 'crack dealers,' and 'crack babies'—images that seemed to confirm the worst negative racial stereotypes about impoverished inner-city residents. The media bonanza surrounding the 'new demon drug' helped to catapult the War on Drugs from an ambitious federal policy to an actual war. The timing of the crack crisis helped to fuel conspiracy theories and general speculation in poor black communities that the War on Drugs was part of a genocidal plan by the government to destroy Black people in the United States. From the outset, stories circulated on the street that crack and other drugs were being brought into black neighborhoods by the CIA. Eventually, even the Urban League came to take the claims of genocide seriously." Michelle Alexander, *The New Jim Crow: Mass Incarceration in the Age of Colorblindness* (New York: New Press, 2010), Kindle 6.

on the uncanny meta-narrative of black performance labor taking place as the real-life stories of Richardson and Ray are layered onto that of Leroy. I go on to analyze a Mapplethorpe photograph of dancer Derrick Cross (1983) to further explore how black dancing masculinities are portrayed in 1980s American culture. Then, cycling back, further demonstrating how intertwined *Fame* and Richardson's career have become, the 2009 revival of *Fame* cites Richardson's company, Complexions, as the greatest contemporary dance company in the world. This chapter thinks through Richardson's high school training alongside the Mapplethorpe image and tropes of youthful dance aspiration in *Fame*, as recounted by Richardson's high school modern dance teacher, Penny Frank, who also acted in the film.

After high school, Richardson spent a year dancing with the Alvin Ailey Repertory Ensemble[24] and then secured a position as a dancer with AAADT in 1987. Chapter 2, "Choreography's Photographic Skin: Sweat, Labor, and Flesh in Alvin Ailey American Dance Theater," questions the relationship between the moving body and the supposed stillness of photographic imagery. Through a reading of surface and stasis, it explores the status of labor as manifested in the particular photo-choreographic context of an Alvin Ailey poster. Placing dance studies into conversation with critical race studies and visual studies, I ask how skin, flesh, mutability, and labor coalesce to present or undermine a multicultural ideology. The moment Richardson began dancing with AAADT, the company had come to stand in for a national dance aesthetic, touring internationally as one of the most recognized companies in the world. AAADT had become one of the US' main national cultural exports. Significantly, promotional posters relied on the virtuosity and masculinity exhibited by Richardson's image. I focus on a poster image for AAADT's City Center season in New York City in 1989, depicting an airborne Richardson with dancer Elizabeth Roxas in choreographer Donald McKayle's 1959 *Rainbow 'Round My Shoulder*, a modern dance piece about a chain gang in the American South.

I place movement theory and sociohistorical discourses from AfroAsian studies in conversation with visual race studies' preoccupation with the photographic. In doing so, I destabilize assumptions that modern dance (in its focus on the body's movements over a strict adherence to character) is "postracial," on the one hand, and best theorized through concepts of kinesthesia and motion, on the other. I question the relationship between the

---

[24] Now Ailey II.

visuality of skin and the commodified value of black and Asian bodies. How does the photograph's interruption—or "capture"—of movement (paired with its representation of skin) perpetuate or complicate the notion of the laboring raced body? I suggest that this poster image fits into a history of the consumption of racialized bodies. By drawing on concepts of labor, surface, skin, and flesh, I examine the interplay between the photographic surface and the epidermal surface. A reading of surface allows for a nuanced look at the relationship between skin and flesh, labor and form. If flesh is the muscularly active (or flaccidly passive) mediator between skin's surface and bone's structure, then to read photographic skin is to point to the dancing body's fleshly labor as that which moves surface into place. The chapter engages with Anne Anlin Cheng's concept of mutability, Vijay Prashad's discussion of AfroAsian identity and polyculturalism, Krista Thompson's notion of shine, and Elizabeth Grosz and Hortense Spillers's writing on flesh. Emerging as *sweat*, the labor of virtuosity is both revealed and concealed at the level of photographic surface, which I read through Cheng's "mutability of style." I claim that *flesh* (what Spillers identifies as the location of racial wounding) is afforded the potential for redress (as discussed by Saidiya Hartman) through Richardson's muscular labor. Ultimately, this poster urges us to consider how the raced body labors in the service of a multicultural ideology.

Choreographic Falsetto and Difficult Fun

The co-founders of Complexions Contemporary Ballet (1994–present), Richardson and Dwight Rhoden (b. 1962), both danced with AAADT from 1987 to 1994. With Richardson as his muse, choreographer Rhoden created an explicitly heterogeneous platform for contemporary dance that sought to diverge from AAADT's dominant aesthetic of "soul," which privileges heteronormative black masculinity and narratives of triumph. Inquiring into Richardson's dual role as muse and codirector of Complexions brings greater understanding to the type of virtuosity he inaugurated.

The third chapter, "The Muse of Virtuosity: Complexions Contemporary Ballet and Choreographic Falsetto," puts forward the concept of choreographic falsetto in analyzing the queer of color aesthetics of Complexions Contemporary Ballet. In locating the vernacular influences on ballet in Richardson and Rhoden's hybrid style, the chapter comes into conversation with Roderick Ferguson on queer of color analysis, Bettina Brandl-Risi and Gabrielle Brandstetter on virtuosity, André Lepecki on stillness, and Gottschild and Thomas DeFrantz on Africanist aesthetics. In thinking of the role of virtuosity in terms of gender transgression, this chapter posits that hyperkinetic corporeal performance appears to be both a space of license and a space of shame. I claim that virtuosity operates at—and blurs—the border between popular and high art, defining the location of the virtuoso's potential transgression.

By proposing and developing the term "choreographic falsetto," I liken Richardson's virtuosity to that of nineteenth-century virtuoso musicians and composers such as Franz Liszt, on the one hand, and black "post-soul"[25] singers such as Prince, on the other, accounting for a historically and cross-culturally prevalent (if relatively forgotten) aspect of virtuosity, namely, its position at the meeting point of gender, religion, capitalism, and individualism. Brandi-Risi asserts, "Virtuosic performances can provoke skepticism towards a form of excellence that cannot be reliably objectified with the help of prevalent norms," and critics tend to resort to a rhetoric of excess in virtuosity's presence. Like the castrato, the falsetto singer lingers in high notes typically reserved for the female voice. Gabriele Brandstetter writes:

> The ambivalence which characterizes judgment of the virtuoso is related to [the] inability to choose . . . between the ethos of the interpreter and the artificiality of the "performance." This dilemma first finds expression in critiques of the castrato's voice—the virtuoso voice.[26]

Instead of dismissing virtuosity as excess, I mine that excess in order to uncover black street dance influences on concert dance. In doing so, the content of that excess is named, and black and Africanist performance culture is rendered more legible. While Richardson initially attained stardom at AAADT, his contributions to Complexions worked to establish a queer, post-soul aesthetic that lingers in gender ambivalence.

This chapter engages with Ferguson's notion of queer of color critique to investigate the inextricability of gender, race, and class in cultural production. In doing so, I suggest that Richardson's virtuosity in Complexions is born of a queering of classical technique. In dialogue with Ferguson, I put

---

[25] "Post-soul" is a term elaborated on by Francesca Royster in *Sounding Like a No-No: Queer Sounds and Eccentric Acts in the Post-Soul Era* (Ann Arbor: University of Michigan Press, 2013).
[26] Gabriele Brandstetter, "The Virtuoso's Stage," *Theatre Research International* 32, no. 2 (2007): 178–95, 181.

forth the concept of choreographic falsetto to account for black masculine virtuosity that exploits technical skills typically reserved for female dancers in a mode that is received as "forced," "unnatural," and "superhuman." The mechanical, soulful, and freakish coalesce at the site of choreographic falsetto. In thinking of the role of virtuosity in terms of gender transgression, virtuosity in corporeal/nonverbal performance appears to be both a space of license and a space of hiding. In Richardson's performances, we detect a compulsive externalization—of technique, "expression," even mechanics—but also a simultaneous concealment of the mechanics of production. This dynamic of exposure and concealment mirrors a dialectics of queer shame, and such shame is often overcome through choreographic falsetto's extreme reach.

I also call into question a strand of dance theory put forth by Lepecki that privileges stillness as a site of anticapitalist critique. I suggest that hyperkinetic choreography incorporating black vernacular dance (epitomized by Complexions Contemporary Ballet) stages its own critique of capitalism (as founded upon slavery, capture), reappropriating queer shame and racial melancholia to generate affective recognition and artistic agency. Complexions recovers what Gottschild refers to as Africanist influences in American ballet both by inserting into its movement newer diasporic elements such as popping, voguing, and deep house club sensibilities and by extending the work of choreographic predecessors such as Balanchine and Forsythe, who were knowingly and unknowingly working in the Africanist tradition. Complexions' refiguring of Africanist aesthetics resists a sense of diaspora that relies on narrative, preferring a mode closer to what Daphne Brooks calls "Afro-alienation." Drawing from foundational debates on virtuosity by Theodor Adorno and Max Weber, this chapter also engages with contemporary theorizations of the term by the Kulturen des Performativen working group from the Free University (Berlin), musicologist Susan Bernstein, and anthropologist Anya Peterson Royce. I suggest, ultimately, that there is no normal blackness and no normal masculinity. Finally, this chapter points to the sixth chapter on one of Richardson's frequent collaborators, Michael Jackson, the quintessential Black falsetto singer-dancer.

Richardson decided to leave Ailey and form Complexions in 1994. The same year, Richardson left the US to dance in Germany with William Forsythe's Ballett Frankfurt. Chapter 4, "Difficult Fun: The Racial Politics of Improvisation in William Forsythe's Ballett Frankfurt," explores how Richardson and choreographer Forsythe's combined modes of improvisation create a notable shift in their practices to a "black radical tradition." I cite George Balanchine and improvisational traditions as influences on Forsythe. Richardson and Forsythe's collaboration collapses racial and choreographic signifiers, lingering in the difficult space of illegibility. Through concerted practice, such illegibility functions as a refiguring of the relationship between subjectivity and blackness. I trace the way Frankfurt dancers describe an otherwise modernist aesthetic of difficulty as "fun," ultimately positioning the body as the locale of choreographic and ontological agency. In doing so, I traverse the interval between what Forsythe calls a "[staging] of disappearance" and what Fred Moten refers to as the inevitably "improvisatory exteriority" of blackness.

While much of the book works to make legible otherwise illegible queer black masculinities, this chapter understands a certain kind of formal, choreographic illegibility as a site of radical, performative potential for black subjectivity. Forsythe's unique relationship to blackness is manifested through the formal aspects of his choreographic movement and emerges from his American sensibility within the German context of his company. Similarly, Ballett Frankfurt provides Richardson with a space in which he can abandon Ailey's reliance on heteronormative narrativity and concentrate on movement explorations in improvisation. Both artists are influenced by Africanist aesthetics, but this chapter explores how their combined modes of improvisation create a notable shift in their practices. Despite Richardson's hypervisibility, his work in improvisation renders him illegible as he collapses racial signifiers in pursuit of an aesthetics of *difficulty* with Forsythe, approaching what Fred Moten refers to as the "black radical tradition." Richardson's innovation lies in his ability to lend ballet a break-informed impulse, to reconfigure its connective tissue from within. Richardson's career traces a shift in the visual performance of bodily racial epistemology from stereotypical animatedness to its excessive overemphasis and deconstruction, ultimately working in and through the illegible space of the "break," epitomizing Richardson and Forsythe's collaboration.

Common practices in Ballet Frankfurt include improvisational technologies developed by Forsythe, including the "alphabet" method.[27] In addition to his expertise in ballet and modern dance, what Richardson brings into Forsythe's studio are experimentations with vernacular and popular dance improvisation, especially popping and locking. Important themes that emerge from an exploration of Richardson's work at Ballett Frankfurt

[27] According to Ballett Frankfurt dancer Dana Casperson, "'Alphabet' refers to a series of gestural movements based on words; for example, 'H' represents a gesture created by thinking about the word

include authenticity, collectivity, and agency. Central to the racialized sphere of concert dance are questions such as: What does it mean for white choreographers to use hip-hop music? What does it mean for Black dancers to do ballet? Ultimately, Richardson and Forsythe's collaboration collapses racial and choreographic signifiers, lingering in the difficult space of illegibility. Through concerted practice, such illegibility functions as a refiguring of supposed relationships between subjectivity and blackness. I explore the concept of authenticity further by tracing the way Frankfurt dancers describe an otherwise difficult aesthetic as "fun," ultimately positioning the body as the locale of choreographic and ontological agency. In doing so, I traverse the interval between what Forsythe calls a "[staging] of disappearance" and what Moten refers to as the inevitably "improvisatory exteriority" of blackness. This chapter also draws from interviews I conducted with African American dancers of Ballett Frankfurt, including Richardson and Stephen Galloway. What is revealed is a deep practice of improvisation, racial abstraction, innovative costuming (the influential socks-over-ballet-slippers choice), and radical choreographic practices. Working out of Germany, Forsythe and the dancers have a relationship to race as well as choreographic risk that is far removed from the relative aesthetic constraints of American performance, overshadowed by a relatively conservative ethic.

Blackface and Freakery: From *Othello* to Michael Jackson

In 1997, Richardson was called upon by choreographer Lar Lubovitch to star in *Othello: A Dance in Three Acts*, a full-length ballet performed by both ABT and SFB. Like Chapter 2, Chapter 5, "Otherwise in Blackface: American Ballet Theatre and San Francisco Ballet's *Othello*" (the book's most historical chapter), engages with visibility and authenticity, but through the practice of blackface. Recent theorizations of blackface and minstrelsy have looked to instances in performance that eschew explicit applications of burnt cork while engaging in appropriative relationships with "blackness" that read to some as "inauthentic." Susan Manning's notion of "metaphorical minstrelsy" questions early modern dance practices, Daphne Brooks's concept of "sonic blackface" traces influences of black

'hat.'" https://walkerart.org/magazine/methodologies-bill-forsythe-and-the-ballett-frankfurt-by-dana-caspersen.

music on white singers such as Amy Winehouse, and Louis Chude-Sokei locates the complex politics of the work of Bert Williams, who famously engaged in black-on-black minstrelsy. Of Caribbean origin, like Richardson, Williams was a wildly successful early twentieth-century Black performer who was politically active in the struggles of Black people in America. This chapter draws from recent discussions of blackface and minstrelsy to examine Richardson's title role in ABT and SFB's shared full-length production of *Othello* (1997). Continuing the historical practice of maintaining a relatively homogeneous (white) appearance, ABT and SFB rarely hire Black dancers. (Misty Copeland of ABT is one of this era's current exceptions, and her career has received a huge amount of public attention of late.) Lubovitch cast Richardson as *Othello* from outside the ranks of ABT and SFB. Richardson's temporary employment at ABT brings attention to the fact that these American ballet companies only tend to recognize an African American dancer when casting calls for a black character. Subsequent casts of *Othello* (when Richardson is not performing) are painted in blackface.[28] The fact that Richardson is not painted in blackface when he performs *Othello* questions relationships between corporeality and blackness (especially in the absence of spoken text), classicism and the contemporary, technique and appropriation, and casting and authenticity. More specifically, if more troubling, is the possibility that Richardson is performing black-on-black minstrelsy in *Othello*. Paradoxically, what appears to the contemporary eye to be the most outlandish aspect of minstrelsy—namely, blacking up with burnt cork—is, according to Chude-Sokei, its most assimilative, conservative aspect. Chude-Sokei reminds us that minstrelsy is a "constant erasure of the black subject through the hyperbolic presence of blackface."[29] Through interview and analysis, this chapter looks at the way Lubovitch's practice of storyboarding lends the production an episodic scene structure much like that of film. Thus, I invoke Linda Williams's theorizations of melodrama and racial melodrama in film and television to demonstrate how blackface and virtuosity continually complicate the (in) visibility of blackness in *Othello*. This chapter also draws from interviews I conducted with Lar Lubovitch in which he reveals being the only white dancer in an otherwise black company, filling an important gap in modern

[28] The *New York Times* refers to it as "shimmering bronze makeup," and I link such descriptions of surface to Chapter 2 (on surface and photography).
[29] Louis Chude-Sokei, *The Last Darky: Bert Williams, Black-on-Black Minstrelsy and the African Diaspora* (Durham, NC: Duke University Press, 2005), 36.

dance history. I layer this discussion of experiencing racial alienation onto my analysis of blackface in Richardson's casting in *Othello*.

Revisiting Richardson's teen years, Chapter 6, "Bad: Freakery, Iconicity, and Michael Jackson's Ghost," comes into close conversation with Chapter 3. Chapter 6 discusses how choreographic falsetto is also manifested in Richardson's collaboration with Michael Jackson. The quintessential falsetto post-soul singer of the 1980s and 1990s, Jackson is a virtuoso in his own regard. Richardson worked with Jackson seven times over the course of his career, first appearing as a teenager in Jackson's music video, "Bad." By incorporating interviews with Richardson into this chapter, I provide the reader with unique insight into Jackson's process and work ethic. In addition to turning its attention to Jackson's oft-eclipsed dancing, this chapter compares Richardson and Jackson's artistry in terms of virtuosity. Its main focus is an investigation of the term "freak"—the history of the term's origins in ethnological freak shows and how it has evolved into a colloquial term that designates both otherness and hyperability. Richardson is often referred to by fans as a "freak" due to the incredible feats he executes with aplomb. The use of the term in Jackson's case was more derogatory and related more to his personal (rather than artistic) life—his surgical bodily modifications and skin condition, vitiligo (not to mention his alleged child sex abuse crimes). In this chapter we find two kinds of alteration taking place, surgical and technical: the body is transformed by knife and rehearsal. The question of the mechanical comes to the fore in regard to surgery, on the one hand, and dance technique (as technology), on the other.

Joseph Roach points to the social "apartness" of celebrities who possess the "it" quality. Whether signaling hyperability or the grotesque (or in Jackson's case, both), freakery (a term elaborated upon by disability scholar Rosemarie Garland Thomson) signals social marginality, even at the top of the social/class order ("disabled" to "superhero"). Exemplified by both Richardson and Jackson, celebrity often functions such that virtuosity and freakery coalesce, generating a social apartness in which the performer is revered. This reverence recalls Max Weber's concept of the religious virtuoso as discussed in Chapter 3. Celebrity culture (especially of the pop/performer sort) has transposed religious zeal to secular entertainment, encouraging (an albeit mediated version of) a viewing habit that mirrors early sociologist Emile Durkheim's term "collective effervescence."

In discussing the way freaks are often emulated, this chapter also traces a genealogy of appropriation and authenticity from Broadway ("The Great

White Way") to the contemporary music video. Those considered "original" are always inevitably influenced by their predecessors. One example the chapter raises is the trajectory from Fosse's dancing to Jackson's emulation to Beyonce's supposed appropriation in her music videos. In discussing Richardson's Tony-nominated Broadway career, I bring attention to the Broadway appearances of his predecessors Alvin Ailey and Judith Jamison, who embraced (and did not reject) such commercial work from time to time. The fluidity—and financial necessity—Richardson, Ailey, and Jamison find between their concert dance and Broadway work recalls Chapter 1's discussion of LaGuardia and Ailey dance training's preparatory capacity for a variety of professional dance contexts. Richardson and Jackson have in common the Hollywood musical (Broadway musicals adapted for film), including *Cabaret* (Richardson) and *The Wiz* (Jackson); thus, TV, film, and popular culture studies factor heavily in this screen-centered chapter.

Virtuosity across the Atlantic

The book's conclusion, "Desmond Richardson on Tour: Virtuosity's Futures," briefly peers transnationally across the Atlantic to consider Richardson's role in the World Festival of Black Arts (1966–2010) and in performances in Russia and the Ukraine. As a post–civil rights (and post-soul) American representative in the third World Festival of Black Arts (2010) in Senegal, Richardson makes a significant contribution to the way we conceptualize African diasporic performance in this globalized economy, as his virtuosity insists that we account for the queer, the technical, the inventive, and the futuristic. In the conclusion, I point to a history of African American dance and literary artists featured in various iterations of the World Festival of Black Arts, most notably Alvin Ailey, Katherine Dunham, and James Baldwin. As the first president of postindependence Senegal, poet/politician Léopold Senghor (with Aimé Césaire) developed the antiassimilationist, postcolonial term "negritude." The conclusion considers how negritude frames the first World Festival of Black Arts in 1966 and how the francophone African philosophy shifts in valence in 2010, when Richardson appears as a soloist, Afrofuturist virtuoso. The conclusion confirms Richardson's role as an inheritor of Alvin Ailey's legacy.

Eighteenth-century Russia is considered the sociohistorical epicenter of classical ballet. Richardson was invited to perform at the Mariinsky

Theater with Diana Vishneva, and Complexions has appeared on Russian stages numerous times. Evidenced by the company name, Complexions Contemporary Ballet departs from pure classicism yet is wildly embraced by Russian and Ukrainian dance audiences. I suggest in this conclusion that, although Russia is known for racial and gender discrimination (among other violences), it takes ballet very seriously (let us recall the recent Bolshoi incident in which a disgruntled dancer had acid thrown in the director's eyes) and recognizes in Complexions a serious commitment to ballet, no matter how "contemporary." Russian audiences find compelling Complexions' focus on the formal aspects of movement, its utter commitment to the intricacies of choreographic form and movement quality (elements that can go overlooked in the US). There is a paradoxical aspect of this dynamic, as Russia has been embroiled in the conflicts of antigay laws and incidents such as Pussy Riot and Brittney Griner's imprisonments. Richardson's role as a gay icon in the 2013 Life Ball in Vienna overlaps with the time period in which he performs in Russia amid such tense political issues. As we see in Chapter 5, as Bert Williams's renown grew, his involvement in activism increased, and we find a similar dynamic in Richardson's life. The conclusion looks backward in time to contemplate the present moment in light of global dance history. Along with the chapters leading up to the book's conclusion, this allows us to better gauge the influences on—and the impact of—the heterogeneous virtuosity of Desmond Richardson. Ultimately, this book suggests that, for all its aspirational impetus, virtuosity enacts a kind of mourning, a creative outstretching of spirit in an effort to recuperate loss.

1
Fame Nation

Queer Black Masculinities and a US Presidential Scholar in the Arts

Baby, look at me
And tell me what you see
You ain't seen the best of me yet
Give me time
I'll make you forget the rest
I got more in me
And you can set it free
I can catch the moon in my hand
Don't you know who I am
Remember my name, fame
I'm gonna live forever
I'm gonna learn how to fly, high
I feel it comin' together
People will see me and cry, fame
I'm gonna make it to heaven
Light up the sky like a flame, fame
I'm gonna live forever
Baby, remember my name[1]

In 1986 at the age of seventeen, while a student in New York City at the Fiorello H. LaGuardia High School of Music & Art and Performing Arts, the "*Fame*" school,[2] Desmond Richardson earned a US Presidential Scholar

---

[1] "Fame," sung by Irene Cara on *Fame* original motion picture soundtrack, 1980. Songwriters: Dean Pitchford/Michael Gore, Fame lyrics © Sony/ATV Music Publishing LLC.

[2] Further demonstrating how intertwined *Fame* and Richardson's career have become, the 2009 revival of *Fame* cites Richardson's company, Complexions, as the greatest contemporary dance company in the world.

Body Impossible. Ariel Osterweis, Oxford University Press. © Oxford University Press 2024.
DOI: 10.1093/oso/9780190645816.003.0002

in the Arts award, presented by Republican president Ronald Reagan. The award is part of the US Presidential Scholars Program, which Democratic president Lyndon Johnson established in 1964 "to recognize and honor some of our nation's most distinguished graduating high school seniors." In 1965, just a year after forming the Presidential Scholars Program, Johnson also established the National Endowment for the Humanities and the National Endowment for the Arts. Johnson's broader civil rights focus also included the Great Society, the War on Poverty, affirmative action, and the Elementary and Secondary Education Act. In 1979, Democratic president Jimmy Carter extended the Presidential Scholars Program "to recognize students who demonstrate exceptional talent in the visual, creative, and performing arts."[3] That LaGuardia High School is the subject of *Fame* could not be more anticipatory of Richardson's career trajectory. Born in Sumter, South Carolina to a Barbadian mother and African American father, Richardson was raised by his mother in Queens, New York. Richardson explains that he first experienced dance at house parties and as a B-boy who practiced hip-hop cultural forms such as breakdancing, popping, and locking while growing up in Queens, and went on to train in ballet and modern dance at LaGuardia and Alvin Ailey. He developed into one of the most celebrated virtuosos of his generation, dancing professionally with Alvin Ailey American Dance Theater (AAADT), American Ballet Theatre, and Ballett Frankfurt, as well as performing on Broadway and with Michael Jackson and cofounding Complexions Contemporary Ballet. The year Richardson won the Presidential Scholar award, Reagan instated the Anti-Drug Abuse Act of 1986[4] and

---

[3] https://www2.ed.gov/programs/psp/index.html. President Jimmy Carter was responsible for the expansion to the arts. "In 2015, the program was again extended to recognize students who demonstrate ability and accomplishment in career and technical education fields. Each year, up to 161 students are named as Presidential Scholars, one of the nation's highest honors for high school students. . . . *Our mission* is to promote student achievement and preparation for global competitiveness by fostering educational excellence and ensuring equal access." This is also included in their blurb: "For the **arts component** of the program, students who meet the following criteria:
- are or will be U.S. citizens or Legal Permanent U.S. Residents by the application deadline;
- graduate or receive a diploma between January and August of 2018, the current program year;
- demonstrate academic achievement and talent in the visual, creative and performing arts; and
- participate in the National YoungArts Foundation's nationwide YoungArts program." https://www.youngarts.org/faq.

[4] "June 1971: Nixon officially declares a 'war on drugs,' identifying drug abuse as 'public enemy No. 1.'" "October 1986: Reagan signs the Anti-Drug Abuse Act of 1986, which appropriates $1.7 billion to fight the drug war. The bill also creates mandatory minimum penalties for drug offenses, which are increasingly criticized for promoting significant racial disparities in the prison population because of the differences in sentencing for crack and powder cocaine. Possession of crack, which is cheaper, results in a harsher sentence; the majority of crack users are lower income." https://www.npr.org/templates/story/story.php?storyId=9252490.

photographer Robert Mapplethorpe published *Black Book*, featuring nude photographic portraits of Black men. Within the sociohistorical context of the culture wars and the New Jim Crow, this chapter opens with a comparison between Richardson as a 1986 Presidential Scholar in the Arts awardee and the fictional dancer Leroy Johnson from the 1980 feature film *Fame* and culminates with an analysis of Mapplethorpe's photograph of dancer Derrick Cross (1983), to think through how queer and closeted black masculinities are portrayed in 1980s American dance and its representations in film and photography. Each of these three examples bears a unique relationship to the nation: Richardson's award is bestowed on a literal and metaphorical political stage, *Fame* circulates as a widely viewed Hollywood film (influencing American viewers but relatively distanced from actual political players), and Mapplethorpe's images of Black (and white) gay men spark national debates about art, obscenity, homosexuality, and censorship.

Reagan actively defunded many of the programs that Johnson had established, negatively impacting Black and poor Americans. Richardson's award comes six years after Reagan's 1980 attempt to abolish the National Endowment for the Arts (NEA) and three years before the 1989 NEA scandal involving Mapplethorpe and Andres Serrano, among others. Mapplethorpe's images were implicated in the culture wars and targeted by Senator Jesse Helms for being "obscene" and upsetting religious morality and "family values." In 1992, Patrick Buchanan (in)famously declared at the Republican National Convention, "There is a religious war going on in this country. It is a cultural war, as critical to the kind of nation we shall be as the Cold War itself, for this war is for the soul of America."[5] The year 1986, when Richardson won the award, marks a critical moment in the history of the US' ongoing racialized and sexualized violence, as the culture wars and what Michelle Alexander refers to as the "New Jim Crow" (and its extension of Nixon's War on Drugs via such troubling initiatives as the school-to-prison pipeline) came together as Reagan was stripping arts funding and refusing to acknowledge the AIDS crisis. As a virtuosic queer Black dancer in the 1980s and 1990s, Richardson played an important role in disrupting the nexus between criminalization and discipline that describes the way young Black men were being interpellated at the time.

Released in 1980, the film *Fame* is largely about the disciplining of young Black performing artists. The film is a fictional portrayal of teenagers

---

[5] Patrick Joseph Buchanan, "Culture War Speech: Address to the Republican National Convention," August 17, 1992. In Chapter 3 I discuss African American "soul" in relation to Richardson's virtuosity. Buchanan's speech uses "soul" to indicate conservative Christianity, not black soul.

auditioning for and attending the High School of the Performing Arts (which came together with the High School of Music & Art in 1984 as LaGuardia at 100 Amsterdam Avenue at the corner of West Sixty-Fifth Street). *Fame* takes viewers on a ride through the grit and aspiration defining the daily lives of New York City arts high schoolers, dramatizing the range from struggle to hard-earned joy that pervades preprofessional arts training. If scholar Mark Anthony Neal laments he is "looking for Leroy" in his monograph of the same title on illegible black masculinities, I provide some resolution here to his search by suggesting that, in this study of Richardson's celebrated high school years, I have, in effect, *reached* Leroy. Comparing Richardson to *Fame* dancer Leroy Johnson, this chapter reframes debates about race and Reaganism to suggest that teenaged Richardson embodies the crux of the late 1980s and early 1990s American politics of showcasing young black talent in a way that distracts the public from the simultaneous school-to-prison pipeline of the New Jim Crow. Recognition, like criminalization, is a form of policing: to reward black exceptionalism creates the image of a "good" black body as disciplined and masks repressive policing. State disciplining of Black men (*as* black male bodies) emerges as a systemic practice that operates at two opposing poles—the rewarding of exceptionalism, on one end, and the repression of those labeled "criminal," on the other.

Reaganism and the New Jim Crow

Alexander describes the New Jim Crow as a racial caste system that criminalizes Black men and places them in the prison system, reminding us that "the system of mass incarceration is based on the prison label, not prison time."[6] While the media points to black success stories such as those of Barack Obama and Oprah Winfrey, such black exceptionalism exists in relationship to "the current system of control" that "permanently locks a huge percentage of the African American community out of the mainstream society and economy. The system operates through our criminal justice institutions, but it functions more like a caste system than a system of crime control."[7] The War on Drugs and its iteration during Reagan's term and beyond plays a significant role in the New Jim Crow and, according to

---

[6] 17.
[7] 16.

Alexander, is a "backlash to the civil-rights movement."[8] Alexander provides the framework of "mass criminalization" to describe how "mass incarceration" is actually a system that "criminalizes" Black youth even if they are not (yet) placed inside an actual prison. Such a system of criminalizing children is wholly connected to the US educational system, including arts schools and the hegemonic mentalities infusing their administration. She writes:

> There are twice as many people on probation or parole today as are locked in prisons or jails. When people think about the system of mass incarceration, they typically just think about who's in prison at any given moment. But what I hope to draw people's attention to is that this system of mass incarceration is actually a system of mass criminalization. It is a system that criminalizes people at very young ages, often before they're old enough to vote. It labels them criminals and felons, and then strips them of basic civil rights, the very rights supposedly won in the civil-rights movement. And this happens even if you've been sentenced only to probation.[9]

Whether or not a teacher has read scholarship such as that of Alexander, racist educational dynamics can be felt in daily school interactions—for example, in who gets excluded from castings, what is left out of curricula, and how teachers treat students of color. The New Jim Crow depends on funnels such as the school-to-prison pipeline.

Without intentionally progressive teachers pushing the limits of the public school system's norms, African American students in the 1980s would not have been showcased. Richardson credits his own high school modern dance teacher, Penny Frank, with providing him with the foundational concert dance training that would lay the ground for his subsequent success with the AAADT. In addition to historical and cultural analysis, this chapter is informed by ethnographic interviews I conducted with both Richardson and Frank. Frank had danced with the Martha Graham Dance Company and is a cherished, long-time teacher of the Graham technique at both LaGuardia and The Ailey school. Richardson speaks of Frank as a crucial mentor and has maintained lifelong contact with her as one would with a cherished family member. What emerged from my research as I interviewed Frank, who not

---

[8] *New Yorker*.
[9] https://www.newyorker.com/news/the-new-yorker-interview/ten-years-after-the-new-jim-crow?source=search_google_dsa_paid&gclid=CjwKCAiAmrOBBhA0EiwArn3mfEp9n09GfM58D H3djeynrFOUmUw3rlliK_CBOYxmf7u27c-LTa_ceBoC98AQAvD_BwE.

only was Richardson's Graham technique teacher but also played a fictional dance teacher featured in *Fame* alongside Debbie Allen, was the discovery that, over a number of years, Frank deliberately chose talented Black dancers to coach and put forward for the Presidential Scholar in the Arts award. Frank taught at the high school for forty years, beginning in 1968 (the year Richardson was born). As a Jewish woman who experienced anti-Semitism in her youth, Frank's insistence on identifying black talent was a tactical way of instilling and nurturing an antiracist agenda during the otherwise racially violent sociopolitical landscape of Reaganism, an era especially vicious toward Black gay men. Frank had an admirable example in Karel Shook, the white co-founder of the Dance Theater of Harlem (DTH) with whom Frank studied at one point. Shook made it his career to train Black dancers in ballet, and his DTH co-founder Arthur Mitchell was once his student. Tracing such training genealogies helps dispel colonial myths of "discovering" talent. While progressive white educators like Frank (and Shook before her) were intentionally creating opportunities for deserving Black dancers who may have otherwise been overlooked due to racism, the Reagan administration's perpetuation of the New Jim Crow criminalized many Black men, confining them to the prison industrial complex. Not only did Frank choreograph the solo Richardson danced to win his Presidential Scholar award, but also Michael Gore (whose given name was Michael Goldstein) cowrote many of the songs in *Fame*. (The song "Fame" itself is sung by Irene Cara, who is Puerto Rican and Cuban American and plays *Fame*'s Coco Hernandez.) Omitted from the writing on *Fame* is the reality that Jewish writers, directors, producers, and teachers were often scripting the black experience in 1970s–1980s American arts and entertainment.[10] Interventions by such Jewish players in the arts and entertainment industries disrupted the economy of recognition and legibility structured by Reaganism in the relative absence of the possibility of self-representation by Black queer dancers themselves. Keeping in mind that *Fame* was not scripted by insiders from within the African American community, the film represents a more pervasive tradition of Jewish creative teams writing black experiences for Black—and white—performers

---

[10] And as far as philanthropy is concerned, the board of directors of the AAADT (where Richardson famously danced shortly after graduating from LaGuardia) is largely Jewish. While questions of blackface and minstrelsy factor more heavily into Chapter 5 (on *Othello*), it is important to keep in mind that celebration and mimicry via flattery live troublingly close to caricaturing, objectification, and cultural theft. Jewish performers played a role in the proliferation of minstrel shows earlier in American history.

to play; think *Porgy and Bess* and early twentieth-century minstrel shows. As Eric Lott[11] would suggest, blackface minstrelsy (an undoubtedly violent practice by today's standards) was born of white (and Jewish) admiration for African American culture. But blackface minstrelsy only worked to reinforce racist imbalances of power. Attitudes and approaches have evolved over time, but despite the best of intentions, what ensues with *Fame* is a film that both celebrates and caricatures blackness—and more specifically, black masculinity as raw talent. Teachers like Frank offer a more progressive approach to race, working tactically (but on a smaller scale) within the educational system.

Politically, the creative team behind *Fame*, and even more so Richardson's teacher, Frank, represented a liberal and increasingly racially inclusive sector of the public of the time. Concurrently, Reagan was imposing a wholly racist agenda. Not yet scripted into American entertainment at the time of *Fame*'s release, what coalesces during Reagan's presidency is an egregious disregard for Black—and Black gay—lives in the US. The dance world experienced a huge amount of loss due to AIDS deaths in the 1980s and 1990s. Reagan's apathy toward the AIDS crisis and its effects on gay men of color directly affected many men in and beyond Richardson's dance community, not to mention men involved in the making of *Fame*, including Gene Anthony Ray, who played Leroy; Louis Falco, the film's choreographer; and Christopher Gore, who wrote the *Fame* screenplay.[12] The culture wars were part of a much larger context of violence: what seemed at the time to be an instantiation of artistic censorship was taking place alongside the New Jim Crow and the AIDS crisis; Reagan was effectively disenfranchising Black and LGBTQ+ Americans. In the 1980s and 1990s, converging with the celebration of Black athletes, the black male dancing body was mobilized in the US to represent something aspirationally "American." But just as pop singers like Prince and

---

[11] *Love & Theft: Blackface Minstrelsy and the American Working Class (Race and American Culture)*.

[12] Ray, Falco, and Gore all died of AIDS. Louis Falco also went to the High School of Performing Arts, as it was called then. He died of AIDS in 1993. He was part of the Limón company and also danced with Alvin Ailey and Donald McKayle. He was known as a virtuoso in his own right. As related to the *Othello* chapter, Falco played opposite Nureyev in Limón's *Moor's Pavane*! He was a virtuoso and had a company of technical virtuosos. He choreographed for Prince. "During the prolific 1970s, Falco's approach to choreography raised more than a few eyebrows among New York dance critics. Falco Company performances became increasingly more difficult to categorize as noted by Clive Barnes in a 1973 *New York Times* review. 'This is a lovely company that annoys, more or less equally, the modern-dance traditionalists and the modern-dance avant-garde. I find this company outrageous but fun.'"

Michael Jackson (for whom Richardson danced[13]) played with gender expectations, there was some room for Black male dancers to work around the heteronormativity demanded of the sports world; artists were granted more freedom of queer expression than athletes. While I enter into this discussion more robustly in the following chapters, Richardson was, in his youth, benefiting from a kind of gendered and sexual "passing," as he could easily be read as "straight" by high school (and even future Ailey) audiences. No matter how he identified in his private life, his sexuality was unannounced and publicly closeted. Furthermore, even though the athleticism required of dancers often exceeds that of athletes, far more money circulates in sports, and athletes are marketed and compensated much more than dancers. Richardson, like Leroy and even Mapplethorpe's *Derrick Cross*, was celebrated for his athletic appearance, exemplifying *Fame*'s trope of "living forever" while numerous queer Black male dancers around him were dying of AIDS and Black men across the US were being targeted by the New Jim Crow. This is not to say that Richardson's award is in any way undeserved; quite the contrary, Richardson's indisputable excellence offers a palliative, no matter how uncalculated (or systemically aligned with the very conditions that produce racist violence), to the otherwise necropolitical conditions Reagan perpetuated for Black men.

Championing Black youth in the arts generated in the national imagination the illusion of reparation and a utopic, multicultural future, as if virtuosic dance had the power to transform memories of a racially violent past into an imagined future of hope, for it is hard to locate political stasis in the face of physical motion. As a young dancer of the highest caliber, Richardson's position was one of both exception and representation, impossibility and prototype. Examining this youthful moment in Richardson's life reveals that, although images of black masculinity are often entangled with assumptions of violence, the presidential awarding of Black teen talent exposes a nationalistic summoning of Black teen excellence as an attempt to erase from our consciousness Reagan's concurrent violence toward and disregard for Black lives. This troubling paradigm insists that blackness needs to be legible as either criminal or exceptional. Celebrating young Richardson on the national stage marks virtuosity as exceptionalism, confirming the impossibility of its neutrality. Virtuosity thus functions in this regard as a kind of violence, as a

---

[13] Richardson danced for both Prince and Michael Jackson. Prince appears in Chapter 3 and Jackson figures prominently in Chapter 6.

confirmation that Black men must be disciplined subjects of the state. Later in Chapter 3, this book explores how Richardson generates more agency over his dance and directing career and develops his style and virtuosity to more clearly promote a queer aesthetic; in that way, he works beyond the excellence of his youth (as legible) to reveal virtuosity's potential for illegibility and queer excess.

Interpellating Leroy: Talent and Violence

Richardson's early forays into dance discipline bear an uncanny resemblance to those of *Fame*'s central character, Leroy. A public arts school, LaGuardia is inevitably a site of state disciplining, with a goal of virtuosity in mind. Returning to *Fame* as a representational artifact of arts education through the vehicle of popular entertainment allows for an understanding of Richardson's virtuosity as a mode that followed a path from childhood street dance, to teen training in ballet and modern concert dance, to professional virtuoso, reminding us that virtuosity does not emerge "out of nowhere" and most often develops in relationship to institutional structures. Scrutinizing *Fame* also sheds light on how virtuosity, albeit a goal intertwined with violence in its attainment, can afford a professional artist a certain degree of freedom and escape later in their career. As demonstrated through a range of Black student experiences (and their representation onscreen) from Leroy to Richardson, LaGuardia finds itself at the meeting point of the logics of the school-to-prison pipeline, black respectability, and black exceptionalism. Early in the film, *Fame* presents us with audition scenes. Significant in terms of educational policy, intentional or otherwise, auditions carry a crucial function in that, when treated as the most important criteria, they prevent racist admissions decisions that can ensue when test scores and grades are privileged over dance ability.[14] Much more recent LaGuardia admissions

---

[14] "Admissions to these schools hinge on a standardized test that some feel creates disproportionate barriers to populations that are already underrepresented. In a statement, Richard A. Carranza, chancellor of the city's department of education, said that while he was proud of the students receiving acceptances, the numbers pointed to a glaring issue. 'Diversity in our specialized high schools remains stagnant, because we know a single test does not capture our students' full potential,' he said in an emailed statement. 'I am hopeful we'll move towards a more equitable system next year.' Eight of the nine specialized high schools admit solely on the basis of the Specialized High School Admissions Test, or SHSAT, and the ninth, the Fiorello H. LaGuardia High School of Music & Art and Performing Arts, admits students by audition. In an email, Amy Stuart Wells, a professor of sociology and education at Columbia University, called the city's one-exam admissions policy 'the new Jim Crow of public education.' Wells, who serves as the executive director of Reimagining Education

policies came under fire for placing more weight on grades and test scores; such a reversal negatively affects black and Latinx admissions. Richardson clarified that dance was the focus upon entry in his 1980s experience and that the school provided an academic tutoring program, once admitted, for those who needed to improve grades.

In *Fame*, Leroy initially attends the audition merely to accompany his friend, Shirley Mulholland, but he emerges as the dancer ultimately admitted to the school. Leroy is presented as unprepared, and he is not wearing the expected concert dance training attire of the time. Richardson was also unprepared, as he tells me he arrived to his own LaGuardia audition in a full formal suit. While Leroy entered the building dressed too casually, Richardson arrived too formally, corresponding to the range of images defining legible blackness, from criminality to respectability. At the outset, Leroy's blackness is associated with violence, as he is forced to leave his knife at the entrance upon arrival. Relying on the clichéd adage of framing the arts as a possible alternative to gang violence, the school administrators checking in auditioners tell Shirley and Leroy, "This is the High School for Performing Arts. We don't cut each other up here."[15] Through the character of Leroy, *Fame* deploys a seemingly contradictory image of Black teen masculinity, as Leroy is both celebrated for embodying heretofore "undiscovered" talent and painted as potentially violent, with a tendency toward knife fights. Embedded in this juxtaposition is, in fact, an overrehearsed trope of black excellence as only ever imaginable as "natural"—that Black teens and men are otherwise violent and that talent is born of the same uncontrollable "wildness." Whether or not Leroy has a knife is insignificant; instead, what unfolds in this early *Fame* scene is an example of the ubiquitous Fanonian knee-jerk interpellation of Black subjects. Alexander describes how Black youth are interpellated into criminality and how such hailing functions to uphold what she elaborates on as the New Jim Crow:

> For black youth, the experience of being "made black" often begins with the first police stop, interrogation, search, or arrest. The experience carries social meaning—this is what it means to be black. . . . The process of marking

for a Racially Just Society at the university's Teachers College, emphasized standardized testing is not a sufficient metric upon which to make such decisions." https://www.nbcnews.com/news/latino/unconscionable-latino-black-student-numbers-nyc-elite-public-high-schools-n1166741.

[15] *Fame* script, 4.

black youth as black criminals is essential to the functioning of mass incarceration as a racial caste system. For the system to succeed ... black people must be labeled criminals before they are formally subject to control. The criminal label is essential, for forms of explicit racial exclusion are not only prohibited but widely condemned.... At its core, then, mass incarceration, like Jim Crow, is a "race-making institution." It serves to define the meaning and significance of race in America.[16]

Here Alexander identifies the "process of marking black youth as black criminals" and Neal frames that marking as entangled with visuality, that "black men are seemingly bound to and bound by their legibility."[17] The same kind of legibility that renders Black men "criminals" is, in keeping with the logic of fetishism, precisely that which renders them sexually desirable to mainstream heterosexual culture, regardless of race. What Neal points to in his study of "illegible" masculinities, as exemplified by Leroy's dance persona and presentation in *Fame*, is that the more one strays from legible black masculinity, the more susceptible he is to gendered violence. (Alexander would remind us, though, that a norm of racial violence against Black men in general already defines America's overarching ideology.) This thinking on gendered violence is in keeping with Judith Butler's early writing on normative and subversive gender performance (after *Paris Is Burning*), namely, that we perform our genders, no matter if we are interpellated into heteronormativity or choose queerness, and our everyday gender performances can subject us to sexual or gendered violence.[18] The crux of Neal's argument is that the only kind of black masculinity that is legible to a racist society is a violent one; yet, he is also pointing to the danger of embodying queer masculine gender presentations.

In *Looking for Leroy: Illegible Black Masculinities*, Neal suggests that the predominant "legible" image of black masculinity is one of violent men deserving of violence:

That the most "legible" black male body is often thought to be a criminal body and/or a body in need of policing and containment—incarceration—is

---

[16] Kindle 248.
[17] Kindle 6.
[18] See Judith Butler, "Gender Is Burning," *Bodies That Matter*.

just a reminder that the black male body that so seduces America is just as often the bogeyman that keeps America awake at night.[19]

Not simply alluding to a broader notion of black masculinity, Neal points specifically to the "black male *body*," reminding us of the physicality and stereotyping that occurs in readings of black masculinity: the body is somehow inextricable from black being. Intertwined with—and even standing in for—black ontology, embodiment thus comes to define black masculinity in the mainstream cultural imagination. Richardson's teen years are reflected through Leroy, at least insofar as Leroy is depicted as a Black teenager without formal dance training who rises to the top of his class, excelling as a hugely talented dancer. While there is a lot about Richardson's teen appearance that could fall under Neal's categories of legibility (brown skin, athletic physique), he is rather lanky as compared to the muscular build he develops during his tenure with the AAADT. Richardson's relative legibility during his Ailey years is further explored in the next chapter on the relationship between black masculinity and photographic surface. It is later in his career (during the formation of Complexions in the mid-1990s) that Richardson begins to exploit illegibility, more openly aligning his sexual identity with his dancing; distinctly, this tends to occur more at the level of movement style than physical appearance. While a teen at LaGuardia, Richardson is in a youthful, liminal phase, not yet fully embodying what Neals refers to as the legible threat of black male adulthood. Seventeen when he received the Presidential Scholar award, Richardson's masculinity, like that of Leroy, appears heteronormatively athletic and a little bit queer, what comes to be a formula for black masculine acceptance in American pop culture. While there is no doubt that the Presidential Scholar in the Arts award is a national announcement of talent—a "coming out," as it were—it is a coming out that (at least in the 1980s) operates to keep closeted any potential sexual coming out. Being named a Presidential Scholar cannot even be likened to an example of homonationalism[20] because it is not (in cases such as Richardson's) a celebration of homosexuality on a national stage. Instead, private lives and public displays are kept separate. Tangled in a dialectic of danger and attraction, black masculinity that reads as straight with a queer edge becomes embraced by the mainstream insofar as queerness is seen to

---

[19] Mark Anthony Neal, *Looking for Leroy* (Postmillennial Pop) (New York: New York University Press), 4–5, Kindle edition. See Patricia Hill Collins for further reading on "containment."
[20] See Jasbir Puar.

temper the threat of black heterosexual virility, a perpetuation of historically racist, irrational fears of miscegenation. After all, "virtue," "virility," and "virtuosity" share a Latin root in "vir," which means "man" and indicates masculine strength.

Only about a decade older than Richardson, Gene Anthony Ray—the actor who played Leroy—was also an actual High School of the Performing Arts[21] dance student, and they shared a teacher in Frank.[22] The parallels between Richardson and Leroy—and Richardson and Ray—could not be more marked, and interviewing Frank and Richardson reinforced the uncanny meta-narrative of black performance labor taking place in their overlapping circumstances. Richardson's story bears much in common with Leroy's story, and my research into Richardson's artistic approach and ensuing success and friction within a particular cultural context of production makes legible the nuances of queer black masculinity that Neal laments as illegible. As this chapter moves through the culture wars' coalescence of Reaganism, the New Jim Crow, and the AIDS crisis, we will come to find that it is Richardson's—more than Leroy's—masculinity that, at the level of representation, is rendered less legible, albeit later in his career.[23] While Neal's writing on legibility resonates with Leroy's character on some levels, his claim that "This cat is gay" is not supported by the film.[24] The young white ballerina in *Fame* lusts for Leroy: "I dig his black ass." *Fame* is actually quite clear about its hypersexualizing of Leroy's straight masculinity, and the film relies on that trope to suggest that black talent is inextricable from virility. Neal writes, "I would like to suggest that Gene Anthony Ray's Leroy represented the foundation for a queering of black masculinity in contemporary popular culture."[25] What Neal points to is what I believe to be, instead, a lack of familiarity with—and a lack of images circulating of—heterosexual boys, teens, and men in dance. In other words, dance—not (homo)sexuality—is the illegible factor here. In fact, we are made to believe that Leroy gets the white teen-aged ballerina pregnant, leading her to anguish over an abortion, a choice rendered less conflicted due to race: Leroy's blackness simplifies the pregnant

---

[21] Which, as we learned earlier in this chapter, joined with the High School of Music & Arts in 1984 to form LaGuardia.

[22] Sadly, not uncommon for men in the dance world at the time, Ray became HIV positive and died of AIDS in 2003.

[23] Neal, Kindle, 1–2. At least in the film's narrative, Leroy is legible as heterosexual. Nevertheless, Neal writes, "Leroy represents a black masculinity that was 'illegible' to many." Neal, Kindle, 3–4.

[24] *Fame* script, 25.

[25] Neal, Kindle, 3.

dancer's choice—abortion over "life." In high school, Richardson is young enough to largely avoid the trappings of heterosexual masculine imperatives. In both *Fame* and Richardson's actual high school experience, discipline is equated with that which can replace both violence and virile hypersexuality. When controlled by white supremacist state policies, though, discipline itself becomes its own kind of masculine, patriarchal violence.

What Alexander comments on as respectability politics' "'get tough' tactics" resonates with cultures of discipline in much dance training, especially as it concerns Black youth:

> Given this history, it should come as no surprise that today some black mayors, politicians, and lobbyists—as well as preachers, teachers, barbers, and ordinary folk—endorse "get tough" tactics and spend more time chastising the urban poor for their behavior than seeking meaningful policy solutions to the appalling conditions in which they are forced to live and raise their children.[26]

Much dance training is rife with tactics of shame as it pertains to even the slightest perception of a lack of discipline (unstable technique or performance, messy hair, "body fat"), and with the added dimension of race in schools like LaGuardia, "get tough" tactics can get really tough. While Michel Foucault's example of the soldier as a "docile body" rests within a militaristic framework, a dancer like Richardson, educated through the state's public education system, is subjected to a kind of racialized Foucauldian docility and disciplining. As such, Richardson is educated during high school through the state training apparatus of dance. Herein lies an example of *Fame*'s representation of a teacher delivering a "get tough" work ethic:

---

[26] Alexander, Kindle, 266. "Mass incarceration [has] been influenced by what Evelyn Brooks Higginbotham has called the 'politics of respectability'—a politics that was born in the nineteenth century and matured in the Jim Crow era. This political strategy is predicated on the notion that the goal of racial equality can only be obtained if black people are able to successfully prove to whites that they are worthy of equal treatment, dignity, and respect. . . . The basic theory underlying this strategy is that white Americans will abandon discriminatory practices if and when it becomes apparent that black people aren't inferior after all. . . . This strategy worked to some extent for a segment of the African American community, particularly those who had access to education and relative privilege. . . . In many cases, the relatively privileged black elite turned against the black urban poor, condemning them and distancing themselves, while at the same time presenting themselves as legitimate spokespeople for the disadvantaged." Kindle, 63.

> Don't think talent's enough
> to get you through.
> You gotta have a strong technique,
> a good agent, and most of all, thick skin.
> Now you're part of an underprivileged
> minority, and you're going to suffer.
> Pulled tendons, shin splints,
> swollen toes, smelly tights...
> Cattle calls, the humiliation,
> the rejection...
> Melodic dictation theory, keyboard
> harmony, piano, piano literature...
> ...music history, orchestration,
> conducting, symphonic band...[27]

The tough *Fame* teacher's statement, "Now you're part of an underprivileged minority," mobilizes racial rhetoric to suggest that artists, like racial minorities, must "suffer," and deservedly so. While Richardson exuded a sense of discipline and work ethic while in school, Frank tells me that Ray, like his character Leroy, was not concerned with adhering to standards of respectability politics or black exceptionalism. And *Fame* unabashedly put on display Leroy's disobedience and other black stereotypes of deviance throughout the film. The complexity of Leroy's youthfully buoyant edge is that, in rejecting respectability politics, his character ends up perpetuating frenzied images of black masculinity as rife with indiscretion and mischief. The Black subject of the New Jim Crow is not ultimately challenged by Leroy; instead, disobedience toward the white supremacist order is portrayed as an overrehearsed stereotype of blackness as messy rebellion. As a historical counterexample, the Black Panthers easily complicated the opposition between disobedience as "black" and obedience as "respectable." Civil disobedience is closely associated with the free speech movement on college campuses; when the Black Panthers insist on their right to bear arms, they insist on legal disobedience, organizing themselves to reject their assigned status in society. In other words, leading up to the historical moment of *Fame* is the Black Panthers' significant work of organization as protest, exemplifying disobedience as structured. *Fame* becomes a microcosm wherein black rebellion within a white institution is played out: the film

---

[27] *Fame* script, 12.

frames Leroy within a good-versus-bad paradigm of liberal politics of recognition. Richardson's experience at LaGuardia was one of a Black teenager (albeit a "respectable" student) in a white institution, setting the stage for him to later cofound his (and Dwight Rhoden's) company, Complexions Contemporary Ballet, which exists independently, outside state-driven imperatives.

The Geography of Fame: Classicism's Ticket

The *Fame* narrative does not fully distance itself from Reaganism's stereotypes of black masculine violence and messiness and suffuses Leroy in what I am calling *skeptical excesses*, while Richardson demonstrates throughout high school efforts a counterpoint, *meritorious excesses*. I identify meritorious excesses as technique, style, and stage presence, which coalesce toward the development of virtuosity. Meritorious excess is rewarded. Especially as pertaining to race, the national discourse of merit has veered in various directions over time: President Johnson created affirmative action in the 1960s and in 1965 "issued E.O. 11246, requiring all government contractors and subcontractors to take affirmative action to expand job opportunities for minorities,"[28] at which point discourse shifted from "merit" to "preference."[29] Richardson's Presidential Scholar award exemplifies the awarding of merit (not preference) two decades after affirmative action was introduced, exemplifying rhetorical oscillation between the ideologies of merit and preference. *Fame* would have us think that it is work ethic that distinguishes virtuosity from disobedience, but that both qualities are possible responses to talent and the institution. Where Richardson's story diverges from the character of Leroy is at the level of virtuosity. Further discussed in Chapter 3, I make a distinction between charisma and virtuosity and between talent, skill, and virtuosity: talent is latent, skill is obtained, and virtuosity is something beyond technical mastery that is developed over time. In other words, talent cannot be equated with virtuosity. Virtuosity requires both technique and artistry.[30] Whereas Richardson becomes a virtuoso, Leroy is portrayed as merely having talent. Leroy is framed as a "natural" with much potential and hypersexualized heterosexuality. The portrayal of Leroy's charisma is caught

---

[28] https://www.aaaed.org/aaaed/History_of_Affirmative_Action.asp.
[29] As discussed in Hartman, *Culture Wars*, 104.
[30] See Introduction and Chapter 3 for a discussion of the role of artistry in virtuosity by Anya Peterson Royce.

up in the film's suggestions that he is charming yet undisciplined, violent, and hypersexual. A major difference between Leroy and Richardson could be distilled to the distinction between charisma and virtuosity—think charm as opposed to technique. While in *Fame*'s narrative Leroy's charisma is linked to the idea of his uncontrollable virility (as in a "cute guy"), Richardson's virtuosity points to a more abstracted attraction (as in the "incredible dance"), and fetishism is thus displaced from personhood to the performance product of dance itself. Whereas Leroy is objectified and fetishized in *Fame*'s narrative, if anything becomes exposed to objectification and fetishization in the example of Richardson, it is more likely to be the dance he produces. The erotic of virtuosity is such that the virtuoso generates an aura of attraction through—and of—their technical brilliance and unique performance. The heightened state felt by the audience in the presence of virtuosity is alternatingly described as spiritual, enlightened, or otherwise exalted. Charisma, and its representation onscreen, lies in the realm of charm and flirtation and often conceals insufficient skill (think of trickster politicians or religious leaders). What charisma looks like in the dance studio is distraction; virtuosity (and its attainment) looks like focus. If charisma alone conceals a lack of skill, virtuosity conceals the virtuoso's labor. (In Chapter 3 I discuss more fully how virtuosos' performances inherently rely on a degree of charisma, that idiosyncratic excess that adds a dimension of uniqueness to performance that would otherwise be merely technically brilliant.) In comparing Leroy and Richardson, various dimensions of fetishization emerge: racial, sexual, and that of Marx's commodity. The fetishizing of blackness occurs hand in hand with sexual fetishization, and in such configurations the sexualized "black body" is rendered an object to be consumed like a commodity. In the sense that labor is concealed in Marx's writing on commodity fetishism, virtuosity itself often functions as a commodity to be fetishized, as the virtuoso's labor is most often concealed—a virtuoso's job is to make difficult performance "look easy." Leroy is fetishized racially and sexually, but Richardson's relationship to fetishization is more complex, as it is his virtuosity more than his person that is fetishized. Queer Black dance virtuosos such as Richardson are subjected to a certain degree of racial and sexual fetishization along with the fetishization of their virtuosity but, unlike Leroy, have the ability to mobilize their virtuosity in the service of artistic invention and professional agency. As his artistry develops over the years, Richardson comes to embody resistance as escape *through* virtuosity.

During my discussions with Frank, I learned that Richardson came to LaGuardia with obvious talent but really had to work for his eventual virtuosity. Richardson did not arrive to high school as a virtuoso, nor was he perceived as a troublemaker; in fact, Frank emphasizes his strong work ethic and "good family," elaborating that she became good friends with Richardson's mother after the awards ceremony.[31] Frank does, however, reveal Richardson's capacity for invention in the midst of error, and self-advocacy in the midst of misnaming. Frank shared that they went to Washington for the performance and that Richardson ended up improvising much of his dance at the Capital but nonetheless gave a stellar performance. (Chapter 4 fully engages with Richardson's late 1990s practice of improvisation when working with William Forsythe in Ballett Frankfurt.) Frank says that when Reagan mispronounced Richardson's middle name, Serandei, during the awards ceremony, Richardson corrected him in the moment: "Reagan called out, 'Desmond *Se-ren-dee* Richardson' and [Desmond] responded, '*Su-ron-die*.' Can you imagine?" Frank concluded, "I thought, he's going to be just fine." In *Fame*, Leroy's recognition is born not of virtuosity, but of charisma. He is framed as noticeable, charming, and in possession of excess sexuality and the potential for violence. As it turns out, Leroy is a big talker with big dreams, and ultimately it is Richardson (not Leroy) who fulfills them. Dialogue in *Fame* includes, "Leroy. What are you doing here?" to which Leroy responds, "You ever heard of Alvin Ailey? . . . / He wants me to join his company."[32] We are meant to believe this is a fabrication. It is Richardson, not Leroy, who ends up being hired by Alvin Ailey.

During Richardson's schooling, LaGuardia relocated from Times Square to Lincoln Center, from midtown Broadway's "Great White Way" to the Upper West Side's geographic hub of concert dance. LaGuardia, as it turns out, would go on to train dancers in styles that would prepare them for careers in both traditions. Representative of what is colloquially referred to as an "uptown" (as opposed to "downtown") dance aesthetic, the high school's dance training methods share much in common with (and often prepare students for) neighboring conservatories such as the School of American Ballet, Juilliard, and the Alvin Ailey American Dance Center. Of course, Richardson would go on to train at the Ailey School and dance professionally with AAADT. Here I only use the terms "uptown" and "downtown" insomuch

---

[31] From interview with Frank.
[32] *Fame* script, 48/56.

as they were used in the everyday dance world vernacular of New York City for many decades. "Midtown" is not often colloquially used in dance, but keeping in mind Broadway dance, one could say that LaGuardia, at the time of Richardson's schooling, was training dancers for midtown and uptown careers. A more accurate description of the institutional training provided by conservatories north of midtown's Times Square would be something to the effect of "Western classically based concert dance" or "ballet-and modern dance-informed proscenium dance training." Nevertheless, we find examples of such training south of Times Square and north of Lincoln Center (in fact, the Dance Theater of Harlem has been largely omitted from discussions of "uptown dance"). "Downtown dance" has been used to point to practices that embrace the Judson Dance Theater and other postmodern traditions, and at this point such geographic and stylistic designations only work to further perpetuate (largely internal) dance-based stereotypes. Marking the precise meeting point of "high art" and commercial dance, the Lincoln Center dance conservatories I mention train dancers for professional concert dance companies as well as Broadway careers. They share a sense of excellence and competition based on technical mastery of ballet, modern dance, and jazz (with the exception of the School of American Ballet, which is solely ballet focused). Post-Judson pedestrianism, improvisation, and conceptualism are often assumed to be downtown dance's domain; while that myth may have held some truth in decades past (certainly during the *Fame* era), we locate what Hans Thies Lehmann calls "postdramatic theatre" in various geographic sites across New York and internationally. (Lehmann's "postdramatic" refers to works that consciously reject, disavow, or question Western theatrical conventions such as drama, presentation, narrative, proscenium, and technique.) Significantly, both racialized assumptions and realities pervade the uptown/downtown divide: even though uptown dance was racially exclusionary (especially ballet schools and companies), downtown dance is also equivocated with whiteness. This has much to do with the disproportionately white racial makeup of practitioners of Judson and other downtown endeavors. While the racial dimensions of the scene have not been elaborately historicized, Ramsay Burt and others have discussed the few Black dancers of the Judson movement. What sets Ailey apart from LaGuardia and other neighboring dance conservatories is its centering of black culture and diasporic forms. The Ailey School's training methods—which emphasize virtuosity as versatility—can prepare a dancer for a professional arena that often refuses to embrace dancers of color. As aspirational sites of training, conservatories can afford to train more students of color than the concert stage will include. We find that, upon completion of such training, it is the recognition of Western classical technique in a dancer's wheelhouse that affords them the perception of legitimacy in the eyes of otherwise skeptical viewers.

Richardson's mastery of ballet is one aspect of his training that has been commended by all who have gone on to hire him into their companies and productions. So often in dance, being able to display such technique (ballet and sometimes modern dance) leads to an endorsement as "refined." As related to various art forms, the discourse of refinement is troubling in its racialized connotations, as it suggests an absence of excess. Perceptions of refinement shift as time passes. Whereas Richardson's virtuosity, especially when reproduced by other dancers in his company, Complexions, was initially received as excessive, even vulgar, his style became a prototype for younger dancers to emulate over the next two decades, thus becoming normalized across the concert dance landscape. The question of proper proportions in the presence of racial, sexual, and virtuosic excesses connects, perhaps unexpectedly, Richardson to Robert Mapplethorpe and the Black gay men he photographed. Mapplethorpe is also an artist whose reception shifted over recent decades from designations of vulgarity to Classicism. The damagingly conservative values of anti-blackness and homophobia perpetuated by Reaganism affected not only education, dance, and film but also—and perhaps most infamously—the visual arts.

Let us recall that Mapplethorpe's *Black Book* was published the same year Richardson received the Presidential Scholar in the Arts award: 1986. On a federal level, it was as if in the same breath the White House was celebrating Richardson while beginning to label Mapplethorpe's photographs of Black dancers as "obscene." By analyzing Richardson's virtuosity alongside Mapplethorpe's photographs of Black men, we discover that, especially as pertaining to queer black masculinity, blackness is necessarily embodied and queerness is necessarily sexualized. Structurally, blackness and queerness are always already excesses. Thus, impossible blackness is disembodied, and impossible queerness is desexualized. Queer black virtuosity is, then, rendered impossible and culturally unacceptable. Richardson is a great example of how queer black virtuosity can indeed exist beyond its cultural impossibility.

What, then, of the actualization of Richardson's virtuosity and Mapplethorpe's homosexual content? While at first one would be hard pressed to locate a through line between Classicism and obscenity, what we find is that, by placing reception of Richardson's dance career beside that of Mapplethorpe's photographic career, Classicism, when haunted by excess—or by excess as blackness or homosexuality—is labeled "obscene." This is when virtuosity shifts from erotics to sexuality, from the realm of fantasy and the imaginary to the material and corporeal. But the shift from erotics to sexuality marks a moment of re-embodiment because virtuosity involves a kind of decorporealization in which labor is erased and the body starts producing impossibilities, as if the body itself becomes impossible. The phenomenon of technique in excess is further explored in Chapter 3, which suggests that inherent to perceptions of virtuosity is an excess of excellence—not simply mastery of technique, but something more than mastery. And that excess at the crux of virtuosity is often referred to as vulgar or obscene. In dance, designations of Classicism are often only reserved for Europeanist ballet. In photography, Western portraiture epitomizes a parallel example. Mapplethorpe's *Black Book* is a book of nude portraits of Black gay men by a photographer who is a white gay man. The book's contents, as well as Mapplethorpe's related exhibitions, fueled the 1989 culture wars' obscenity debates and censorship scandals. Even more cacophonous than voicings of potential objectification of Black men by a white photographer were responses of shock and wrath about the phallocentric visibility (and visuality) of nude Black men, as if work of *or about* black male bodies was inherently upsetting to the mainstream. The usual—but no less troubling—dialectics of attraction and repulsion and desire and threat are brought about in the reception of Mapplethorpe's images, and to an extent Richardson's performances (especially later in his career), and we find that Richardson and Derrick Cross (the dancer who posed for Mapplethorpe in 1983) betray an athletic muscularity that viewers find sexually attractive and potentially dangerous, as American audiences, art patrons, and politicians have been trained by the media to fear images of black masculine virility and strength. Sexual attraction here signals a return of virtuosity's repressed; if expressed, it falls into vulgarity. Embedded in such irrational fear is a racism that fears comparative sexual inadequacy as well as defenselessness in the face of imagined physical rage.

As for Richardson and Cross, further consideration of their muscularity reveals that they are both trained dancers and that their physicality is a result of aesthetic pursuits, no matter how athletic. The photograph of Cross pointedly brings together discipline and, not so much transgression, but transition—perhaps undressing due to the heat of dance rehearsal,

Figure 1.1 Leroy in the "Red Light" scene of the film *Fame*, 1980 (See color plates).

or shifting from rehearsal mode to evening hours or sexual activity. He is wearing the rolled-down tights of a committed dancer, and his torso and arms are bare. Does the viewer perceive the unraveling of discipline or the disciplining of potential sexuality? I would suggest that the photograph *Derrick Cross* brings together what I defined earlier as *meritorious* and *skeptical excesses*. Of note is that Leroy rejects tights in *Fame* and instead dances in short shorts.[33] One of his dance teachers comments, "Look, Leroy, I told you, if you don't have tights, you don't dance. Now go!"[34] In the 1986 Young Arts Festival photograph, Richardson is also dressed in black tights (and a t-shirt). While Neal associates Leroy's bare legs with homosexuality, a closer look at sexual dynamics in dance training and *Fame* reveals that Leroy's shorts are part of the heterosexual "bad boy" persona constructed by the film. Indeed, he is portrayed as hypersexual, but with an interest in women, not men. A further reading of Leroy's costuming could suggest that he cannot afford to purchase tights and therefore wears everyday athletic shorts. Herein, the film sexualizes the low-class body, and sexualization, racism, and classism intersect. As mentioned earlier, Richardson shared with me that, assuming a certain formality surrounding his LaGuardia audition, he arrived in a green suit jacket and pants and had to borrow dance

---

[33] "Leroy refused to wear dancing tights throughout the series, choosing instead to wear shorts that always highlighted his muscularity and, ironically, heightened his sexual availability." Neal, Kindle, 3–4.

[34] *Fame* script, 24.

46 BODY IMPOSSIBLE

Figure 1.2 Desmond Richardson in National YoungArts Week 1986 (See color plates).
Photo courtesy of National YoungArts Foundation.

wear from another student that day. To that end, outfit mishaps also indicate the teenaged naivete of entering a new path of study. Mapplethorpe's photograph *Derrick Cross* expresses homoerotic desire for Cross by focusing on the sheen and musculature emphasized by pelvis-hugging tights. Whereas shorts would obscure the region, Cross's defined buttocks and genitalia are suggestively outlined by his tights and further highlighted by Mapplethorpe's photographic technique, including his attention to light. As it pertains to dance, one should avoid an easy correlation between queerness and a lack of discipline. While gay and queer dancers may be positioned outside mainstream society, they often compose the majority in concert dance circles, and that majority values discipline. Moreover, let us not forget the cliché (and oft troubling reality) of straight men in ballet and modern dance as gaining sexual access to women (sometimes through force) who are otherwise left alone by gay men. Cross communicates something between pose and repose, or availability and refusal—the initiation or interruption of physical motion. His fisted hands signal a range from tensing in frustration to figuratively holding onto a thought—anger or a cherishing.

The resulting musculature of a trained male dancer's body is often likened to that of ancient Greek sculptures, the Europeanist pinnacle of the "classical" body in Western culture. The classical, in this tradition, birthed a certain concept of beauty itself. Adding another layer to the complex dynamic of Richardson's and Cross's (via Mapplethorpe's) reception is the culturally habitual mode of fetishizing classical male nudes. Also often referred to as prototypes (like Richardson in dance), classical Greek forms are fetishized for their muscularity. Such fetishizing is what vindicates Mapplethorpe to some extent, as critics cite his classicism (his seemingly sculptural treatment of the photographed male nude) as a reason to obstruct his censorship. In similar fashion, the *New York Times* (as I elaborate on in Chapter 3) calls Richardson the "saving grace" of Complexions' otherwise obscene ("vulgar") choreographic aesthetic. In the end, mainstream journalists value classicism, but any excess of technical and charismatic brilliance is seen as (even unknowingly) queer and ultimately obscene. To be classically brilliant yet racially and sexually Other is to cause quite a stir: legibilities clash, as legible classicism is upset by another kind of legibility (and its non-fulfillment)—the legibility of the Black-man-as-threat (an assumption only made possible through, paradoxically, a classical Europeanist treatment of musculature). The latter form of legibility is situated in contradistinction to being "seen."[35] Just as there is a cultural undecidability between desire and threat as pertaining to black male bodies, we ultimately detect national fluctuation about perceptions and deployments of "classicism" and "obscenity." Not merely ambivalent in its dynamic, the ricocheting between terms is found to be strategic, depending on whether one is defending art or defeating (and demeaning) Black men. As Robert Reid-Pharr writes:

> It is important to remember that some of Mapplethorpe's fiercest and most articulate critics have been gay African-American intellectuals, especially Kobena Mercer and Essex Hemphill, who argue that Mapplethorpe's much-celebrated technique, his ability to photograph (black) bodies as if they were marble or bronze sculptures, actually continues a centuries-long tradition of separating black physicality from black subjectivity. Thus when confronted with Janet Kardon's celebratory claim in the "Perfect Moment" catalogue that

[35] In current vernacular, "being seen" is likened to being understood, a sense of recognition.

Mapplethorpe's black models are "startlingly volumetric, occupying their space so convincingly that the photographer might be holding a chisel instead of a camera," the response of these African-American critics has been to remind us that there is nothing particularly novel about Mapplethorpe's aesthetic. Paying attention only to surface and volume, or what Kardon calls "the dark terrain" of black bodies, has often been the way that African-Americans have been treated in both American art and culture.[36]

While Derrick Cross (in the photograph *Derrick Cross*) exudes mastery over his body's movement in Mapplethorpe's image, he spirals his torso such that his face is turned away from the camera and our gaze. This could be read as a refusal, preventing us from assuming any kind of subjectivity in particular, but it could also be interpreted as a denial of subjectivity choreographed by Mapplethorpe. Kobena Mercer revised his initial critical stance on Mapplethorpe's work to say:

> In returning to my earlier essay I want to suggest an approach to ambivalence not as something that occurs "inside" the text (as if cultural texts were hermetically sealed or self-sufficient) but as something that is experienced across the relations between authors, texts, and readers, relations that are always contingent, context-bound, and historically specific.[37]

Thus, Mercer would suggest that the Western classical treatment of Mapplethorpe's subjects is not entirely objectifying nor entirely such that his models have total agency over their reception. While Helms, under Reagan, would insist on Mapplethorpe's "obscenity," recognition of his classicism redeems him in the eyes of many; significantly, valuing Western classicism often goes hand in hand with designating images of blackness and homosexuality as "obscene." Further demonstrating what Mercer identifies as the contingency of ambivalence, exhibitions such as *Robert Mapplethorpe and the Classical Tradition* may be titled as such more to avoid censorship than to ideologically conceal the works' black and gay content. Would museums have had the same success had they named the same exhibit *Robert Mapplethorpe*

---

[36] Robert Reid-Pharr, n.p.
[37] Kobena Mercer's "Skin Head Sex Thing," 237.

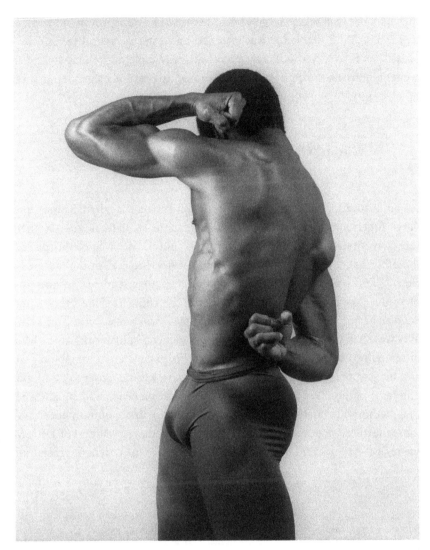

Figure 1.3 *Derrick Cross*, 1983 (See color plates).
© Robert Mapplethorpe Foundation. Used by permission.

and Homosexuality, for example?[38] The Mapplethorpe obscenity trial of 1990 (just after Mapplethorpe's 1989 death) regarding the Contemporary Arts Center in Cincinnati's exhibition *The Perfect Moment* focused on five photographs of gay BDSM culture, and the jury ultimately acquitted the

---

[38] https://www.guggenheim.org/exhibition/robert-mapplethorpe-and-the-classical-tradition-2.

museum and its director, largely because the works were proven to have "artistic value," and that value was attached to Western classical technique.[39] Classicism thus served as a convenient veil for Mapplethorpe's gay and black content, blurring the controversy just enough to prevent a legal designation of "obscenity."[40]

From "Gay" to "Queer": Before, during, and after the AIDS Crisis

As an institution and a film, respectively, LaGuardia High School and *Fame* functioned as straight spaces, hegemonically heterosexual in their representational demands on Richardson and Leroy. Mapplethorpe, on the other hand, came out as a gay man in 1969, the year of the Stonewall riots,"[41] and was out during his photographic career. Unlike the closeting of young Richardson at school and within the context of the Presidential Scholar award (and Leroy in *Fame*), Mapplethorpe's relationship to sexuality was such that his own sexuality was evidenced in his work. At the level of sexuality, there was proximity between his gay male photographic gaze and his gay, presumably desired, subjects; there was no closet to be found. The same national closet that celebrates Richardson censors Mapplethorpe. Mapplethorpe is unabashed in his presentation of and commitment to homosexual life. It has been historicized that Mapplethorpe was part of a BDSM scene in New York and had sex with Black men, some of whom graced the

---

[39] For a thorough discussion of the trial and events of 1989–1990 (including how "obscenity" definitions from *Miller v. California* factored into *The Perfect Moment*'s legal saga), see Richard Meyer's *Outlaw Representation: Censorship and Homosexuality in Twentieth-Century American Art*, 213–15.

[40] In his majority opinion, Chief Justice Warren Burger outlined what he called "guidelines" for jurors in obscenity cases. These guidelines are the three prongs of the Miller test. They are:

(1) whether the average person applying contemporary community standards would find the work, taken as a whole, appeals to the prurient interest;
(2) whether the work depicts or describes, in a patently offensive way, sexual conduct specifically defined by the applicable state law; and
(3) whether the work, taken as a whole, lacks serious literary, artistic, political or scientific value. https://mtsu.edu/first-amendment/article/1585/the-miller-test.

Also, while I'm not espousing a theory of visual arts "virtuosity," one could say that it was Mapplethorpe's "virtuosity," his excessively outstanding technique and artistry, that saved his work from an obscenity label, legally speaking.

[41] https://www.bookforum.com/print/2301/robert-mapplethorpe-s-archive-reveals-a-restless-and-radical-young-artist-15806.

pages of *Black Book*. One could take him to task for so starkly portraying a sharp distinction between his whiteness and his Black subjects, just as white, lesbian filmmaker Jennie Livingston was accused by some (including bell hooks) of objectifying Black and Latinx members of the voguing and ballroom culture in the making of her documentary, *Paris Is Burning*. However, a redemptive reading of Mapplethorpe's creative endeavors would suggest that he was paying homage to a community of Black gay men dear to him, in anticipation (knowingly or unknowingly) of the AIDS crisis's ravaging effects.[42] Some of the men portrayed in Mapplethorpe's photographs, as well as so many dancers in Richardson's milieu, were killed by AIDS and, moreover, by Reagan's decidedly inhumane lack of response to the epidemic. Not only was 1986 the year Richardson was named a Presidential Scholar and the year that Mapplethorpe published *Black Book*, but it was also the year Mapplethorpe received his HIV diagnosis; he died of AIDS in 1989, the same year his work was being targeted and attacked at the center of the culture wars.[43] The distance between Mapplethorpe's white identity and his Black subjects no doubt creates a paradox of exposure such that the increased visibility of his work afforded by his whiteness also raises questions of authenticity and subjectivity and makes him and his curators targets of the government's censorship. For context, examples of remarkable but less widely circulated art and writing by Black gay men about (and largely for) Black gay men in the 1980s includes the likes of Marlon Riggs's 1989 film *Tongues Untied*, Isaac Julien's 1989 film *Looking for Langston*, and the poetry of Essex Hemphill that inspired and was incorporated into both Riggs's and Julien's experimental works (now considered "classics" of queer underground culture). While Richardson himself was not stricken with AIDS, nor is this book meant to serve as a biography, to study his image and those of Mapplethorpe is to further ascertain how black masculinities are—especially by those from outside black communities—constructed, celebrated, and denigrated in American culture.

As previously noted, both Richardson and Cross (Mapplethorpe's muse) embody cultural ideals of masculine musculature and virility.

---

[42] In *Paris Is Burning*, voguer Willi Ninja, "the mother of the House of Ninja," shares that he wants to bring voguing to Paris itself, with a goal of international fame. Sadly, Ninja died of AIDS in 2006. Ninja worked with Madonna, and Madonna (who is white) received both criticism and praise for bringing light to the underground black and Latinx gay dance culture of voguing; some claim it was appropriation for material gain, and others appreciate her embrace of the culture.
[43] The Mapplethorpe Foundation contributes to the HIV/AIDS cause; they also generously provided photo rights for this chapter.

Seventeen-year-old Richardson as a Presidential Scholar and sinewy, strong Cross epitomize youth and the spirit of immortality of *Fame*'s insistent adage, "I'm gonna live forever!" To that end, Mapplethorpe's *Black Book* functions on some level as an archive of black gay beauty, hope, and health at the dawning of the AIDS epidemic. Photography's trace is more materially indelible than that of dance performance, but if the pursuit of fame is chasing anything, it is chasing immortality. As an art form, photography, more than dance, captures a kind of immortal finitude.[44] In the late 1980s and early 1990s, the impossibility of living "forever" became all too stark a reality in the black gay imaginary and the dance world at large. What differentiated the aesthetic of *Fame* from that of *Black Book* is that the film circulated in the populist realm of Hollywood cinema, while the book was a product of "high art." As pertaining to the pursuit of black artistic excellence, *Fame* emphasizes grit, while *Black Book* channels grace and "refinement." Although the film and the book both portray Black subjects who are, presumably, financially struggling artists and practitioners of embodied fields such as dance, fitness, and BDSM, they are nonetheless intended for discrete audiences. *Fame* delivers youthful song, dance, and resilience, and *Black Book* integrates classicism and eroticism. Whether or not Mapplethorpe was objectifying his muses was of no concern to the US government. Instead, they took advantage of the static dimension of the photographic to objectify Mapplethorpe himself, targeting a gay artist by misusing the rhetoric of "pornography" as accusation. In other words, blackness, "obscenity," and "pornography" all functioned as rhetorical tools to disparage Mapplethorpe and his work, for the conservative, religious Right was intolerant of that which it feared—blackness and homosexuality. While merely erotic and nude, the elements of blackness and homoeroticism in the photographs resulted in the inaccurate yet strategic labeling of Mapplethorpe's images (largely devoid of penetration or explicit sex) as "pornographic."[45]

The year 1986 also marks a moment in LGBTQ+ history just before a discursive shift from "gay" to "queer." While many in the black gay male community remained committed to "gay" as an identity marker, and still do today, Queer Nation's declaration for NYC Pride in 1990 reflected a newfound embrace of the reappropriation of the once-derogatory label "queer"

---

[44] A paradox formulated by Roland Barthes in *Camera Lucida*.
[45] While in *Self-Portrait* (1978) Mapplethorpe penetrates himself with a whip, most of his black gay nudes are not pornographic.

for sociopolitical purposes of identification. Queerness becomes central to Richardson's later career, when he progresses from a gay but artistically and publicly closeted Ailey company dancer to Complexions' out and queer co-artistic director putting forward queer aesthetics. "Queers Read This" was published as an anonymous leaflet for the 1990 NYC Pride Parade:

> How can I tell you. How can I convince you, brother, sister that your life is in danger: That everyday you wake up alive, relatively happy, and functioning human being, you are committing a rebellious act.... Since time began, the world has been inspired by the work of queer artists. In exchange, there has been suffering, there has been pain, there has been violence. Throughout history, society has struck a bargain with its queer citizens: they may pursue creative careers, if they do it discreetly. Through the arts queers are productive, lucrative, entertaining and even uplifting. These are the clear-cut and useful by-products of what is otherwise considered antisocial behavior. In cultured circles, queers may quietly coexist with an otherwise disapproving power elite. At the forefront of the most recent campaign to bash queer artists is Jesse Helms, arbiter of all that is decent, moral, christian and amerikan [sic]." ... I hate Jesse Helms.... I hate Ronald Reagan, too, because he mass-murdered my people for eight years.... I hate the "respectable" art world; and the entertainment industry, and the mainstream media, especially the New York Times.... Well, yes, "gay" is great. It has its place. But when a lot of lesbians and gay men wake up in the morning we feel angry and disgusted, not gay. So we've chosen to call ourselves queer. Using "queer" is a way of reminding us how we are perceived by the rest of the world.[46]

In a pivot from "gay" to "queer," QUEER NATION, which was started by ACT UP activists, rejected the allusion to happiness of the word "gay" and railed

---

[46] From "QUEERS READ THIS," the leaflet produced in 1990 anonymously for the NYC Pride March. The forward from the 2009 reprint reads as follows: "QUEERS READ THIS was distributed as a leaflet at the June 1990 Pride march in New York City. Anonymous queers offer this republication of QUEERS READ THIS as a contribution to the militant queer tendency. We are excited to find a text almost 20 years old that so eloquently expresses the deep anger and the desire for conflict that we feel every day living in a straight world. The authors define straightness as different from heterosexuality. Straightness is a force in the world and inside each of us that we must purge (p2). Straightness is normality. The norm for queer people is to take oppression lying down. These authors urge us to fight back. They ask why, when we are being bashed and killed, we freak out at angry queers who carry banners that say BASH BACK (p15). Of course, we could not agree more. The cultural references in this leaflet are, at times, outdated, but the rage is timeless. - July, 2009." The saying "We're here, we're queer, get used to it" comes out of QUEER NATION.

against the violence of Helms and Reagan. Because of its active defunding of the arts and apathy toward AIDS victims, the Reagan administration was met with shared disdain by white and black LGBTQ+ communities. "QUEERS READ THIS" also takes to task a certain kind of respectability politics of the art world (not to be wholly equated with black respectability politics also discussed in this chapter). To clarify, what "QUEERS READ THIS" finds problematic is the "'respectable' art world's" imperative of closeted sexual identity, especially given the fact that LQBTQ+ artists fuel creative industries. Richardson's career traces an arc parallel to that of the national "gay" to "queer" shift in that his teen sexual identity during his Presidential Scholar awarding is not publicly discussed, his tenure at the AAADT (as discussed in Chapter 2) includes an LBGTQ+-positive work life in the studio but a relatively closeted expression onstage, and Complexions (the company he cofounds with Dwight Rhoden, his partner at the time) is openly queer in its rehearsal life, performance content, and newspaper interviews (not to mention interviews for this book). In 2013, Richardson was crowned the king of the Vienna Life Ball, a globally visible HIV/AIDS charity that emphasizes gay and queer pride and performances of opulence and virtuosity, and he has since discussed his sexuality in the *New York Times* and beyond. Richardson has expressed to me that his increasing comfort with publicizing the extent of his commitment to LBGTQ+ rights and gay pride coincided with his rise in success and recognition. As we find in numerous arts careers, it is not always safe to come out as gay or queer until having received a certain level of public accolade, at which point activist artists feel more empowered to use their position and visibility as a platform. Even though Complexions generated queer aesthetics and nurtured queer artists, the company followed a journey in which their work at the company's inception was more radical and transgressive. To that end, it embraced the queer radicality of QUEER NATION's antiassimilationist demands. However, as Complexions performed more works over the next two decades, its aesthetic acquired a less radical resonance in that, instead of pushing boundaries as it once had, it had become emulated to the degree that it had influenced an increasing amount of mainstream concert dance choreography. To some degree, it has become the new "classical." As we will see in Chapter 3, exciting, novel types of virtuosity emerge in their specific historical moments, but once they have become the prototype for subsequent choreographies (and dancers' styles), their lack of novelty renders them trite, overrehearsed, or even "vulgar." Reaganism's racism and homophobia could have rendered

Richardson a target of violence, but Richardson's deep exploration and development of his virtuosity exceeded national ideological expectations of both disobedience and respectability. Thus, while his Presidential Scholar in the Arts award afforded him artistic recognition, it was Richardson's later, more mature stretching of his virtuosity that carried him from legible respectability to more illegible queer creativity and vision. If *Fame*'s Leroy is Reagan's easy target, then Cross in Mapplethorpe's 1983 photograph marks an ambivalent midpoint of subjectivity along a spectrum that finds at its extremity resistance and escape through virtuosity in motion in Richardson's dancing, especially in the decades following his Presidential Scholar in the Arts award.

The next chapter further explores photographic image making within—and beyond—the AAADT. It closely analyzes the AfroAsian politics of the surface—the photographic skin—of a Jack Mitchell photograph that served as the final image Alvin Ailey himself chose for a publicity poster before dying of AIDS complications. The AAADT, while internally supportive of Black gay lives, functioned as a closet, as its dancers, director, and artistic content had to remain within the boundaries of the performance of the nation. Recognized as the most successful dance company in the world, AAADT had to uphold a certain national representation of Americanness. While heteronormative performances of Americanness as African American or multicultural were found to be acceptable for a company in such wide circulation, Americanness as expressed through black gay masculinity—or any other LGBTQ+ identities for that matter—was off the table. The next chapter marks a significant moment in Richardson's dance career just before creating queer space through Complexions Contemporary Ballet—his rise to fame through and eventually beyond the embodiment and performance of athletic black masculinity and the development of his unique and internationally admired virtuosity on the Ailey stage.

2
Choreography's Photographic Skin

Sweat, Labor, and Flesh in Alvin Ailey American Dance Theater

The black-and-white photograph by Jack Mitchell depicts airborne Desmond Richardson with company dancer Elizabeth Roxas in choreographer Donald McKayle's *Rainbow 'Round My Shoulder*. An almost identical photograph from the same studio session with Mitchell is featured on a poster for Alvin Ailey American Dance Theater's (AAADT) 1989 City Center season in New York City. *Rainbow* is a modern dance piece about a chain gang in the American South. Originally choreographed for McKayle's own company in 1959, the piece was revived for the Ailey company in 1972 and 1980 and has remained in their repertoire ever since. Based on a historical piece that, in turn, comments on the past, this poster highlights the meeting point of multiple historical moments, including the early twentieth-century American exploitation of African American prisoners (which it depicts), mid-century American modern dance (which it exemplifies as performance), and the futurity of virtuosic millennial contemporary dance aesthetics (which it foreshadows). It marks a breakout moment in Richardson's career and the trajectory of AAADT. Seen here at the young age of twenty, two years after joining the company, Richardson embodies a shifting Ailey aesthetic as it emerges in the late 1980s and early 1990s. This poster announces Richardson's status as a star in the making and a prototype for dancers to come.[1] Only dancers highly trained in classical ballet or modern dance can attain the height and line of Richardson's leap. Richardson's rise, documented in this poster, coincides with a specific time in AAADT's history when the company was on its way to becoming the most successful dance company in the world. While rooted in choreography reflecting a range of African American experiences, the company

---

[1] Already a company of highly skilled dancers, Richardson stood out from the group from his first moments with AAADT.

Body Impossible. Ariel Osterweis, Oxford University Press. © Oxford University Press 2024.
DOI: 10.1093/oso/9780190645816.003.0003

CHOREOGRAPHY'S PHOTOGRAPHIC SKIN 57

Figure 2.1 Desmond Richardson and Elizabeth Roxas in Alvin Ailey American Dance Theater's production of *Rainbow 'Round My Shoulder*, choreographed by Donald McKayle (See color plates).

Photograph by Jack Mitchell, 1989. Courtesy of the Alvin Ailey Foundation and the Smithsonian National Museum of African American History & Culture.

under the direction of Alvin Ailey was racially diverse and often put forward an aesthetics of nationalistic "multiculturalism" to continue to prove itself as worthy of international export. This image's rendering of AfroAsian kinship satisfies the Ailey company's 1989 ethos of "diversity" and also

Figure 2.2 Alvin Ailey poster, 1989. Desmond Richardson and Elizabeth Roxas in Alvin Ailey American Dance Theater's production of *Rainbow 'Round My Shoulder*, choreographed by Donald McKayle (See color plates).
Courtesy of the Alvin Ailey Foundation.

delineates an era in which the company began to champion the type of virtuosity exhibited by Richardson and Roxas. This poster sells the idea of multicultural unity by inadvertently endorsing clichéd notions of the flirtatious Asian woman (with hair flying every which way and a flexed hand reaching for Richardson's groin)[2] and the hyper-hetero-masculine Black man. The stereotypical Asian female and black male bodies put forth in this image urge the viewer to consume a kind of multicultural heteronormativity. By focusing this chapter on this poster image in particular, I distill a crucial moment in AAADT's history in which Richardson defines an emerging aesthetic of virtuosity, inaugurating what I call the "virtuosic turn" in American concert dance.[3]

The last promotional image chosen by Alvin Ailey before his untimely death due to AIDS complications in December of the same year, this photograph by Mitchell differs greatly from current Ailey poster images, which are in color, feature glistening skin, and rarely reference the Asian body. In what follows, I examine the interplay between the photographic surface and the epidermal surface, drawing on Marxist and choreographic concepts of labor, the surface quality of sweat, and the distinction between flesh and skin. Situated under an overarching investigation of the visual economy of race in American multiculturalism in the late 1980s and early 1990s, this chapter questions how the dual deployment of black and Asian dancing bodies in the AAADT operates in a circuitry of aesthetic consumption. Throughout, I interrogate the relationship between the body in motion and the photograph's supposed stasis in the public context of the photo-choreographic poster. By way of skin and surface, I propose a consideration of how a phenomenological approach to dance can account for race and visuality, especially as pertaining to the discourse of "flesh." If flesh is the muscularly active (or flaccidly passive) mediator between skin's surface and bone's structure, to read choreography's photographic skin is to point to the dancing body's fleshy labor as that which moves surface into place. Occurring at the level of flesh and manifested visually as perspiration on the skin, the Ailey dancer's labor operates in the service of a nationalistic, racialized aesthetic ideology, far from phenomenology's naïve evocations of a universally embodied mode of experience.

---

[2] This gesture evokes the over-rehearsed stereotype of the black male phallus and American representations of the threat of (and fascination with) the black penis and/as sexuality. This issue is further addressed in Chapter 3.

[3] 1990s–2010s (=/-).

Labor and Racial Fetishism

Labor is the spectral presence driving *Rainbow*: the piece calls upon the labor of dancers to evoke the labor of a chain gang. Chain gangs were composed of prisoners who were compelled to perform labor for very little compensation if any at all. Lyrics to the main spiritual in *Rainbow* are, "I've got a rainbow, huh / Tied all around my shoulder, huh / I'm goin' home, huh / My Lord, I'm goin' home."[4] McKayle explains, "Rainbow was the prison slang for the tool used to break rock for road beds."[5] Thus, the piece's title, *Rainbow 'Round My Shoulder*, at once connotes the sense of an ethereal utopic beyond ("I'm goin' home")—or heaven as "home"—and the actual tool used on the chain gang. Like McKayle's choreography and that of much of the AAADT repertory, spirituals epitomize an African American aesthetic of overcoming in the midst of laborious conditions. "'*Tol' My Captain*," writes McKayle of a song in *Rainbow*, is

> a chain-gang song from the prisons of the American South, a song of men who must do forced labor, breaking rock in the hot sun under the watchful eye of an overseer leaning on his rifle. . . . The songs from the southern chain gangs were unique. They were an accompaniment to heavy physical work and their uneven musical structure paralleled the rise and fall of the pickaxes swung by the men as they sang.[6]

The loss of the sonic dimension of the photographic image is especially palpable in dance photography.[7] Without actual music playing, however, dance photography invites a focus on visual and corporeal aspects of the image. Of importance in this poster of *Rainbow* is the relationship between the theme of labor in the piece and the relative lack of labor exhibited in the image, and how such labors are revealed or concealed on the racialized surfaces of skin and photograph. I call the coalescence of these two surfaces (corporeal skin and photographic surface) "photographic skin."

---

[4] McKayle, 115.

[5] Ibid. "Their varied musings were personified in the dream figure of a woman, a composite of all their longings, all their fantasies, alluring, tender, nurturing, and always just out of reach" (McKayle, 115). "Mary, now my wife, entered . . . as if emerging from a dream. . . . She tries to heal the scars of injustice" (116). "The men must return to their labor" (115).

[6] 114.

[7] While Moten refers to the "scream" in images of racial violence such as that of Emmett Till, I refer here more to actual pieces of music that accompany certain dance pieces. Nevertheless, the songs are inevitably layered over history's "screams" and more abstractly sonic elements.

Having premiered in 1959, *Rainbow*'s inception marks the precise historical moment that dance scholar Mark Franko locates as the onset of the "formalist perspective" in American modern dance and ballet.[8] He argues:

> By the 1960s, with the ascendancy of Merce Cunningham and George Balanchine as preeminent choreographers in modern dance and ballet, the critical precedent for formalism was established. Following on the repressive atmosphere of fifties America, this formalist perspective encouraged forgetfulness of the relation between dance and labor.[9]

Thus, *Rainbow* was created just along the cusp of 1950s-era exposure of labor in dance and the 1960s formalist approach, which dispensed with explicit aestheticization of the relationship between dance and labor. In his effortless technical bravura, Richardson epitomizes the physicality of formalism. However, in the context of AAADT's repertoire (which calls for narrative and emotional expression), Richardson's formalist abilities are paired with modernist expressionism (as called for in Martha Graham's, Alvin Ailey's, and Donald McKayle's choreography). After Hannah Arendt, Franko distinguishes between work and labor such that "*Work* is conventionally thought of as a productive activity, whereas *labor* is the force that accomplishes it. . . . Labor, in Arendt's terms, is more like dance than work: it is an action, a process."[10] Thus, when I refer to "labor," I refer to dance as process—danc*ing*, not to be mistaken for "work." In concealing dance's labor by putting forth a sweat-free image of effortlessness, this photograph reifies racial and sexual fetishism of black male and Asian female bodies, inviting a racialized and sexualized gaze that celebrates difference in the precarious realm of the "multicultural," a realm that undermines antiracist projects by operating under the guise of liberal acceptance. In its aestheticization of manual labor, *Rainbow* begins to depart from modern dance practices of the 1930s in which (as Franko explains) "dance contributed to political struggle" and was connected to the "labor force."[11] *Rainbow* refers not to the 1930s labor movements forming Franko's discussion; it is meant to recall a historical struggle that predates the 1930s. While *Rainbow* is not devoid of political

---

[8] 8.
[9] 8.
[10] 2, my emphasis. Franko's project "explores how work in the 1930s was configured by dance, and how dancers performed cultural work. The performance of work constituted a new direction in American theatrical culture between 1929 and 1941" (1).
[11] 2.

relevance, it is not necessarily a piece meant to incite direct political action. Through choreography with formalist and modernist influences, the piece performs historical memory. As evidenced in the song's lyrics, *Rainbow* lends the idea of labor a spiritual dimension of the possibility of release from the strife of oppression. The African diasporic tradition of singing spirituals during or about labor suggests that, unlike the relative optimism of 1930s labor movements, the history of African American labor is such that there is often no possibility for justice or alleviation in the physical realm. Song and dance connected to the spiritual dimension at one point offered some of the only potential for release. To this end, the Ailey company has maintained a commitment to further depicting the spiritually liberating dimension of song and dance in the African diaspora.

Dance scholar Thomas DeFrantz extends the idea of labor[12] in *Rainbow* to include pleasure, by writing:

> The brawny black men who "play" laborers in *Rainbow* . . . revise conceptions of "work" through their presence on opera house stages. These men may look like laborers, but are, in fact, artists; the pleasure their bodies in motion provide for them and us is the labor of their trade.[13]

While the exhilaration of performing onstage may indeed grant a dancer momentary pleasure, this pleasure may in fact hinder the performer's ability to objectively ascertain the degree to which she is complicit in a visual economy of exploitation, no matter how subtle or naturalized. As such, the professional dancer traverses a fine line between commodity and tactical agent, embodying neither completely. We cannot underestimate the immense effort required of the professional dancer; the physical toil on the dancer's body can lead to pain and injury, and there are politics of contractual labor to consider when writing about dancers and their often-pleasurable jobs. Nevertheless, the pleasure that DeFrantz points to is of great importance to any study of Ailey and Richardson in that inherent to virtuosity is a sense of delight in one's own performance—the pleasure of execution and expression in the presence of an audience. Any labor that goes into a dance performance by Richardson or the Ailey company is indeed part of the work of

---

[12] DeFrantz uses the word "work" (not labor), but within this context, he seems to mean something closely aligned with what Franko calls "labor" and refers to as "laborers" in *Rainbow*.
[13] 36.

artistry and cannot be equated with the labor of a chain gang. Indicative of the spirit of virtuosity, what we find in this photograph of Richardson and Roxas is a sense of ease in the face of very demanding dance movement. After all, virtuosos make difficult feats look easy.

The AAADT's increased emphasis on the exhibition of technical mastery and flawless dancing at the moment this poster's photograph was taken tended toward an aesthetic of effortlessness, of concealing the labor required to execute such high-flying leaps and extensions. The Ailey formula of freedom afforded by (concealed) labor parallels the logic behind much technical dance training, such as that found at the Ailey School, where students learn classical ballet, modern techniques such as Graham and Horton, and diasporic techniques such as Dunham.[14] While less chronicled, there is a photographic impulse behind much dance training. It is not uncommon to hear a ballet or modern dance instructor utter, "I should be able to take a photograph at the height of your jump and find you in the perfect position." As Richardson had trained at LaGuardia and the Ailey School, the idea of photographic capture inevitably informed his dancing, especially during performance and photo sessions. As such, the poster becomes one of several goals and outputs (if not "products" in Marx's sense of that which creates surplus) of dance performance. Richardson's pose personifies the photographic compulsion of capture—the trope of "release" granted by technique—motivating much technical dance training. And *Rainbow* itself proposes the idea of freedom from and through labor. The idea that one could be photographed at any moment while dancing adds a dimension of self-consciousness that extends and exceeds the logic of the studio mirror. Whereas the studio mirror is a tool for self-reflexive correction, the photograph is both a static threat and a potential channel toward fame. With the hegemony of social media's demands of dance and dancers, the phone video is today's equivalent of that which generates photographic anxiety and a sense of an audience beyond a live audience.

The attention toward suspension in the dance photograph facilitates an analysis of the movements—sociocultural and historical—informing the piece itself, movements otherwise occluded by overdetermined emphases on choreography alone. Interrogating instances of suspension within an otherwise kinetic art form impels us to better understand how an image

---

[14] These techniques refer to those of Martha Graham, Lester Horton, and Katherine Dunham, respectively.

itself "moves" and performs, reflecting social "movements" that produce its very possibility. Given the art form's movement imperative, most dance scholarship addresses the body in motion as opposed to the photographic image. However, much of our dance consumption occurs at the level of the still image—the poster, the billboard, the photograph: images deployed as marketing tools with the specific purpose of attracting audiences and selling tickets. With the more recent advent of social media, much dance advertisement now circulates online and is viewed onscreen. At the time of this AAADT poster, dance performances were largely advertised in print material, in public spaces, and on moving buses. As Franko has written of an earlier era: "The glib or articulate texts and images disseminating dance in print media testify to the secondary circulation of embodied feeling."[15] "More than prosthesis" to live performance, the dance poster relies on viewers' affective responses to two-dimensional representations of three-dimensional performances.[16] And they do so in the service of a marketing agenda, to entice potential audiences through an image that is meant to stand in for a whole without giving away the entirety of a performance's contents. Accompanying the visual and spatial senses,[17] the "embodied feeling" circulated by print media is suggested by the dance poster's unique ability to evoke corporeal movement, kinetic presentation, and its transfer of "feeling."[18] To study a photograph of Richardson in detail is to understand how the cult of the virtuoso in a kinetic art form often relies upon the suspension and capture provided by a nonmoving image. In this particular poster example, the idea that the still photograph essentially suspends a moment in time happens to coincide with a "suspended" leap, midair. It is this suspension that makes the photograph available to repetition, to a kind of repeatability that "captures" movement for public viewing. In the context of

---

[15] *Labor*, 12. "The burgeoning of dance writing and the rise of dance photography and graphics in the thirties indicate that theatrically produced dance was a knowledge-generating practice" (12).

[16] Ibid.

[17] Although it could be tempting to engage here with recent work in critical race studies/diaspora/ photography on the "sonic" or "haptic" dimension of the visual (as in Saidiya Hartman and Tina Campt's seminar in 2009), theorizations such as that of Fred Moten engage with either (1) extremely violent images such as that of Emmett Till or (2) work in the black radical tradition, and I would not place Ailey (or his posters) in either category. Laura Marks's theory of haptic visuality proposes the idea of "touch"—that a moving image can touch you and you it; however, I find that (especially in light of dancing bodies—photographed or live) "touch" then becomes metaphorical and disrupts/ confuses actual touch that occurs so often in dance. Moten's "sonic" also becomes metaphorical to some degree, and (furthermore) could be confusing in light of "actual" musical scores/sounds playing during dance performance.

[18] See Mark Franko's critique of John Martin's term "metakinesis" and its irrational and nationalistic components (61).

AAADT, photographic stillness only perpetuates an otherwise extremely kinetic aesthetic that privileges motion over stasis. Not only is such kinetic movement evoked through the dance photograph's otherwise static medium, but also the photograph highlights for audiences the criteria with which to determine excellence in AAADT's repertoire. That Richardson hovers at the height of a jump with muscular joy and nonchalance educates us in virtuosity's signifiers, if not its resulting emotional effect. Richardson is often described in *im*material terms, hailed for his tremendous energy and charisma, and this photograph captures him in the height of a jump, in a climactic moment that mimics the affective force of his live performances. The impact of this image is found in the juxtaposition of photographic suspension and choreographic motion.

In *Rainbow*, Richardson and Roxas are called upon to embody similar virtuosic extremes—their high-kicking legs, technical precision, and emotional extroversion draw from ballet, Graham, and Horton techniques. Roxas was a ballet dancer in the Philippines before dancing with AAADT. Thus, while her early training was less steeped in modern dance than that of Richardson, it was similarly haunted by the photographic. The company does not consistently include Asian dancers among its ranks, and at the time of this poster, Roxas was one of two. During the 1970s and '80s, when Ailey himself was alive, the company appeared headed toward a more diverse exploration of polycultural dynamics of race.[19] In fact, this 1989 poster represents a moment during Roxas's tenure with Ailey in which the company could have done much to explore representations of AfroAsian solidarity. Instead, since the mid-1990s, the company's productions have focused more exclusively on mainstream representations of blackness.[20] Succeeding Alvin Ailey as artistic director, Judith Jamison wanted to center blackness and black experiences more fully, at a time when she could afford to do so. The Ailey company exhibits a mastery of Western and African diasporic forms that inherently dispel historical stereotypes of Black dancers as "primitive" or one-dimensional (and contemporary stereotypes of Black dancers as engaged in a never-ending hip-hop battle). AAADT has always celebrated blackness in addition to racial diversity, but, like any poster of an athletic body in motion, there is a minor risk of objectifying dancers, making them available for sexually and racially fetishistic consumption. If in American dance the Asian

---

[19] There is an Ailey company photograph from the 1970s that displays an explicitly racially heterogeneous company.
[20] With the exception of Donald Byrd, and perhaps Ulysses Dove.

feminine body is called upon to conjure the "exotic," the sexual, and the precise, the black masculine body has been called upon to exhibit what DeFrantz calls a "hypermasculine stance."[21] DeFrantz writes, "The sexualized 'black buck' and 'Jezebel' imagery that Ailey and his dancers inhabited, largely by their presence as muscular men and glamorous women on public stages, satisfied racialized desire even as it encouraged it."[22] In fact, Roxas's role was originally played by Mary Hinkson in 1959 (Richardson's role was played by McKayle himself). While casting Roxas (as opposed to an African American woman more similar in appearance to Hinkson) could be interpreted as a generous acknowledgment of her dancing abilities before race, the choice also risks capitulating to the popular American habit of casting Asian women to stand in for general ambiguity (or worse, an empty vessel). That Roxas is not meant to be racially specific in her tripartite role as mother/spirit/lover could leave space open for her fetishization. The virtuoso, however, no matter how attractive in stillness or in motion, possesses power in and through her skill: there is agency in her virtuosity, and such agency is more accessible in live performance.

"Liberalism of the Skin"

The West has a vexed relationship with black bodies, both championing and degrading the Other in visual economies of stage, screen, and print. In the performing arts and entertainment, from blackface minstrelsy to the commercial hip-hop industry, "the black body" has, in the American imagination, come to stand in for effortless exuberance, on the one hand, and effortful "soul," on the other.[23] The body of the Other (especially that of "the black body") has become a platform for America to exercise its dualistic consumptive habit of commodity fetishism and racial fetishism.[24] A system of body-as-commodity, slavery is the unspoken foundation of American capitalism. In Karl Marx's formulation of the commodity, human labor is abstracted and concealed. Though the nation's dominant mode is to repress its violent history, images of laboring black bodies have been naturalized—visible to the degree that they have been overexposed, therefore rendered invisible. This

---

[21] 37.
[22] Ibid.
[23] See dance scholar Brenda Dixon Gottschild on "soul."
[24] See Anne Cheng on racial fetishism in Baker article.

poster of *Rainbow* allows us to bring together questions of corporeal representation, dance movement, and commodity at the level of surface and skin. What would it mean to apply an analysis of both the aesthetics and rhetoric of "skin" in this example of choreography's photographic skin?[25]

> Historian Vijay Prashad discusses multiculturalism's tendency to "delimit social groups" through culture as opposed to obvious references to skin. He writes, "Liberalism of the skin, which we generically know as multiculturalism, refuses to accept that biology is destiny, but it smuggles in culture to do much the same thing . . . to create and delimit social groups."[26] As opposed to "liberalism of the skin," Prashad explains, *defiant* skins come under the sign of the *poly*cultural, a provisional concept grounded in antiracism rather than in diversity. Polyculturalism, unlike multiculturalism, assumes that people live coherent lives that are made up of a host of lineages. . . . [It] is a ferocious engagement with the political world of culture, a painful embrace of the skin and all its contradictions.[27]

In using this image, the Ailey company capitulates to the logic of multiculturalism, one that promotes differentiation and delimitation as opposed to what Prashad refers to as *poly*culturalism's antiracist project. Prashad suggests that "liberalism of the skin" (multiculturalism) can be disrupted by engaging with cultural contradictions. In keeping with such a suggestion, race scholar Anne Anlin Cheng offers a reading of skin and surface that lends Prashad's political discussion of polyculturalism's "defiant skins" an aesthetic dimension. She reads skin and surface to arrive at cultural analysis. Cheng's work exemplifies recent debates lying at the intersection of critical race studies, visual studies, and studies of the senses.[28] Cheng suggests that surface *performs*, and she examines the way skin participates in such performance. Her study of skin focuses on modernist fetishism as it relates to the photography and film of Josephine Baker. She writes, "There is a predicament of embodiment and visuality that fetishistic and democratic recognition share. And it is the crisis of visuality, rather than the allocation of visibility, that constitutes one of the most profound challenges for American democratic recognition and civil imagination."[29] Cheng suggests that civil

[25] Prashad.
[26] xi.
[27] xi–xii, my emphasis.
[28] Thompson, 2009.
[29] 68.

rights efforts to render visible otherwise "invisible" African American subjectivity have been operating superficially at the level of the visible (skin), and this allocation of visibility is both static and differentiating. Instead, she urges us to reconsider our ways of seeing and sensing to account for critical *visuality*, as a practice of engaging with surfaces in motion that may exceed the immediately *visible*.

According to Cheng, racial fetishism employs a mode of partial recognition similar to the concealment of labor that Marx identifies with commodity fetishism. Sharing Prashad's concern with identity politics' easy embrace of diversity, Cheng writes,

> Racial fetishism ... continues to inform contemporary American racial dynamics in various ways, from egregious racial stereotyping in legal and popular commodity cultures to the different though equally troubling effects of identity politics, in which an affirmative political or social identity often seems to reassert the stereotype it was meant to rectify in the first place.[30]

This poster brings to mind Cheng's latter conception of the racial fetish as that which inadvertently engages in stereotyping by affirming social identity. By deploying this poster image for promotional use in 1989, what was the company that calls itself one of the "most acclaimed international ambassadors of American culture"[31] envisioning as—and for—the nation? What does it mean that, as the Ailey company gained notoriety and exposure, it leaned increasingly on an exclusively black company (sometimes erasing from its ranks Asian dancers)? As one of the most virtuosic dancers of our time, Richardson's dancing exceeds stereotypical expectations of race because of his versatility, his mutability of style. However, this poster captures Richardson and Roxas in a system of racialized "meanings" that compulsively tries to situate them within a liberal project of multiculturalism. No matter how unintentional, Roxas is called upon in this poster to perform the liberal affirmative work of "diversity."[32]

---

[30] 38.
[31] AAADC website.
[32] As an antidote to such liberal logic found in both the socioeconomic and scholarly realms of the 1990s and contemporary neoliberal culturalism, Prashad explains, "AfroAsian work tries hard to cultivate the epistemological and historical archive of *solidarity*. The memory of the interactions, now being erased by neoliberal culturalism, has to be unearthed. This will allow us to better analyze the way in which ethnicities are mobilized by power to rub against each other" (Steen xxi, my emphasis).

CHOREOGRAPHY'S PHOTOGRAPHIC SKIN 69

In *Rainbow*, "Desmond Richardson [is] the youth who recalls his sweetheart and mother."[33] As the dream character, Roxas evokes multiple personas throughout the piece, including a love interest, a mother figure to Richardson's character, and what McKayle calls a "symbol of freedom for the imprisoned men."[34] Roxas's character "was at once free . . . then a rooted being," and this double sense of rootedness and freedom is indeed mimicked in her pose in the poster image.[35] The pairing of Richardson and Roxas paints the Ailey company as a utopia of AfroAsian kinship when, in fact, the Asian female's body in the actual piece (let alone the company ranks) is meant to operate as a dream figure, as a specter that almost lies beyond the possibility of objectification, whether epidermal or fleshy. Roxas flings her body into an ecstatic stance of abandon, signaling upward to Richardson, sending him into an airborne leap, as though Roxas herself has engendered his sense of freedom. While a function of nontraditional casting, Roxas is called upon to transfer the model minority myth onto Richardson: her body acts as a magic wand of ability. As such, this image emphasizes a multicultural concept of diversity, as opposed to reflecting more profound AfroAsian solidarity. Despite *Rainbow 'Round My Shoulder*'s preoccupation with labor, this poster risks presenting a troubling notion of the model minority's efficiency—a sweatless façade of labor's output, an invitation for Afro to *become* Asian.

Roxas playfully tosses up her long mane of hair, smiling toward Richardson. While this image might seem haphazard, even frenzied in its connotation of a wild mane, hair is in fact subjected to a similar sense of discipline as legs or feet at the Ailey School. In company performances, throughout the repertoire, any time a dancer's hair is not in a tight bun, she is expected to whip it with aplomb. As a student at the Ailey School, during a rehearsal period for a dance choreographed by company member Andre Tyson—a contemporary of Richardson—I was invited to a hair-whipping workshop. Because the piece in question called for the deliberate motion of hair in conjunction with arcing head and neck movements, Tyson wanted to make sure our hair—as much as our arms and legs—satisfied the rhythmical demands of the piece, arriving to its destination on the proper count and not a beat later. Indeed, Roxas was responsible for conducting this very hair-whipping session, as she

---

[33] Kisselgoff.
[34] 115. Cheng's discussion of mutability refers mainly to formal mutability, and as an exercise it could be generative to find relationship to character, as in mutability of character or personality *within* a single piece.
[35] McKayle, 115.

had become the expert in this regard. At the time, as was also the case with most of the other Asian women training at Ailey, my hair was almost waist-length, in keeping with the Roxas aesthetic. To possess extreme flexibility, honed technique, and long hair was to satisfy expectations for the Asian female dancer in the Ailey repertoire. If Asian female flexibility is one stereotype, the inflexibility of the black male body is another. Yet, in AAADT in the years surrounding 1990, Richardson's flexibility and control were exploited to the same degree as that of the two female Asian dancers, Roxas and Dana Hash.

Flesh

The virtuosity indicated by this image of Richardson and Roxas is born of fleshy labor. To initiate its analysis via the question of skin and surface is to point to the way AAADT generates interest through an alluring image. Entering into a discussion of flesh, I wish to further develop my investigation of the racialized body in dance, a body that exceeds its photographic capture. Moreover, the photograph-as-poster presents us with a fetishizable object of one of dance's most fetishized "positions," the split-legged leap, evoking the type of image to which the dancer's imagination compulsively returns. In other words, if phenomenology seeks to register and render experience through the sensorial, in space and time, the phenomenological experience of many a dancer working toward a choreographic goal is inevitably informed by images of dance icons such as Richardson. Moreover, how might Richardson and Roxas's own phenomenological experiences of dancing affirm or depart from the racial fetishism generated by this multicultural image? According to Richardson, dance is both an effort and a "calling." He shares with me that there is a degree of pain associated with rigor but that the satisfaction of performing for others stops him short of referring to dance labor as distressing. Moreover, he repeatedly expresses a belief in a sense of responsibility toward his talent. While dancer's labor has been referred to by some as ephemeral and thus wasteful, Richardson considers it a "waste" not to explore the limits of his talent.[36]

---

[36] The word "ability" could replace "talent" here, and doing so would raise a valid issue as related to the area of disability studies. While it exceeds the scope of this chapter, discourses of talent and ability need to be carefully considered as pertaining to disability performance culture. One might say that,

At its most reductive level, skin is the body's outer membrane, that which encases flesh. As Elizabeth Grosz (after Maurice Merleau-Ponty) reminds us, flesh is not entirely internal. She writes:

> Flesh is . . . being's most elementary level. Flesh is being's reversibility, its capacity to fold in on itself, a dual orientation inward and outward. . . . Flesh is reflexivity, that fundamental gap or dehiscence of being that Merleau-Ponty illustrates with a favorite example, the "double sensation," an example that clearly illustrates the various gradations between subjectivity and objectivity.[37]

Grosz emphasizes certain aspects of flesh that could be especially pertinent to interrogations of racial subjectivity, namely its dual qualities of inwardness and outwardness, and subjectivity and objectivity. Indicated by skin and supported by bones, flesh is not wholly internal. Therefore, as a mediator between bodies and the world, flesh plays a pivotal role in sensory understandings of the external, and is all too personified by the dancing body, at once experiencing its own kinesthesia and projecting it outward toward an audience. Furthermore, it could be said that Merleau-Ponty's "double sensation" is what allows for experience itself. Although Merleau-Ponty does not extend his argument to the question of race, one could argue that "double sensation" is the preconceptual (or phenomenological) formulation of Du Bois's "double consciousness" or Fanon's psychoanalytical interpolation ("Look, a negro!"). Blackness and racial subjectivity are always predicated on such duality—or on an abject indiscernibility between subjectivity and objectivity.

Flesh's relationship to surface enters into Cheng's discussion of the Josephine Baker film *Princesse Tam Tam* with the following statement: "The metaphor of bare skin thus comes to stand in for the materiality of exposed flesh."[38] Cheng thus distills the crux of representation. And just as bare skin stands in for flesh's materiality, a suspended image (the AAADT poster) stands in for a whole dance (*Rainbow*). Cheng states that Baker's "nakedness never stands alone." Even in its relative matte quality (lit but not shiny),

especially given the history of freak shows in the US, withholding the performance and visibility of bodily "talents," lacks, and dis/abilities could function as a productive biopolitical strategy.

[37] *Volatile Bodies*, 100.
[38] 60.

Richardson's bare skin "never stands alone," adorned by its own outlining of musculature and its tracing of an action. In this sense, both sweat and its lack can function as skin's adornment. One of Cheng's most provocative arguments marks the erosion of the distinction between Baker's skin and its ornamental costume and surface quality. In its sheen and gloss, Baker's skin is at once her own and extraneous; it is its own supplement. Cheng writes:

> The distinction between the organic and the synthetic blurs in such a way as to render Baker's skin itself costume, prop, and surrogate.... Is the fabric or animal skin on which she leans extraneous ornamentation or ontological companion?... [This] effect... has to do with what Bill Brown calls the indeterminate "ontology of modern objects," the inability to fully separate the animate from the inanimate.[39]

That Baker's breasts are often exposed, while meant to titillate at the crossroads of racial and sexual fetishism, can be partially attributed to cultural (French) context, one comfortable at once with exposed skin and with colonial exploitation. Whereas the skin-meets-flesh of Baker's breasts presents us with a muscularly inactive bodily attribute, Richardson's exposed musculature in the *Rainbow* photograph similarly indicates the place where skin gives way to flesh while introducing the possibility of actively engaged flesh (muscle). While sweat is indeed absent from the image, effacing labor in one sense, that Richardson's muscles are clearly engaged in the photograph points to the active—fleshy—mobilization of his own skin. Thus, bodily technique, muscular execution, and virtuosity become sites of agency (albeit complicated ones) for the dancer. Cheng refers to skin in motion as a "mobile outline." She writes:

> The only authentic thing we can locate in [Baker's] performance is the virtuosity of movement—a virtuosity that does not allow Baker to transcend racial, gender, or national differences, but that, counterintuitively, precisely reveals those distinctions to be built on transferable disembodiment and disarticulation.[40]

---

[39] 60.
[40] Ibid.

"Baker's supposedly African and primitive choreographic diction," Cheng continues, "is in fact a collage of various styles. . . . [The] scene of discrimination is thus . . . a scene of stylistic *in*discrimination."[41] It is often stylistic indiscrimination—rather than skin color—that serves as a racial marker. According to Cheng, "Racial legibility has less to do with the visibility of skin color than with the visuality of style"—style can "out" someone.[42] That ontology can be structured through a mutability of form—that the dancing body can, paradoxically, establish its being through the donning and shedding of multiple styles—is a radical notion that contests both discriminatory racial readings of surface as color and racial studies that attempt to combat such exclusionary tactics by narrating a figure's singular subjectivity based on surface. The relationship between flesh and skin in dance can be further complicated by noting the role of rehearsal in generating a sense of "muscle memory" in which movement that was once laborious becomes "second nature," naturalized in the body of the performer.

What Grosz and Merleau-Ponty omit from their discussions of flesh is the racial. While Hortense Spillers agrees with Merleau-Ponty in stating that "flesh . . . is that zero degree of social conceptualization," she offers an explanation that accounts for racial violence as injury to the flesh. Spillers writes:

> I would make a distinction . . . between "body" and "flesh" and impose that distinction as the central one between captive and liberated subject-positions. In that sense, before the "body" there is the "flesh," that zero degree of social conceptualization that does not escape concealment under the brush of discourse, or the reflexes of iconography. Even though the European hegemonies stole bodies . . . out of West African communities in concert with the African "middleman," we regard this human and social irreparability as high crimes against the *flesh*, as the person of African females and African males registered the wounding. If we think of the "flesh" as a primary narrative, then we mean its seared, divided, ripped-apartness, riveted to the ship's hole, fallen, or "escaped" overboard.[43]

For Spillers, exploitation of black bodies occurs at the level of flesh. Taking the dancing black body into account, it would seem that labor occurs in the domain of the exploitable—that corporeal beauty is created at the very

[41] 65.
[42] Ibid.
[43] Spillers, 67.

locus of the body (flesh) that is injured in racial violence. What the Ailey company continually rehearses is the resuturing of what Spillers refers to as the African American body's historically "seared, divided, [ripped-apart]" flesh. Such consistent disciplining of the flesh for choreographic purposes imbues the raced body with a degree of agency. In a multitemporal piece such as *Rainbow*, which takes as its subject matter historical labor abuses and continues to be performed today, the contemporary dancer negotiates yesterday's trauma with the high technical demands of today's Ailey aesthetic. In buttressing the Ailey company's overarching aesthetic of spiritual transcendence, Richardson's appearance in this poster image undermines the power of his live performances to "transfer feeling" by (in Spillers's terms) continually liberating otherwise captive flesh.

"No Sweat"

Central to the concealment of labor in this photograph is the absence of *sweat*. Conspicuously absent from this image, perspiration is that abject surface substance that announces exertion, the necessary fluid a dancer must experience when effort works in the service of effortlessness. Richardson recalls being photographed for this poster in a studio, not in a theater, midperformance. The lack of perspiration and message of freedom in this image mirror the Ailey company's view of technique as that which enables an ease of movement. I prefer the term "sweat" to "perspiration," as sweat's varied colloquial usages are in fact more descriptive of dance's labor: to say, "I'm sweating" in rehearsal is to say, "I'm working hard"; to "sweat it" is to worry; and, finally, to say you are "sweating someone" is to admit that you are attracted to them. Thus, no substance more fully encapsulates the coalescence of the logics of protestant labor, capitalist anxiety, and sexual fetishism.[44]

Art historian Krista Thompson's discussion of "shine" speaks to the aesthetic confluence of commodity fetishism and racial fetishism at the level of skin and surface. Thompson traces shiny skin (as that which refracts light) to slaves being greased before auctions and concludes that shine is central to commodity capitalism's logic in which the shinier the object, the easier the sell. According to Thompson, this logic culminates with hip-hop culture's

---

[44] Haunting this entire chapter is the phrase "no sweat," meant to communicate effortlessness, which the Ailey company—especially Richardson—continually embodies.

embrace of "bling," and Thompson cites visual artist Kehinde Wiley's contemporary portraits as a critical example of epidermal bling, or "shine." Only squeaky-clean shine (as in a new diamond) is acceptable in this realm. The shine of sweat is of a different order, that of religion, possession, athleticism, and performance. Sweat is the stuff of the live, rarely championed in photographic images unless linked to commodities selling weight loss or athletic replenishment (think Gatorade or Nike). The element of distance introduced in live concert dance settings further complicates the issue of sweat, as it is often difficult to see sweat from the audience; thus, sweat's relationship to visibility informs its status (or lack of) as an abject or taboo-ridden fluid. Contemporary Ailey posters, which avoid sweat, adhere more to the logic of "shine," of bling, as they render dancers' skin shiny but never sweaty. If, in the early twentieth century, African Americans struggled to attain visibility, Thomson suggests that our current cultural moment renders the black body "hyper-visible." Most provocatively, she asks, "How might the hyper-visibility of bling be another instance of the disappearance of the black subject, a new form of emblazoned invisibility?"[45] Sinewy contemporary Ailey poster dancers, paradoxically, achieve "shine" without the material adornment of "bling's" diamonds or cars. Instead, oil and light coalesce to create skin's consumable surface.[46] By paying comparative attention to surface qualities of the Ailey company's earlier posters featuring matte skin and later posters featuring shiny skin, I suggest that what Thompson calls "shine" coats the body in a preparatory state, readying it for labor or sale, and that sweat evidences labor during or after exertion. If shine is skin's prelabor surface quality, then sweat signals its postlabor condition. Central to this investigation of images is a kinesthetic imagination that allows for a consideration of the choreographic body in spatiotemporal terms, as that which interacts with—and in—the photograph before, after, and during capture.

It is also important to consider the poster of *Rainbow* within its multiple spatiotemporal contexts of staging and circulation. In other words, the image cannot stand in for a live viewing experience of the piece in its entirety; nor can its appearance on buildings and buses with accompanying advertising text be ignored. First of all, as Richardson states, "All photos for the Ailey

[45] 2009.
[46] Whereas in posters such as that of the 2005 film *Rize* the sheen of sweat is used to sexualize and sell the problematically utopian idea of dancing one's way out of the "hood" or as a substitute for black-on-black gang violence, this poster of Richardson and Roxas has a classically matte sculptural quality, celebrating the muscular without exposing supposedly abject bodily fluids.

Company are done in the studio. At that time we had to make it as though we were in performance."[47] Thus, in the photographic studio (which, in this case, is also a dance studio, as evidenced by the tape securing the Marley floor) Ailey himself directed the scene and chose the moment to capture for the image's marketing purposes. If in a performance of *Rainbow* the dancer must perform as if in a narrative of bondage and freedom, in the confines of the photographer's studio, the dancer is asked to perform "as though in performance," adopting a larger-than-life expression of overcoming or effervescence. Thus, if a similar image of *Rainbow* were photographed during performance (as opposed to in a studio environment), we might see skin coated in sweat. As choreographer McKayle states, in performances of *Rainbow*, there was "sweat running down their faces."[48] DeFrantz writes, "*Rainbow* is known as one of the sweatiest dances . . . because of its demands on the men."[49] When skin is coated in sweat, the religious, the capitalistic, and the aesthetic coincide. A dancer's sweat conjures both the Protestant work ethic and the black Christian celebration of sweat as what Anthony Pinn calls "a sign of intense contact between the divine and the human in spirit possession and in spreading the word of God."[50] "Sweat marks the body as a biochemical reality meant for labor," explains Pinn, "or . . . as a sign of Black bodies seeking to press against such boundaries."[51] In this arid poster, we get neither laborious biochemical reality nor its resistance. Instead, AAADT's is a message of effortless transcendence.

Ultimately, this image urges us to think about how American dance can put forth more deeply investigated images of AfroAsian solidarity without resorting to literal casting, didactic narrative, or the effacement of labor at the level of surface. To expose the labor concealed by this image is to acknowledge shared experiences of physical labor, effort, and exploitation, largely effaced by mainstream American performance. Nevertheless, Richardson generates his fame by laboring in the service of AAADT, dancing in and through an aesthetic of African American overcoming. Images such as this *Rainbow* poster mark a moment in history when Black men in concert dance could point to—but not exceed—an accepted level of athletic heterosexual expressivity. It is only through establishing a reputation for invested artistry

---

[47] Interview with the author, November 2009.
[48] 120.
[49] Discussion with the author (email).
[50] 21.
[51] Ibid.

and rousing virtuosity at AAADT that Richardson gained the recognition needed to form his own company. It is upon us to consider how renderings of choreography's photographic skin work to encourage or undermine antiracist approaches to dance. The type of racial fetishism made available by Richardson's virtuosity in this poster is precisely that which he works to subvert by cofounding Complexions Contemporary Ballet.

3
The Muse of Virtuosity
Complexions Contemporary Ballet and Choreographic Falsetto

In earlier epochs, technical virtuosity, at least, was demanded of singing stars, the castrati and prima donnas. Today, the material as such, destitute of any function, is celebrated.

—Theodor Adorno[1]

As in sport or athletics, the achievement by a virtuoso dancer raises the achievable standard for everybody else. And this is what Baryshnikov, more than any other dancer of our time, has done—not only by what he can do with his body (he has, among other feats, jumped higher than anyone else, and has landed lower), but what he can show, in the maturity and range of his expressiveness.

—Susan Sontag[2]

What is it in the falsetto that thins and threatens to abolish the voice but the wear of so much reaching for heaven?

—Nathaniel Mackey[3]

Desmond Richardson has been labeled "one of the great virtuoso dancers of his generation."[4] Having danced in a range of performance contexts, from the companies of Alvin Ailey American Dance Theater (AAADT), Ballett

---

[1] 1991, 32.
[2] 1987.
[3] 1997, 62–63.
[4] Dunning, 1995, n.p.

Frankfurt, and American Ballet Theatre to Hollywood films, Broadway musicals, and the tours of Michael Jackson and Madonna, Richardson holds a unique position as one of America's most visible and admired African American concert dance artists.[5] An expert in styles as seemingly disparate as breakdancing and ballet, Richardson has honed his ability in a way that has allowed him to traverse a cultural landscape ranging from the popular to the avant-garde. It is rare for a concert dancer to achieve star status—one he shares with the likes of predecessors Mikhail Baryshnikov and Sylvie Guillem and contemporaries such as Misty Copeland. Like Baryshnikov, Guillem, and Copeland, Richardson exerts a high degree of control over his own career and is unafraid to venture into commercial settings from time to time. If we locate the inception of what I term the "virtuosic turn" in Williams Forsythe's 1980 choreographies for Ballett Frankfurt, it is through Richardson that the 1990s' shift really takes hold. He has become a prototype for young conservatory dancers, as well as audiences of *So You Think You Can Dance*, which he frequented as a guest artist. Transcending boundaries of style, Richardson is an exception, earning widespread acceptance in the face of the exclusion of other dancers of color. Richardson's popularity exemplifies a cultural practice of consumption demanding of the Black male dancer the projection of charisma, athletic ability, and muscularity. As this chapter reveals, when viewing black masculine performance, audiences are more inclined to embrace virtuosity's inherent queerness when it is offset by such markers of virility.

Cofounders of Complexions Contemporary Ballet (1994–present), Richardson (b. 1968) and Dwight Rhoden (b. 1962) both danced with the AAADT from 1987 to 1994.[6] With Richardson as his muse, choreographer Rhoden created an explicitly heterogeneous platform for contemporary dance that sought to diverge from AAADT's dominant aesthetic of "soul," which privileges heteronormative black masculinity and narratives of triumph. Inquiring into Richardson's dual role as muse and co–artistic director of Complexions brings greater understanding to the type of virtuosity he inaugurated in American dance in the 1990s. I develop the idea of "choreographic falsetto," to place Richardson's virtuosity in conversation

---

[5] An earlier version of this chapter appeared as an article in *Dance Research Journal* 54, no. 3 (December 2013).

[6] From this point forward, I will refer to Complexions Contemporary Ballet as "Complexions." The company's name has changed several times, from DR2, to Complexions: A Concept in Dance, to Complexions, to Complexions Contemporary Ballet.

with a range of references, from nineteenth-century virtuoso musicians and composers like Franz Liszt and Black "post-soul" singers like Prince. In doing so, I locate virtuosity at the convergence of gender, religion, capitalism, and individualism. While Richardson initially attained stardom at AAADT, his contributions to Complexions worked to establish a queer, post-soul aesthetic that lingers in gender ambivalence. On the heels of Robert Joffrey and Gerald Arpino and Bill T. Jones and Arnie Zane, Richardson and Rhoden continued the work of other gay male-identified choreographer-muse partnerships that introduced heterogeneity into American concert dance. Certainly, the Bill T. Jones/Arnie Zane Company has been more vocal about confronting homosexuality in its work (which emerged in an experimental domain far from the confines of ballet), whereas Joffrey Ballet and Complexions—even while fostering queer aesthetics—have sustained traditional heterosexual *pas de deux* pairings carried over from classical ballet. Moreover, unlike Jones's unmasked politics and use of theatrical and poetic text onstage, Complexions relies almost entirely on the dancing body. The company's heterogeneity is one of technique, not media. As discussed in Chapter 1, Richardson began as a B-boy, immersed in popping and locking in his childhood neighborhood in Queens, New York. His classical ballet and modern dance training did not begin until high school at the School of Performing Arts (the setting for *Fame*) and the Alvin Ailey American Dance Center.[7] While virtuosos throughout music history have also composed or directed, it was their performing that earned them the label of "virtuoso." Liszt, Niccolò Paganini, Wolfgang Amadeus Mozart, Michael Jackson, and Prince are but a few wide-ranging examples. A commonly noted attribute of such virtuosos is their improvisatory prowess—their capacity for tactical invention. Improvisation within performance otherwise reliant on composition not only generates formal heterogeneity but also functions as an essential mode through which the virtuoso stands apart from the collective. Richardson refines his brand of virtuosity through a diverse practice of improvisation within the otherwise formal confines of concert dance choreography. His improvisational style—one that combines ballet and modern dance from the "high art" concert dance realm with black vernacular forms

---

[7] It is now called the Fiorello H. LaGuardia High School of Music & Art and Performing Arts. Richardson's embodiment of the endpoint of the potential, imagined success of Leroy from *Fame* inadvertently answers the question driving Mark Anthony Neal's *Looking for Leroy: Illegible Black Masculinities* (2013). On the other hand, Rhoden's first dance style was hand dancing (also called the hustle), which has greatly influenced his partnering choreography.

such as popping and voguing—has greatly influenced the movement style that defines Complexions' choreography. Performing on concert dance's proscenium, Richardson continually alludes to hip-hop's cipher and voguing's runway, sites that ever summon the emergence of a soloist.

Virtuosity

As dance cultures coalesce and intermingle, it becomes increasingly important to create discourse around virtuosity, highlighting the term's own exclusions while paying heed to culturally specific contexts of production. Discourses of virtuosity are linked to connotations of excess, and an examination of the formal and sociocultural aspects of virtuosic performance reveals underrecognized heterogeneity in which we detect vernacular influences on "high art." Class-based perspectives maintain virtuosity's instability, as virtuosity is applauded when seen to further "high art" but condemned when deployed in popular or lowbrow settings.[8] Whether applauded or criticized, the virtuoso makes known a great deal about cultural taste. The curious relationship between disciplined perceptions of virtuosity's excess and the disciplin*ing* of the racialized body is such that audiences are often taught to be weary of abundant movement while simultaneously expecting it of Black dancers. In increasingly heterogeneous societies, taste (and its omissions and repulsions) can evidence a lack of exposure to the same degree that it can demonstrate an audience's familiarity with a particular art form. Virtuosity simultaneously defines and obscures the border between popular and high art. Any disdain for the virtuoso occurs in opposition to another beholder's celebration. The virtuoso, ever idiosyncratic and often marginal, is never wholly abject. Because Richardson's virtuosity is predicated on a gendered, heterogeneous combination of dance forms emerging from multiple historical and cultural contexts, from classical ballet to hip-hop, it deserves to be analyzed through scholarship deriving from—and commenting on—various eras of performance, especially nineteenth-century Europe and the contemporary US.

---

[8] To give you an idea of how Complexions' audiences are painted (by the *New York Times*) as uneducated, consider the following excerpt from a performance review: the work "never adds up to anything much, but it's pleasant enough to watch and, like everything else on this program, well danced. For Complexions' cheering audience, that is apparently enough" (Sulcas, 2008, n.p.).

82 BODY IMPOSSIBLE

From the beginning, popular and critical reception of Complexions has been defined by extremes: the remake of the film *Fame* (2009) cited Complexions as "the best dance company in the world,"[9] while *Time Out New York* placed the company on its "Worst of 2009" list.[10] Over the past decade and a half, the *New York Times* has repeatedly lambasted Complexions' choreography while reserving just enough breath to hail Richardson as "the saving grace of this company."[11] What is it that lends Richardson the power to consistently redeem Complexions' otherwise offensive aesthetic? And what kinds of choreographic practices have led Complexions from occupying a position of avant-garde experimentation in the 1990s to a space of mainstream appreciation after 2000? Richardson has been referred to by critics as "a welcome blessing"[12] and as "a dancer of magnificent stature, power, and effortless charisma who makes Mr. Rhoden's busy choreography look legible and even interesting."[13] The following passage is from a *New York Times* review of Complexions by Claudia La Rocco:

> The extent to which Mr. Rhoden packs—and overpacks—phrases, cultivates warp-speed delivery, and hyperextends every possible hip jut and arabesque is, thank goodness, something special to Complexions. The eye is so overwhelmed that long before this overlong program concludes . . . all you can do is stare blearily at the stage, praying that each whiplash partnering sequence or gratuitous split will be the last.[14]

La Rocco's resistance to Complexions reflects a widespread ambivalence to the very concept of virtuosity in the latter half of the twentieth century. It also points to a certain discomfort generated for some in the face of such virtuosity's seemingly interminable climax. Complexions strings together continuous passages of movement composed of what might otherwise appear briefly within another's coda. The legs sensually hyperflex, emanating from the pelvis, and the climax of heightened (and maintained) momentum coalesces with images evoking sexual ecstasy and exaltation. Thus, the unabashed sexuality of Complexions' dancing—not merely excess

---

[9] Burnett, 2009.
[10] Kourlas, 2009–2010.
[11] Sulcas, 2008, n.p.
[12] Kourlas, 2009.
[13] Sulcas, 2008, n.p.
[14] 2007, n.p.

movement—makes such virtuosity in this context especially vulnerable to accusations of vulgarity. As a concept more at home in the master-driven period of individual genius, the notion of virtuosity appears undesirable to many contemporary artists and critics. In its embrace of presentational hyperkineticism, has Complexions overstepped an unspoken line of acceptable activity? La Rocco's overwhelmed response to Complexions' abundance of movement mirrors Bettina Brandl-Risi's assertion that virtuosic performances can "provoke skepticism towards a form of excellence that cannot be reliably objectified with the help of prevalent norms."[15] A member of the Kulturen des Performativen working group that convened at the Freie Universität Berlin in the early 2000s, Brandl-Risi offers the concept of "spectatorial virtuosity," a mode of reception that "oscillates between expertise and enthusiasm."[16] Within Brandl-Risi's frame, La Rocco does not exhibit spectatorial virtuosity in the context of Complexions' performance. Brandl-Risi goes on to explain, "Virtuosity demands and generates evaluative practices that are based on excessive reactions. In this respect, virtuosity stands in contrast to . . . aesthetics that refer to the solid quasi-concreteness of the artwork or creative process as evidence for achievement."[17] Because it inevitably insinuates affective excess, virtuosity cannot easily satisfy established critical vocabularies, especially those that privilege the integrity (the precise repeatability) of the composition.

Studies of virtuosity have yet to engage with African diasporic aspects of Western concert performance and the co-constitutive sociocultural paradigms of race, gender, and class. Two of the most important characteristics of the type of virtuosity epitomized by Richardson are versatility and velocity. Thinking through virtuosity in the context of Complexions makes evident the relationship between ability, hybridity, and perceptions of excess in contemporary performance, especially that which eschews the supposed boundary between art and entertainment. Richardson's dancing embodies a virtuosity of versatility—exceptional execution and stylistic hybridity, both of which bring about discursive challenges for critics who are less versed in African American culture. I propose culturally contextualized deployments of the term "virtuosity" in order to counter assumptions of its universality, and suggest an analytic approach that accounts for the term's entanglement with excess, ambivalence, and a history of the cult of the individual.

[15] 2010, n.p.
[16] Brandl-Risi, 2010, n.p.
[17] 2010, n.p.

To distance the concept of virtuosity from its diluted colloquial uses, it is important to differentiate between ability, skill, and virtuosity, such that virtuosity not only signals inherent ability and technique (skill) honed over time but also relies upon charisma, generates excess, and deserves to be analyzed over the course of an entire work and even across the span of a performer's career. Identifying virtuosity is a curious practice of critical assessment. The virtuosic artist refuses to be placed into the realm of the vulgar, the offensive, or the transgressive. The fine balancing act of remaining just slightly imbalanced—an excess that is not offensive, an affect that hardly transgresses—defines virtuosity's precariousness. While the notion of individualism is fundamental to virtuosity, the virtuoso's apartness exists in relation to the group, always indicating otherness. The Kulturen des Performativen[18] working group understands the virtuoso "as a new artist type who, since the seventeenth century, has influenced not only artistic concepts but also the very notion of performance in various cultural, social, and political domains," and it defines virtuosity "as the potentially excessive enhancement of artistic practice," suggesting a distinction between artistry and virtuosity that recalls anthropologist Anya Peterson Royce's cross-cultural study of virtuosity in dance and performance, *Anthropology of the Performing Arts: Artistry, Virtuosity, and Interpretation in a Cross-Cultural Perspective*.[19] Royce argues that the "aesthetic of dance... is composed of two parts: virtuosity and artistry,"[20] with artistry referring to fulfillment of the work at hand and virtuosity referring to a barely graspable excess that cannot be accounted for within the work alone.

Rather than propose an exhaustive definition of virtuosity, I would like to call attention to gendered and religious dimensions of the term that have been circulating in Western thought for centuries, then proceed with a consideration of race in virtuosity's inherently nonnormative performances. The *Oxford English Dictionary* has charted virtuosity's expansive coverage of a range of masculinities, from the virile to the effeminate. Virtuosity's frequent associations with effeminacy since the seventeenth century tend to be linked to a "suspicious" or "falsifying" production of skill, an "excessive attention to technique."[21] The figure of the falsetto rests at the crux of virtuosity's

---

[18] 2010, n.p.
[19] 2004.
[20] 2004, 21.
[21] Also of note is "virtuoso's" connotations of (1) collection and accumulation (see 1700 example) and (2) suspicion (see 1921 example); "virtuosity" is often used in conjunction with the word

connotations of excessive technique and transgressive gender performance. Of note is the fact that the Italian word *evirato*,[22] which is a synonym for *castrato*, shares a root ("vir," which means "man") with "virtuoso" and "virtuosity." In contrast to the castrato's anatomical (surgical) alteration, the falsetto in contemporary American culture tends to represent a mature, sexually yearning man. The falsetto singer is posited as boyish, feminine, and inauthentic ("false") in European traditions yet hailed as virile or spiritually closer to God in African American soul and post-soul singing. Seemingly disparate, the gamut of these associations is reflected in various recurring definitions of virtuosity.

At no point does virtuosity signal restraint, unless applied externally to aesthetic systems that do not inherently invoke the term. While Royce suggests instances of virtuosity in non-Western performance and claims that it is a "necessary part of any aesthetic system,"[23] I prefer to interrogate how the term itself has been cultivated in European and American arts journalism, as traced by musicologist Susan Bernstein:

> The virtuoso is a sociohistorical figure that emerges within the confines of a specific history of music, of the economics and politics of entertainment and spectacle, and of journalism. . . . The virtuosi provide the cultural reporter with subject matter, while the virtuoso's success is a function of journalistic advertising and good press coverage.[24]

Bernstein errs toward virtuosity's derogatory connotations of cheapness and vulgarity, observing how it (particularly nineteenth-century European virtuosity) rests at the ever-troubled distinction between art and entertainment. Having been thrown about in the media, the term itself has been rather evacuated of meaning, prey to the "you know it when you see it" variety of signification. For Bernstein, performer-composer-conductor Liszt functions as the quintessential embodiment of virtuosity. Resonating with Brandl-Risi, Bernstein suggests, "Like the rhapsodic, the virtuoso is simultaneously the

---

"performance" to connote cunning or convincing of a suspicious/falsifying nature, and the connotation of collection and excess suggests that virtuosity usually refers to doing too much. "Virtuosity" has also been used to connote effeminacy (seventeenth century; *Oxford English Dictionary*).

[22] "(It.). Unmanned. 18th-cent. type of male singer whose boy-sop. v. had been preserved by castration. Same as castrato." https://www.oxfordreference.com/view/10.1093/oi/authority.20110803095803598.
[23] 2004, 21.
[24] 1998, 12, 11.

possibility and the impossibility of composition. Liszt holds the key both to its preservation and to its destruction, wielding the power of its success and failure, its existence and disappearance."[25] Richardson's multifaceted role as dancer and director distills what Bernstein suggests and what Theodor Adorno and Max Weber complicate more fully. Bernstein and Adorno use the term to describe both performance and conducting (and certain shifts between them), pointing to the virtuoso's power over performers and audiences.

Adorno mourns an era in which performers' virtuosity fulfilled a musical function—one evaporated by the virtuosity of the conductor, a figure fetishized even in his absence:

> Not for nothing does the rule of the established conductor remind one of that of the totalitarian Fuhrer. Like the latter, he reduces aura and organization to a common denominator. He is the real modern type of the virtuoso, as bandleader as well as in the Philharmonic. He has got to the point where he no longer has to do anything himself; he is even sometimes relieved of reading the score by the staff of musical advisers. At one stroke he provides norm and individualization: the norm is identified with his person, and the individual tricks which he perpetrates furnish the general rules. The fetish character of the conductor is the most obvious and the most hidden. The standard works could probably be performed by the virtuosi of contemporary orchestras just as well without the conductor, and the public which cheers the conductor would be unable to tell that, in the concealment of the orchestra, the musical adviser was taking the place of the hero laid low by a cold.[26]

Adorno holds the performer's virtuosity (that of the musician) in higher regard than what he points to as the newfound "modern" virtuosity of the conductor—one structured upon fetish. The cult of the conductor signals the decline of individualism and nuance in the performance of orchestral music, bringing about undifferentiated performances and recordings as well as the passive listener—"radio ham"—of music listened to by the masses. Adorno points to Weber's 1948 writings on virtuosity and charisma. Weber's lament also privileges a more archaic type of virtuosity, asserting that "religious

---

[25] 1998, 100.
[26] 1991, 39.

virtuosos," very much in keeping with the anthropological logic of magic, possess the individuality and charisma to incite a local, dedicated following that resists the adulteration and lack of "musicality" of institutionalized religion. In contrast to Bernstein's virtuoso, who is produced by mass-mediated journalistic discourse, Weber's virtuoso lies outside the mainstream and harbors a marginal form of power. Whether situated in religion and politics or in music and performance, questions of power, circulation, and fetishism permeate theorizations of virtuosity. Weber's application of performance terminology to religion is not merely metaphorical: charismatic (religious) virtuosos include "sacred dancers." For Weber, charisma and virtuosity signal an individual as distinct from the collective. Such individuals possess leadership qualities but are not necessarily authoritarian or fascist, as in Adorno's "totalitarian Fuhrer." According to Weber:

> The sacred values that have been most cherished, the ecstatic and visionary capacities of shamans, sorcerers, ascetics, and pneumatics of all sorts, could not be attained by everyone. The possession of such faculties is a "charisma," which, to be sure, might be awakened in some but not in all. It follows from this that all intensive religiosity has a tendency toward a sort of status stratification, in accordance with differences in the charismatic qualifications. "Heroic" or "virtuosic" religiosity is opposed to mass religiosity. By "mass" we understand those who are religiously "unmusical"; we do not, of course, mean those who occupy an inferior position in the secular status order. In this sense, the status carriers of a virtuoso religion have been the leagues of sorcerers and sacred dancers.[27]

Weber's "'virtuosic' religiosity" suggests that, just as virtuosity can be a necessary component of the structuring of religious status, religiosity is often inherent to performing arts virtuosity.

The type of adulation showered upon Richardson resembles the religious virtuoso's spiritual following. In his book *It*, on the charisma of "abnormally interesting people," performance scholar Joseph Roach suggests that deity worship has been replaced by celebrity fandom.[28] Because dancers rarely amount to full-fledged celebrities in the pop cultural sense (as in, despite his renown in the dance world, Richardson will never be as famous as

[27] 1948, 287.
[28] 2007, 1.

Michael Jackson), Richardson's position as a dance virtuoso corresponds to Weber's religious virtuoso in terms of relative degree and status. Just as the religious virtuoso stands apart from the widely followed institutionalized religion of the masses, the dance virtuoso circulates less extensively through mass-mediated outlets than a pop cultural icon. Furthermore, Richardson's virtuosity captures the convergence of the word's associations with the arts and religion. Richardson has continually danced in companies whose styles derive from the depiction and expression of black spirituality in American culture. At AAADT, in pieces such as Ailey's *Revelations* (based on African American spirituals), he was called upon to depict personae in the midst of religious rapture or yearning. At Complexions, he and Rhoden often stage the conflict between religion and sexuality, the sacred and profane.

Choreographic Falsetto

In the falsetto tradition, there can be tremendous power, as well as vulnerability—a crack in the macho posture, the expression of need.
—Francesca Royster[29]

In order to do justice to their mission, the holders of charisma, the master as well as his disciples and followers, must stand outside the ties of this world, outside the routine occupations, as well as outside the routine obligations of family life.
—Max Weber[30]

Dancing with Complexions was one of my first professional dance company jobs in New York City. At the time, the company operated as a pickup company, reassembling when other companies were off-season. I can recall the stir caused by the company's few performances, which gathered dancers from companies as diverse as AAADT, Ballett Frankfurt, Philadanco, Dance Theater of Harlem, Dayton Contemporary Dance Company, and American

---

[29] 2013, 117–18.
[30] 1948, 248. Throughout his study, Weber emphasizes the virtuoso's status as set apart from conventional family life: for Weber, the virtuoso is at once nonnormative and in the realm of the spiritual and magical. For example, he also writes, "The rule of the status groups of religious virtuosos over the religious community readily shifts into a magical anthropolarity; the virtuoso is directly worshipped as a Saint, or at least laymen buy his blessing and his magical powers as a means of promoting mundane success or religious salvation" (Weber, 1948, 289).

Ballet Theatre and presented a community of virtuosos who rejected narrative in favor of an abundance of kinetically charged movements that felt futuristic and transgressive. Having initially trained at San Francisco Ballet, I found myself more suited to modern dance, continuing at Martha Graham and then as a scholarship student at Alvin Ailey. After two years, it became clear that the Ailey training company, in the words of one of my teachers there, "didn't need another Asian girl." Thus, I sought dance employment outside the Ailey establishment. Complexions was accepting of unconventional (dance) body types and more interested in movement style and creativity of approach. Reflecting on the company's early years, Rhoden tells me, referring to race, sexuality, and body type, "You're a misfit. You had so much facility, but you might not have had the perfect body for a ballet company. We love the curves." As a dancer, Complexions felt to me like the creative home I had never imagined, composed of a multiracial sensibility and a heterogeneous dance palette, and dictated by a demanding, idiosyncratic style that boldly disobeyed the ballet of my youth while simultaneously paying heed to its discipline, rigor, and lines. What amalgamation, you ask, bore a dance company that embraced a young, queer, mixed-race woman with a somewhat unconventional dancer's body and a love of extreme movement?[31] Herein I trace how, through Richardson, Complexions and its prehistory changed the dance landscape such that yesterday's "misfits" became tomorrow's prototypes.

At AAADT, Richardson was paired with Rhoden in Ulysses Dove's 1989 *Episodes* in a memorable sequence of masculine union and competition. With great urgency, Richardson runs onto an otherwise bare, darkened stage in a diagonal corridor of light; Rhoden follows him, halting their forward propulsion with a soaring jump (legs bent into a diamond shape, arms diagonally reaching upward), and they punctuate their duet with a whirlwind series of unison turns and cuts (contemporary pirouette sequences slashed by diagonal reaches and deep *grand-pliés à la seconde*). A charged, yet sparse, percussive electronic score by Robert Ruggieri drives their movement. An important influence on Rhoden's choreography, Dove's piece represents a rare instance of homosexual imagery in the AAADT repertoire. *New York Times* critic Anna Kisselgoff reflects the relatively closeted dynamic of the company, never one to parade its director Alvin Ailey's gay identity. She avoids any word indicating homosexuality while alluding to its

---

[31] I now identify as nonbinary and use she/they pronouns.

representation in a description of a later duet in *Episodes*: "A male duet for Wesley Johnson 3d and Dereque Whiturs fleetingly expresses a new relationship, but more so in pirouettes than in literal imagery. The heterosexual couples resume."[32] Dove has described *Episodes* as a piece about choices at a crossroads in a time haunted by the specter of HIV and AIDS. The late 1980s and early 1990s were a period of sexual and racial ambivalence in American concert dance history. The loss of life due to AIDS was felt on a visceral level, as many dancers and directors died from the disease. Even today, concert dance remains a relatively closeted sphere, one in which explicit celebration or representation of homosexual and queer politics is avoided for fear of audience aversion and funding retraction. Complexions moves beyond AAADT's suppression of queer and homosexual identity, and it does so mainly in its showcasing of Richardson's versatility—his queering of concert and vernacular techniques: ballet queers popping while voguing queers ballet. Nevertheless, ambivalence (more than explicit homosexual politics) dominates their aesthetic. Complexions' stylistic homages to voguing perform a recuperative function, celebrating a queer, masculine form built upon AIDS' losses. The word "complexions" in the company name demonstrates Richardson and Rhoden's emphasis on plurality and ambivalence—racially, sexually, and formally. Refusing to adhere to the label of a "black" or "African American" company (which AAADT still claims), Richardson and Rhoden allow for an entire range of racial representation while also nurturing dancers from multiple dance and sexual backgrounds. In his influential study "Black Masculinity and the Sexual Politics of Race," scholar of black diasporic aesthetics Kobena Mercer focuses on artists who linger in "the messy and murky realm of ambivalence, in which black male subjectivity becomes the site upon which a contest of competing psychic and social forces is played out."[33] Due to his ability to project both strength and vulnerability, Richardson is often called upon to embody such competing forces, which are further extended onto the ensemble in Complexions' work.[34]

Applied to Complexions, American studies scholar Roderick Ferguson's concept of "queer of color analysis" uncovers queer histories of vernacular

---

[32] Kisselgoff, 1989.
[33] 1994, 164.
[34] In this section, I inherently address Richardson's flexibility. I prefer not to conflate multiple senses of the word "flexibility." While it has become de rigueur to refer to contemporary dancing bodies as post-Fordist or "flexible" laboring bodies, I find it imperative to differentiate between chosen artistic professions and those of the decidedly nine-to-five (and/or "flexible") sort. Today's post-Fordist economy has harnessed concepts of "flexibility" and "specialization" for globalized, profit-driven

and concert dance forms and their coalescence at the level of composition. Taking his cue from Mikhail Bakhtin,[35] Ferguson resists canonizing heterogeneity, opting instead to discuss "material heterogeneity" in order to "expose the gender and sexual diversity within racial formations."[36] In other words, according to Ferguson, "Queer of color analysis has to debunk the idea that race, class, gender, and sexuality are discrete formations insulated from one another."[37] Inquiries into arts practices such as those of Complexions satisfy what Ferguson calls "inquir[ies] into the nonnormative components of racial formations," thus challenging "restrictions of normative epistemes" and moving "beyond identity politics."[38] Richardson and Rhoden live with a certain level of comfort in their sexuality in everyday life, but they did not until recently deliberately announce a queer identity in their dance.[39] While their choreography has been, at times, burdened by echoes of queer shame, Richardson and Rhoden's project is better framed through a recognition of their active presentation of ambivalence. The queerness we find in the formal aspects of Complexions' choreography (movement, stylistic influence, and

---

ends. Even "virtuosity" from arts discourse has been used to characterize ideal post-Fordist operation. Artistic terminology is appropriated by explicitly economic domains ("performance" is a perfect example), but that does not mean that when the arts reappropriate such terms they signify as they once did within their original arts contexts. We must keep in mind that a dancer such as Richardson is trained in a conservatory environment, ever willing to partake in the rigor and discipline required to develop technique. He certainly had the option of attending university and choosing an alternate career. Nevertheless, despite agency and control over his own career, his is not a career born solely of the goals of financial gain. Significantly, Richardson represents a recurring impulse in African American dance traditions—one that evokes, but is not identical to, Weber's "protestant ethic and the spirit of capitalism"—namely, that of possessing the "gift" of talent and of being "chosen" to dance. Certainly, similarities between the labor of dance and the labor of the post-Fordist worker abound and, without question, dance reflects and speaks back to the globalized economy at large, but a study of American dance practice has more to gain by drawing out the religiously inflected, spiritual dimension of dance culture. A return to Weber illuminates the inherently, if commonly overlooked, religious (and also racialized and gendered) character of the virtuoso. Although Richardson is indeed flexible (in the sense of sinew and loose limbs, as well as versatility), moving beyond the temptation to indulge coincidence and graft one meaning of flexibility onto another provides us with the space to shift from an overemphasis on the secular dimensions of the economy to rediscover Weber's solo figure of the religious virtuoso. Moreover, I find the term "mutability" (as elaborated upon by Anne Anlin Cheng [2008]) to be much more productive in terms of describing a widely trained dancer's versatility, as "flexibility" already carries such specific anatomical and aesthetic meaning in the dance studio.

[35] 1982.
[36] 2004, 21.
[37] 2004, 4.
[38] Ferguson, 2004, 29.
[39] There are so many nuanced dimensions to a dancer/choreographer's experiences or "identity": while the dance world is very queer-friendly on many levels, one does not exist in a single community or social sphere (one can experience relative acceptance in one sphere while experiencing prejudice in another setting). Also, Complexions' more recent piece based on David Bowie songs has celebrated queer identities, and men dance en pointe in the piece.

execution) performs a kind of magic, transforming the trauma of racial memory into a genre of affirmation. Rhoden states, "I think I'm making a statement of 'love is love is love' through the movement."[40] Poet, novelist, and literary scholar Nathaniel Mackey detects in Al Green's falsetto a similar insistence on love, one that emerges from—and transforms—a history of racialized violence: "All his going on about love succeeds in alchemizing a legacy of lynchings."[41] Moreover, by dancing instead of singing, Richardson quite literally embodies Mackey's suggestion that black falsetto simultaneously exceeds and reinvigorates discourse:

> Like the moan or the shout, I'm suggesting, the falsetto explores a redemptive, unworded realm—a meta-word, if you will—where the implied critique or the momentary eclipse of the word curiously rescues, restores and renews it: new word, new world. . . . What is it in the falsetto that thins and threatens to abolish the voice but the wear of so much reaching for heaven?[42]

In his extreme reaching and hyperflexible heights, Richardson's dancing beyond the grasp of the "worded" incites utopic potentiality. Rhoden's declaration of "love is love is love" is one of gender acceptance but also one of stylistic acceptance, encapsulating the extent of Richardson's range.

Just as Richardson and Rhoden have welcomed dancers of various backgrounds and appearances into their company, they embrace multiple dance styles in a way that lends the African American practice of "versioning" a sense of postmodern citationality. By developing the concept of versioning, dance scholar Thomas DeFrantz offers a theorization of heterogeneity that allows for a queer of color analysis that moves beyond overdetermined identity categories. In his book *Dancing Revelations: Alvin Ailey's Embodiment of African American Culture*, he extends dance scholar Brenda Dixon Gottschild's delineation of Africanist dance culture by introducing "versioning [as] the generational reworking of aesthetic ideals," or "a . . . strategy of African American performance."

> At once postmodern and as ancient as the hills, versioning is a way to tell an old tale new or to launch a musty proverb into the contemporary moment.

---

[40] 2010, n.p. Rhoden, interview with the author, 2010.
[41] 1997, 62.
[42] Mackey, 1997, 62–63.

Born of transplanted modes of African orature, it has given rise to decades of popular music styles and dances, from ragtime to hip-hop, from the cakewalk, a nineteenth-century parody of European ballroom processionals, to the running man, a subtle satire of celluloid superheroes.[43]

That African American performance has always commented on its past is a concept that reveals Complexions' multifaceted influences. Complexions' versioning is postmodern in that its citational mode is abstract and nonnarrative, as opposed to narrative or spoken. In Complexions, the concert dance forms of ballet and modern dance absorb and (re-)present glimpses of diasporic dance forms such as popping and voguing, typically encountered in subcultural or popular settings (club, ballrooms, music videos). Framed differently, the choreography can also be seen as an African diasporic reinterpretation of Europeanist forms. Because Rhoden's emphasis is on dance techniques and not popular narratives, such reworking differs somewhat from what DeFrantz describes as the parody and satire of much versioning. As opposed to humor, Rhoden's aesthetic is one of rigor and finesse, manifested by Richardson's command of otherwise very difficult movement. In rehearsal, the Complexions dancer is asked to mathematically insert, reorder, and distort movement while losing herself to a sensation of extreme physicality. Rhoden and Richardson's intricate versioning practice cultivates both precision and ecstasy, a kinesthetic alchemy of muscular exactitude and emotional intensity.

The founding of Complexions in the mid-1990s stages a shift in American concert dance from a soul to a post-soul aesthetic (one that occurs alongside other developments in contemporary dance). Precipitated by Dove's *Episodes*, AAADT's dominant soul aesthetic gives way to Complexions' post-soul experimentation, allowing for gender ambivalence and its formal corollaries. A scholar of race, gender, and performance, Francesca Royster astutely marks this transition in popular music, citing a departure from soul's heterosexual masculinity and "unified blackness."[44] If soul embraces Black Power, post-soul's post–civil rights aesthetic lingers in "blaxploitation" and individual eccentricity. In *Sounding Like a No-No: Queer Sounds and Eccentric Acts in the Post-Soul Era*, Royster writes:

---

[43] DeFrantz, 2004, 82.
[44] 2013, 9.

How has Post-Soul eccentricity been forged from the fires of Soul? Soul is seen as the aesthetic and philosophical embodiment of Black Power—an ideal of a unified blackness and beauty. Soul feels like a recovery project that centers heretofore suppressed black physicality and sexuality: Isaac Hayes's gold chains and bare chest, James Brown's hard-earned sweat, Angela Davis's Afro, the righteously bold stance of Pam Grier bearing a machine gun. Soul feels like the crooning seductions of Teddy Pendergrass, Roberta's warmth and Aretha's gospel shout. Soul claims its roots in the shared cultural memory of black history.... Soul privileges and polices heterosexuality and masculinity, and it reflects a Christian influence at its base (i.e., Soul's link to gospel), along with the embrace of a both sensual and procreative sexuality.... Post-Soul eccentricity, on the other hand, asks, what happens after the basic needs of family and community are met? What if the clothing of unity is too tight? What if the rhythms of the black body are less distinctly steady or comfortable? Post-Soul eccentricity draws on the contemporaneous development of the aesthetic of punk, which takes castaways and garbage and refashions them in all of their dirt.[45]

In voice, dress, and personality, the musician Prince typifies post-soul eccentricity. In keeping with Royster's observations, essayist Hilton Als writes:

Before Prince, black popular music had been limited by its blackness, which is to say its fundamentally Christian, blues-inflected, conservative attitude toward everything pushed in Prince's early shows with his backing band, the Revolution, and in his records: girl-on-girl action, genuine female empowerment based not on suffering but on a love of the body, a racially and thus sonically mixed world.... Prince's best songs, like those of a

---

[45] Royster, 2013, 9–10. In an important passage, Royster distills Michael Jackson's falsetto singing: "Jackson's voice takes us from familiar to unfamiliar spaces; he is at once nostalgic and future seeking, combining soul man falsetto and jazz scatting along with his refusal to fully occupy the space of meaning and familiarity. For example, we might link Jackson's falsetto voice to the tradition of the male falsetto in Soul, blues, and gospel music. Singers like Frankie Lymon, Jackie Wilson, Smokey Robinson, Marvin Gaye, Al Green, Prince, and more recently D'Angelo all use a high masculine vocal range and yet are often connected to (sometimes) heterosexual masculine seductiveness. In the falsetto tradition, there can be tremendous power, as well as vulnerability—a crack in the macho posture, the expression of need. In Jackson's voice, there were these aspects of the tradition, as well as something else—the suggestion of being on the verge of something we haven't yet heard, a spirit of fugitivity, claiming what Nathaniel Mackey calls 'the obliquity of an unbound reference' both forged by and breaking away from histories of black struggle. Jackson's vocal and often highly theatrical embodied performances capture the contrariness and resistance of the eccentric, pushing our expectations of gender and racial authenticity" (2013, 117–18).

number of black artists before him (Aretha Franklin, James Brown, Stevie Wonder), have always been an admixture of the sacred (gospel) and the profane (sex).[46]

Prince's break from the soul-inflected sounds and artistic choices of his early career to the more explicit presentation of the gendered tension between sex and religion in his later career (after breaking with his record company and gaining more agency over his own vision and career) greatly resembles Richardson's move from AAADT to his own company. The aesthetic correlation between Richardson's dancing and Prince's singing is rendered overtly in Rhoden's choreography at the end of the 1990s.

Choreographed by Rhoden in 1998, Solo is danced to an echoey a cappella Prince song of the same name. It encapsulates the crux of Complexions' work—its location at the intersection of sexuality and religion, race and identity, virtuosity and versatility, individual and collective. Richardson appears in a militaristic Roman flap skirt, evoking gender ambiguity, much like the choreography itself, in which Richardson is in muscular command of his grand movements while introducing emotional vulnerability through fluid sinew. Costuming aligns with choreography, and Richardson proceeds to undiscipline and rediscipline ballet's militaristic training; break and flow ensue. Calling to mind qualities of Prince's yearning falsetto singing, Richardson's dancing epitomizes choreographic falsetto: the deliberate use of otherwise feminine-identified movements in the service of a queer masculinist aesthetic. Brilliantly executing typically feminine hyperextensions with a sense of masculinist athleticism and bravado, Richardson performs what has become a signature of Rhoden's choreography: deliberately distorted *penchés* (in which the leg extends to the back beyond a 180-degree arabesque line and the hip inverts in a deconstructive treatment of ballet), sinewy torso movements, and effortlessly produced turns punctuated by explosive jumps. Prince's song lyrics are a play on words, and "solo" alternately reads "so low" in the lyrics' text, just as "no one" alternately reads "no. 1," echoing notions of the virtuoso as simultaneously abject and championed.

> So low, the curb looks like a skyscraper
> So high, the stars are under me
> So quiet, I can hear the blood rushing through my veins

[46] 2012, 63.

> So low, I feel like I'm going insane
> The angels, they watch in wonder
> When U made love 2 me
> Through the rain and the thunder
> U cried in ecstasy
> And U were so kind
> I felt sorry 4 all creation
> Because at the time, no 1 was lucky
> no 1 was lucky, no 1 was lucky as me
> And now U're gone and I just wanna be still
> So silent, I'll just let my senses sleep
> It's gonna be so hard 2 hear my voice
> If I ever learn once more 2 speak
> I'm so lost, no 1 can find me
> And I've been looking 4 so long
> But now I'm done
> I'm so low, solo, my name is No 1

Solo's calculated lyrics were cowritten by playwright David Henry Hwang, known for his interest in issues of queer of color identity.[47] In *Solo*, Richardson is at once confident and vulnerable, autonomous and subjected, visible and invisible. Paradoxically, the most vulnerable movements in the solo—rippling upper body undulations and the way Richardson's head reverberates between his hands—actually disclose the most normative of black masculinist vernacular influences in Complexions' work, popping and locking. The influence of Richardson's individual movement style permeates Rhoden's choreography. The pause-and-go interruption of inserting pops into ballet technique mirrors an articulation of subjectivity as that which is always already fragmented. "Liquid" transitions (championed in hip-hop) insinuate flow and mutability. In *Solo*, popping between soaring balletic leaps and powerful leg extensions transforms movements typical of heteronormative masculine posturing in hip-hop dance into a subtle exploration of queer experience. "*Solo* is about anonymity," Rhoden says, "someone who is grappling with himself and acceptance of who and what he is."[48] Mirroring the paradoxical nature of the concept of the virtuoso, here one of the least

---

[47] Hwang, 1994. Lyrics.
[48] Mendoza, 2009.

anonymous performers executes an abstract tale of anonymity. Emotional vulnerability is translated through a choreographic palette executed with tremendous skill. Moreover, Solo presents the tension between the identity of the performer and the content of the performance, which recalls the prevalent observation that virtuosity makes it difficult to distinguish between performer and performance. To stage Richardson in a solo is to stage the question of virtuosity itself—a concept most at home in the context of solo performance.

While Richardson's choreographic falsetto most resembles black post-soul falsetto singing, we find a historical precedent for associating the high male voice with virtuosity. In Europeanist thought, the dilemma of the virtuoso (as one who lends his interpretation a degree of excess) finds its historical foundation in the qualitative—and certainly gendered—ambivalence exhibited by the castrato. Similar to the castrato's embrace of the high end of the tonal spectrum (albeit via biological refashioning), the falsetto too lingers in high notes typically reserved for the female voice. Gabriele Brandstetter writes:

> The ambivalence which characterizes judgment of the virtuoso is related to [the] inability to choose . . . between the ethos of the interpreter and the artificiality of the "performance." This dilemma first finds expression in critiques of the castrato's voice—the virtuoso voice.[49]

Adorno also comments on castrati, bemoaning the decline of technical virtuosity: "In earlier epochs, technical virtuosity, at least, was demanded of singing stars, the castrati and prima donnas. Today, the material as such, destitute of any function, is celebrated."[50] Both the castrato and the falsetto singer complicate an easy division between the organic and the artificial, the "male" and the "female." Like sung falsetto, Richardson's dancing betrays a corporeal movement quality, on the one hand, and a sense of artifice, on the other. We are at once confronted with human and machine, as Rhoden's choreography intentionally lays bare—and glorifies—glitches that occur during transitions from one extreme movement to another. When Richardson performs such demanding—and typically feminine—feats, his exploitation of the mechanics of technique functions in the service of spiritual, otherworldly yearning. As Brandstetter states:

[49] 2007, 181.
[50] 1991, 32.

The virtuoso is a revenant of a different notion of art and technology; he is a magician whose actions appear to contravene the boundaries of the physically possible while at the same time concealing from delighted audiences the nature of his transgression.[51]

In this case, Richardson's "transgressions," the technically achieved yet affectively extraordinary qualities of his performance—those that exceed the call of the work—both conjure affective excess and conceal many of the mechanics supporting his movement.[52] "Transgression" here refers to technique and composition, and Brandstetter's use of the term provides an opportunity to note that artistic virtuosity's engagement with form merely indicates sociopolitical transgression. Like instances of contained transgression (as in the Bakhtinian carnivalesque, but different from, say, legal transgression), virtuosity can operate conservatively, maintaining the status quo.[53]

Virtuosity's pejorative connotations reflect larger sociocultural anxieties about technology's potential subsumption of the human. "Since the performances of the legendary nineteenth-century theatrical and musical virtuosi," explains Brandstetter, "the majority of criticism ... has been pejorative, so that the term 'virtuoso' became, to a certain extent, the polar opposite of the 'true artist.'"[54] Brandstetter explains that the pejorative notion of virtuosity is linked to assumptions that the virtuoso's performance is "soullessly mechanical."[55] Easy associations between the "soulless" and the "mechanical" are undone by taking into consideration virtuosity that works

---

[51] 2007, 178.

[52] Reflecting on the falsetto singing of Michael Jackson, an example of a post-soul eccentric, Royster invokes Roland Barthes's embodied concept of the "grain of the voice." As a dancer, Richardson would seem to lay bare his body and its muscular workings to offer us a glimpse into the "grain," the otherwise obscured "body" of the singing voice. Nevertheless, I would suggest that corporeal performance (the dance of the choreographic falsetto dancer) does not necessarily reveal more of Barthes's "grain" than the falsetto singer. Royster writes: "Barthes talks about the 'grain' of the voice—the aspect of authenticity that speaks of a combination of body (the 'muscles, membranes, cartilage,' the rasping of the throat, the state of the vocal cords) and its relationship to the symbolic: 'The "grain" is the body in the voice as it sings, the hand as it writes, the limb as it performs.' While Jackson's voice conveys the embodied nature suggested by Barthes' notion of 'grain,' it does so in a way that reconstructs our notion of a stable or 'authentic' physical self, particularly in terms of age and gender. In this way, Jackson forces us to think about the ways that the grain of the voice can be counterintuitive, and never fully describable or known" (2013, 120).

[53] Paolo Virno (1996) co-opts "virtuosity" from artistic discourse, using it to refer to politics, but in his work the performer/dancer functions as a mere metaphor. An engagement with Virno is perhaps better suited to scholarship that takes up performance and/or artists whose project it is to measure the efficacy of their work through sociopolitical change.

[54] 2007, 179.

[55] 179.

in the service of soul and post-soul aesthetics. In *The Black Dancing Body*, Gottschild writes:

> Soul represents that attribute of the body/mind that mediates between flesh and spirit. It is manifested in the feel of a performance. It has a sensual, visceral connotation of connectedness with the earth (and the earth-centered religions that distinguish West and Central African cultures) and, concomitantly, a reaching for the spirit.[56]

In *Solo*, Richardson self-flagellates and stretches for something beyond himself, demonstrated by high-reaching arms and soaring leaps. He thus embodies Gottschild's soul, reaching for the spiritual while still situated within the realm of the earthly, but ventures into Complexions' characteristic post-soul theme of the lone figure in tension with the exaltation of the group or in conflict with himself. Richardson and Rhoden avoid presenting a definitive stance toward sexuality in such pieces, opting instead to leave the tension between sexuality and religion unresolved. Although he claims not to follow any faith, Rhoden attended Catholic school and has always been interested in the concept of "devotion."[57] Important to Rhoden is the "contradiction of religion plus sensuality," and he has "an appreciation for counterpoints, opposites, and contrast."[58]

Speed and Stillness

In addition to a demanding hybrid movement style, speed is central to Complexions' virtuosic aesthetic. Ever preoccupied with journalism's role in engendering virtuosic performance, Bernstein makes an insightful observation about journalism's and virtuosity's shared embrace of acceleration and speed. Commenting on the effect of the printing press, she writes:

> This escalation of print means an increase in the number of information sources as well as a generalized information acceleration—an ever-rising

---

[56] 2003, 223.
[57] Rhoden, 2010, n.p.
[58] Rhoden, 2010, n.p.

ration between distance and velocity. This acceleration characterizes both journalistic production and its consumption. The overwhelming quality of this acceleration is, of course, one of the most prominent characteristics of the virtuoso, whose technique often aims more at speed than at quality, mistaking speed for skill, difficulty for expression.[59]

While the speed of technology is often reflected in the aesthetics of dance, it does not hold that accelerated movement or sound necessarily lowers the quality of performance. In fact, the discourse of analysis created by Gottschild accounts for diasporic influences of highly kinetic choreography. Centering on dance in the US—more than on transnational circulations of movement style—Gottschild argues that Africanist aesthetics embrace the idea that "the universe is in a dynamic process-in-motion, not a static entity."[60] Somewhat opposed to Weber's Protestant ethic of efficiency, Africanist aesthetics embrace movement, even if it does not contribute to—or represent—maximum capitalist productivity.[61] The politics behind Gottschild's discussion of speed in Africanist aesthetics are such that, while historically, Black performers' sense of speed may have had much to do with "traditional West African [religion and sacred principles] brought to the New World in the Middle Passage," all Americans are inherently implicated in Africanist culture: it is "not a choice," states Gottschild, "but an imperative that comes to us through the culture."[62]

The impulse behind a privileging of stillness in much contemporary dance and its scholarship can be found in the 1960s Judson Dance Theater. While not commenting directly on speed, Yvonne Rainer famously proclaims in her "No Manifesto" (1965), "No to virtuosity!" Although it was written for a particular piece and represents a certain phase of Judson, many have latched onto the manifesto's imperatives as representative of Judson's aggregate aesthetic. Calling for a choreography that works against capitalism's speed and motion, Lepecki writes, "Modernity creates its kinetic being based on a

---

[59] Bernstein, 1998, 15. Furthermore, we can make a poignant link between the "falsetto" and what Bernstein calls "falsification" or plagiarism in journalism: "Sensationalism, plagiarism, manipulation, and falsification are standard stylistic traits of the expanding competitive market for printed matter" (Bernstein, 1998, 15).
[60] 1996, 11.
[61] An argument could be made for an aesthetic corollary to economist Joseph Schumpeter's (2003) concept of "creative destruction" (and a compulsion toward the new in hyperkinetic choreography). How might diasporic choreography not associated with the experimental or avant-garde represent a preoccupation with the new that differs from that of the (experimental or) avant-garde?
[62] 1996, 5.

primary 'accumulation of subjectivity'.... The intrusion of the still in choreography (the still-act) initiates a direct ontopolitical critique of modernity's relentless kinetic interpellation of the subject."[63] Lepecki is informed by German scholar Peter Sloterdijk's *La Mobilisation infinite*, which examines automobiles and traffic in a study of modern movement. In such contexts, regardless of the speed of the vehicle, the human body is virtually still. For Sloterdijk, speed functions as the dominant mode of late capitalism in the context of the body's very stasis. To be clear, Lepecki does not equate stillness with stasis. If we follow Lepecki's formulation that stillness is a choice to move very little or to focus on attention and intensity, we can assume that stasis is, rather, a condition born not of agency but of its very absence. Not necessarily a slowing or a stillness, stasis seems to indicate an inability to incite dynamic change, regardless of speed. Analysis of the contemporary dancer requires a different type of attention to motion and agency than that of the automobile. For the most part, the dancing body is a locus of self-dynamism; unlike the automobile, it is not a dynamism produced by a relation between agent and object. In this respect, the contemporary dancing body is not an automobile; it is auto-mobility.

Jerome Bel evokes what Lepecki calls "choreography's slower ontology."[64] In pieces such as *Jerome Bel* (1995), performers stand onstage in the nude for long periods of time; in *The Show Must Go On* (2001), Bel pairs mass-mediated pop songs and musical show tunes with self-consciously antichoreographic nondance, bringing attention to popular entertainment's failed attempts to represent political movements. Lepecki writes, "Bel ... deploys stillness and slowness to propose how movement is not only a question of kinetics but also one of intensities, of generating an intensive field of microperceptions."[65] Lepecki's concept of "microperceptions" seems to resonate with Brandl-Risi's discussion of the "spectatorial" and difficulties associated more with reception than performance. Furthermore, when paired with "intensities," "microperceptions" (by indicating the impression of minute, barely perceptible movements) point to the internal—the idea that movement could be occurring within the body, unavailable to audience perception. To think of Complexions' hyperkinetic aesthetic in terms of what could be called "hyperperceptions" is to discover that, like stillness, kinetic abundance can also constitute "intensities" that skew audience perception. Requiring

[63] 2006, 58.
[64] 2006, 45.
[65] 2006, 57.

spectatorial virtuosity, hyperperception wholly externalizes the otherwise internal movements or energetics of the microperceived. Ultimately, hyperkinetic choreography such as that of Complexions can also challenge the viewer in generative ways. Rhoden's work brings to light the paradoxical invisibilizing effect of the black body's hypervisibility, echoing art historian Krista Thompson's provocation, "How might the hyper-visibility of bling be another instance of the disappearance of the black subject, a new form of emblazoned invisibility?"[66] We might venture to think of Rhoden's choreography as an experimentation with bling's (otherwise visual) kinesthetic counterpoint, commoditized visual excess aestheticized in motion. Lepecki's "intensities," then, shift from the performer to the viewer's perception.

Furthermore, it is important to reassess Lepecki's argument through a consideration of modernity's simultaneous limiting of movement for those whose agency is most compromised.[67] In other words, the legacy of slavery in the US is such that choreographic qualities like restlessness and kineticism have their aesthetic foundations in diasporic dance traditions as well as in the trope of escape. For American dancers working in the African diaspora, highly kinetic choreography draws from traditions that aestheticize a resistance to stasis or capture. Thus, aesthetics of speed also have the potential to stage what Lepecki calls an "ontopolitical critique." Bel has called himself an artist whose "work is not danced but . . . is about dance."[68] Thus, if current experimental and avant-garde dance following in the tradition of the Judson Dance Theater claims to be dance about dance, a piece such as *Solo* stages virtuosity about virtuosity. For his attention to the phenomenological aspect of dancing—how it feels to dance at the limits of one's technique and expression—Rhoden is often called "a dancer's choreographer." We detect an ontological difference between these two reflexive modes—Bel's dance about dance and Rhoden's virtuosity about virtuosity. Essayist Susan Sontag's 1987

---

[66] 2009, n.p.

[67] Here I remind you of the epigraph that opens this book's Introduction: "Flung out and dispersed in the Diaspora, one has a sense of being touched by or glimpsed from this door. As if walking down the street someone touches you on the shoulder but when you look around there is no one, yet the air is oddly warm with some live presence. That touch is full of ambivalence; it is partly comforting but mostly discomforting, tortured, burning with angered, unknowable remembrance. More disturbing, it does not confine itself to remembrance; you look around you and present embraces are equally discomforting, present glimpses are equally hostile. Art, perhaps music, perhaps poetry, perhaps stories, perhaps aching constant movement—dance and speed—are the only comforts. Being in the Diaspora braces itself in virtuosity or despair" (Dionne Brand, *A Map to the Door of No Return*, Toronto: Vintage Canada, 26).

[68] 2009b, n.p.

musing "Dancer and the Dance" discloses a certain ontological view of the dancer that continues to define the basis of Richardson's virtuosity and much concert dance that lies outside the influence of the Judson Dance Theater. Preoccupied with the meeting point of high and low art, Sontag addresses virtuosity and the figure of the soloist dancer, as follows:

> Dance cannot exist without dance design: choreography. But dance is the dancer. The relation of dancer to choreographer is not just that of executant or performer to auteur—which, however creative, however inspired the performer, is still a subservient relation. Though a performer in this sense, too, the dancer is also more than a performer. There is a mystery of incarnation in dance that has no analogue in the other performing arts. A great dancer is not just performing (a role) but being (a dancer). Someone can be the greatest Odette/Odile, the greatest Albrecht one has ever seen—as a singer can be the best (in anyone's memory) Tosca or Boris or Carmen or Sieglinde or Don Giovanni; or an actor can be the finest Nora or Hamlet or Faust or Phaedra or Winnie. But beyond the already grandiose aim of giving the definitive performance of a work, a role, a score, there is a further, even higher standard which applies to dancers in a way I think does not apply to singers or actors or musicians. One can be not just the best performer of certain roles but the most complete exhibit of what it is to be a dancer. And this Baryshnikov is in our time.[69]

With Baryshnikov as her example, Sontag distills the ontology that makes virtuosity possible in the first place: the dancer is not simply a person onstage (as Bel would have it) but only ever a dancer, before, during, and after performance. In this configuration, the dancer cannot shed her identity as a dancer, and is therefore inherently attached to her technique, her accumulation of—and continually performed practice of—discipline. Unlike Bel's everyday person who happens to find herself onstage, Sontag's dancer is steeped in rigor: she cannot be reduced to a person who knows no more than quotidian habitus, unadulterated by the refinements and flourishes of presentational technique. When Sontag writes, "There is a mystery of incarnation in dance that has no analogue in the other performing arts," she points to what is alternately referred to as liveness, presence, or *mana*. Roach has likened the contemporary charisma of celebrity to Durkheimian *mana* (or

[69] Sontag, 1987, n.p.

force), which is also evoked in Weber's religious virtuoso. The virtuoso who possesses the "it" quality often exists on the periphery of social acceptability. Roach claims there is "often a social apartness [of] those who possess ['it']."[70] Sontag's statement that "dance is the dancer" holds even more weight when applied to abstract nonnarrative dance such as Richardson's that is movement (not character) driven. Another important distinction between these two modes is that Rhoden's "claim" is implicit, not buttressed by the discursive outlets upon which Bel's aesthetic hinges. In interviews, Rhoden is more likely to express an appreciation for dance and a celebration of Richardson, as opposed to an analysis or rationale of his own work. The performance of reflexivity in and around Bel's work is rendered latent in Rhoden's work.

The title of Lepecki's book, *Exhausting Dance*, refers to the idea of stepping beyond dance's habitual compulsion to move—to look beyond what is typically thought of as "dance." However, for Complexions to linger in the type of movement that actually exhausts the performer is to extend and revise the Africanist embrace of motion found in AAADT's trope of overcoming adversity. We detect in Richardson's choreographic falsetto a refusal to submit to exhaustion, to nondance. In terms of temporality, this compels us to ask, does exhaustion mark the moment after virtuosity or does it precede it? In other words, would one have had to experience the pursuit of virtuosity before admitting exhaustion and embracing stillness? It would be impossible to propose such inquiries without keeping in mind Mackey's suggestion of falsetto's redemptive function in black performance. When Complexions stages movement so kinetic and technically demanding that it continually tests the limits of exhaustion, the work comments on the labor through which virtuosic concert dance is produced. Whereas Lepecki calls for the exhaustion of narrative, kinetic dance (epitomized by AAADT or American Ballet Theatre), Rhoden abstracts and exaggerates formal aspects of such choreography, adding to an already accumulative aesthetic. Bel's stillness represents a reaction in a minimalist vein; Rhoden's hyperkineticism represents a reaction in a maximalist extreme. Both are different ways of provoking the viewer to reflect about the structure and function of dance; both are conducting a meta-critique about the form that they are simultaneously enacting. Paradoxically, in a refusal to stage such challenging ensemble choreography, contemporary dance artists advocating for an aesthetics of stillness can end up capitulating to the very type of high capitalist obsession

---

[70] 2007, 11.

with the individual that it eschews. If, as dance critic Roslyn Sulcas[71] says, Complexions' works "are hyperkinetic, flashy exhibitions of physical prowess that mostly scream one thing: 'Look at me up here with my fabulous body doing fabulous things!' " then what of Bel's nude body, penis exposed, facing the audience? Bel, though by different (unaccompanied and unadorned) means, also screams, "Look at me!" By simply presenting the body as an object in the vein of Rainer's Judson aesthetics, Bel calls attention to the theatricality of the performing body's presence in relationship to the audience. If Sulcas suggests that Complexions' dancers invite a relationship of attraction, Bel, after Rainer, invites the viewer to pay heed to her own habits of viewership. Composed of an ensemble of performers all supposedly begging their audience to "Look at [my] fabulous body doing fabulous things," Complexions' group pieces place multiplied demands on the viewer. The viewer is unable to grasp the entirety of activity onstage, cutting back and forth between watching individual dancers and group passages. Thus, the work dictates an act of viewing that is both one of attraction (as in "Look at me!") and one of ontology (as in "Look at me in relationship to yourself, and take note of our coexisting subjectivities").

As Ferguson[72] has suggested, a queer of color analysis interrogates the "nonnormative components of racial formations," and it is precisely by examining the nonnormative—queer and raced, and queerly raced—components of choreographic formations that I am able to propose an alternative to the argument that an "ontopolitical critique" of capitalism must rely on slowness and stillness. As essayist and African American studies scholar Robert Reid-Pharr has stated, "There is no normal blackness, no normal masculinity to which the black subject, American or otherwise, might refer."[73] As a term that inevitably points to that which exceeds the normal and the normative, virtuosity lingers in ambivalence. Even though the ambivalence surrounding virtuosity generates a kind of excess that is already affectively queer, to situate the term in the context of queer of color dance exposes culturally biased judgments of virtuosic performance while providing the opportunity to generate effective ways of distilling culturally specific formal elements of choreography and its execution. After all, as Royster describes, post-soul falsetto's "space of excess turns out to be not one of lack, but an embarrassment of riches," and "these performances recenter the effects of

[71] 2008, n.p.
[72] 2004, 29.
[73] 2001, 103.

Figure 3.1 Desmond Richardson in Dwight Rhoden's *Moonlight* (See color plates).
Photo by Sharen Bradford.

Figure 3.2 Desmond Richardson in the studio (See color plates).
© 2022 Mark Andrew Images.

Figure 3.3 Desmond Richardson in Dwight Rhoden's *Solo*, Complexions Contemporary Ballet (See color plates).
Photo by Sharen Bradford.

racism and gender surveillance back to the body, yet a return to the body with a difference."[74] By defining and exceeding the demands of Rhoden's choreography, Richardson is a virtuoso in every regard, and his post-soul choreographic falsetto disrupts the common assumption that "virtuosity" signals a victory of the mechanical over the spiritual. To recognize Richardson's embodiment of choreographic falsetto in the context of Complexions' practice of versioning is to shine a spotlight on the virtuoso's excess—his refusal to land on any single domain of contemporary performance.

[74] 2013, 10.

Figure 3.4 Terk Waters in Complexions Contemporary Ballet (See color plates).
Photo by Rachel Neville.

Figure I.1a, b, c Desmond Richardson at the barre.

© 2022 Mark Andrew Images.

Figure 1.1 Leroy in the "Red Light" scene of the film *Fame*, 1980.

Figure 1.2 Desmond Richardson in National YoungArts Week 1986.

Photo courtesy of National YoungArts Foundation.

Figure 1.3 *Derrick Cross*, 1983.
© Robert Mapplethorpe Foundation. Used by permission.

Figure 2.1 Desmond Richardson and Elizabeth Roxas in Alvin Ailey American Dance Theater's production of *Rainbow 'Round My Shoulder*, choreographed by Donald McKayle.

Photograph by Jack Mitchell, 1989. Courtesy of the Alvin Ailey Foundation and the Smithsonian National Museum of African American History & Culture.

Figure 2.2 Alvin Ailey poster, 1989. Desmond Richardson and Elizabeth Roxas in Alvin Ailey American Dance Theater's production of *Rainbow 'Round My Shoulder*, choreographed by Donald McKayle.
Courtesy of the Alvin Ailey Foundation.

Figure 3.1 Desmond Richardson in Dwight Rhoden's *Moonlight*.
Photo by Sharen Bradford.

Figure 3.2 Desmond Richardson in the studio.
© 2022 Mark Andrew Images.

Figure 3.3 Desmond Richardson in Dwight Rhoden's *Solo*, Complexions Contemporary Ballet.
Photo by Sharen Bradford.

Figure 3.4 Terk Waters in Complexions Contemporary Ballet.
Photo by Rachel Neville.

Figure 4.1 Desmond Richardson, Francesca Harper, Francesca Caroti, Jone San Martin, and Maurice Causey in *Eidos: Telos* by William Forsythe, Ballett Frankfurt, Opernhaus Frankfurt am Main, 1995.
Copyright Dominik Mentzos.

Figure 4.2 Desmond Richardson, Francesca Harper, Francesca Caroti, Jone San Martin, and Maurice Causey in *Eidos: Telos* by William Forsythe, Ballett Frankfurt, Opernhaus Frankfurt am Main, 1995.
Copyright Dominik Mentzos.

Figure 4.3 Desmond Richardson and Francesca Harper in *The Vertiginous Thrill of Exactitude* by William Forsythe, Ballett Frankfurt, Opernhaus Frankfurt am Main, 1996.
Copyright Dominik Mentzos.

Figure 4.4 Desmond Richardson in *The Vertiginous Thrill of Exactitude* by William Forsythe, Ballett Frankfurt, Opernhaus Frankfurt am Main, 1996. Copyright Dominik Mentzos.

Figure 5.1 Desmond Richardson and Sandra Brown in American Ballet Theatre's *Othello* by Lar Lubovitch.
Photograph by Roy Round.

Figure 6.1 Music video of "Bad" by Michael Jackson.

Figure C.1 *Desmond Richardson.*
© 2022 Mark Andrew Images.

Figure C.2 Desmond Richardson and Diana Vishneva in rehearsal.
Photograph by Nikolay Krusser.

Figure C.3 Desmond Richardson and Diana Vishneva in rehearsal.
Photograph by Nikolay Krusser.

4

Difficult Fun

The Racial Politics of Improvisation in William Forsythe's Ballett Frankfurt

The whole point of improvisation is to stage disappearance.
—William Forsythe[1]

Blackness, in all of its constructed imposition, can tend and has tended toward the experimental achievement and tradition of an advanced, transgressive publicity. Blackness is, therefore, a special site and resources for a task of articulation where immanence is structured by an irreducibly improvisatory exteriority that can occasion something very much like sadness and something very much like devilish enjoyment. To record this improvisational immanence—where untraceable, anoriginal rootedness and unenclosed, disclosing outness converge, where that convergence is articulation by and through an infinitesimal and unbridgeable break—is a daunting task. This is because blackness is always a disruptive surprise moving in the rich nonfullness of every term it modifies. Such mediation suspends neither the question of identity nor the question of essence.

—Fred Moten[2]

By Way of Fun

Desmond Richardson left Alvin Ailey American Dance Theater (AAADT) to form Complexions Contemporary Ballet with choreographer Dwight

---

[1] William Forsythe as quoted in Heidi Gilpin, "Aberrations of Gravity," in Steven Spier (ed.), *William Forsythe and the Practice of Choreography* (London: Routledge, 2002), 122.

[2] Fred Moten, *In the Break*, 255, n.1.

Rhoden in 1994. The same year, he traveled to Germany to dance with William Forsythe's Ballett Frankfurt, returning to New York in the summers to work with Complexions.[3] In the US, employment opportunities for concert dancers of Richardson's caliber and versatility are often limited to companies with classical or mainstream artistic visions, and such companies rarely hire African American dancers. "I knew it was time for a shift in my last year of Ailey," recounts Richardson. "I put my feelers out, and Francesca Harper approached me about working with Forsythe."[4] Harper, whose mother, Denise Jefferson, directed the Ailey School, had worked with Dance Theater of Harlem before joining Ballett Frankfurt, and trained with Richardson during their youth. "I went to the Théâtre du Châtelet in Paris," recalls Richardson, "and after an audition involving much improvisation, [Forsythe] said, 'When can you arrive?'"[5] Despite his quick transition from Ailey to Frankfurt, Richardson had developed a taste for contemporary European dance much earlier, having attended the Internationale Akademie des Tanz in Köln, Germany, for two summers as a teen.[6] An expatriate who danced with the Joffrey Ballet and the Stuttgart Ballet, Forsythe is an American who found support for his contemporary ballet aesthetic within German cultural funding structures.[7] He was resident choreographer of Stuttgart Ballet before becoming artistic director of Ballett Frankfurt in 1984.[8] Forsythe is known for deconstructing ballet technique in the service of an avant-garde aesthetic.[9] His worked has ranged from neoclassical to punk to postdramatic. In the 1990s, his style was highly kinetic, intricate, and distorted, and often called upon Thom Willems's experimental electronic music composed of decontextualized chords and beats.

Richardson was seeking an environment in which he did not need to perform in the service of Ailey's overrehearsed, normative images of blackness. He also sought a context where he was not called on to fulfill the demands of underdeveloped, stereotyped "Black" characters or "Moors" (as in American

---

[3] One such summer between 1995 and 1997, I was dancing with Complexions, along with Desmond Richardson and the Frankfurt dancers he had recruited.

[4] Richardson, interview with the author, 2010.

[5] Richardson, interview with the author, 2010.

[6] Here I mean to say dance occurring in Europe, as we find that Forsythe is actually an American choreographing in Germany.

[7] Like Richardson, Forsythe was raised in New York.

[8] Ballett Frankfurt closed in 2004 (as the city government wanted to fund more classically oriented ballet), at which time he founded a smaller ensemble known as the Forsythe Company. While most opera houses in Germany at the time housed both opera and ballet, Forsythe distanced himself from opera, focusing solely on dance.

[9] This aesthetic has since been referred to by Hans Thies Lehmann as "postdramatic."

Ballet Theatre's *Othello*) or to satisfy the logic of tokenism as the only African American principal dancer in a major American ballet company. Like African American artists Josephine Baker and James Baldwin in Paris, Richardson would find in Ballett Frankfurt a creative experimentation afforded by transAtlantic expatriation. This space of experimentation worked reciprocally for Forsythe and Richardson at Ballett Frankfurt from 1994 to 1997. Both established American dance artists, they found different ways of redefining racial affiliation in the move to a European context: Forsythe would be able to further infuse his work with black vernacular elements of music and dance; meanwhile, Richardson would be able to distance himself from dance that correlated skin color with character or expressive style. In creating work that formally sampled and deconstructed racial signifiers, both artists lingered in the unrecognizable: on the one hand, German audiences may not have perceived American cultural markers in the first place; on the other hand, Forsythe and Richardson intentionally foreclosed the possibility of tracing movement's racial authenticity. There was a freedom afforded by illegibility, and their collaborative aesthetic—never short on producing heightened sensation for the viewer—privileged difficulty, fun, and abstraction.

In mimicking the fragmentation and flow of Forsythe's choreography, Mike Figgis's 1995 documentary *Just Dancing Around* provides glimpses of the dancer's labor as it intersects with what Richardson refers to as "fun."[10] Here I recount a section of Forsythe's ballet, *Invisible Film*, as filmed and rehearsed onstage in the film: A hand slaps the ground: *bang*! Feet pound *stomp-stomp-swipe*, then *clap* from off-camera, downstage. A dancer slides her hand down the top of her own diagonally lunged leg only to skidder back upstage as if to try to escape herself. She blurts an effortful "*ugh*" between otherwise seamless movements. We hear the exhale of a breath (as if squeezed out through muscle tissue) as another dancer, leaning back on his hands, pelvis facing the ceiling, right leg stretched out along the ground, arcs his left leg up and over past his right side. Then, *bang*! Another hand to ground. A duet: *assemblé* into *passé* into a disobedient backward thrust of the butt into a toe *tap*. We hear another *clap* into a *developé penché* into a hinge back onto the dancer's partner, who appears just in time. Cut to Forsythe seated at a downstage table with composer Thom Willems and a music mixing board uttering to the camera, "Now doing the Handel actually makes sense. It's so completely wrong that any more of this [music] would be too

---

[10] Richardson, interview with the author, 2010.

much." Cut to a previous moment in which deep electronic chords and beats resonate through the staged rehearsal, theatrical apparatus exposed: lighting fixtures, sweatpants, huffing, road cases, taped Marley floor. The ball of a socked foot torques: *squeak*! The camera cuts diagonally to a dancer, the epitome of sinew, mass, control, and release. He beats his legs together in an *assemblé* as his straight yet dangling arms cut across space horizontally in opposition to his torso and lower body. He grabs his partner with both hands, arms stretched out, and swings her along the ground in a sweeping arc. He "pops" his shoulder into a liquid flow of arm movements that initiate an upward hip movement. As if disconnected from the rest of his body (yet seemingly emanating from an innermost corporeal source), he inverts his extended leg, upturning his hip, a simultaneous act of reverence for and defacement of classical ballet. It is as if the upper and lower halves of his body disconnect and reconnect, mirroring the relationship between this dancer and his partner. Out of this thread of unending movement emerges a *double coupé pirouette* into a brisk, disjointed extension of the leg reaching overhead: *clap*! This particular episode features Richardson as the latter figure who "pops" and sinews through the movement; it exposes Ballett Frankfurt's working methods; and, with "invisible" in its title, the piece self-reflexively comments on what Forsythe refers to as improvisation's capacity to "stage disappearance."[11]

Given the difficulty of maintaining such a high level of technique during Forsythean improvisation, only a contemporary ballet dancer of the most elite caliber could construe such activity as "fun." In the context of Forsythe's working environment, "fun" is most often used by dancers to describe a collaborative sense of artistic agency in executing a challenge.[12] In this case, the dancer's sense of fun does not mean that an audience is necessarily having fun. Indeed, what is fun for the dancer is often difficult for the audience. Richardson experienced with Forsythe a different sense of what it was to

---

[11] Forsythe's "disappearance" offers an alternative to and inversion of Krista Thompson's "hypervisibility" discussed in Chapter 2 (after Saidiya Hartman) because such hypervisibility is composed of reified, commodified images that get circulated in the media. In contrast, by demanding improvisation based on non-media-produced images and movements that preclude replication by the mainstream, Forsythe forecloses the possibility of the hypervisibility of the black body. As discussed in Chapter 2, Thompson refers to hypervisibility as "invisibilizing," and I would like to make a distinction between invisibilizing and what Forsythe calls disappearance. Whereas invisibilizing suggests being subjected into a position of oppression, here disappearance suggests a mode of escape, a resistance to capture and duplication. Thus, disappearance, for the black dancing body in Ballett Frankfurt, places the performer in a position of agency and control.

[12] Galloway repeatedly referred to the work and process as "fun" during our interview.

have fun than he had experienced at AAADT. As we saw earlier, the type of virtuosity Richardson cultivated with AAADT was geared toward pleasing audiences through an aesthetic of accessibility, representative of a mainstream African American tradition. AAADT's aesthetic is one in which difficult movement seeks to create an easy experience for the audience. Forsythe's brand of difficulty, however, is one that rejects accessibility.[13] To "just dance around" is to be steeped in experimentation. Rather than display effort, Forsythe's is a brand of difficulty that disavows it in some moments and plays with it in degrees at others. On "effort," Forsythe remarks:

> I don't think that work and fun are mutually exclusive. I think we need to dismantle the myth of effort. Don't believe the hype about effort. There are degrees. Effort does not mean one hundred percent [all the time]. There's one percent, zero percent, or a hundred percent effort and a big spectrum in between. Effort has a lot to do with skill and knowing how much and when to use; it [requires] statistical sophistication. And Desmond intuitively knows how to use the right amount of effort.[14]

"Just dancing around" and "fun" are, in large part, discursive performances of nonchalance that attempt to undermine the difficult, risky aspects of the work. Labor-as-fun both embraces and effaces the "difficulty" that defines both the choreography's execution and its reception. Forsythe's aesthetic is one propelled by a modernist aesthetic of difficulty, "that recurring *relationship* that came into being between modernist works and their audiences."[15] But in Richardson's body, Forsythe's difficult choreography will be made differently difficult by virtue of his location in a black vernacular tradition. While some Ballett Frankfurt dancers may insert difficulty rooted in classical ballet, Richardson draws from a sophisticated mix of popping and contemporary dance (among other styles), in addition to classical ballet.

As a poet and scholar committed to his own aesthetics of difficulty and opacity, Fred Moten offers new resources for situating this critical conversation in Richardson's career. Moten refers to the "rich nonfullness" of blackness.[16] As such, "articulation," explains Moten, takes place "by and through

---

[13] My discussion of difficulty here should not be mistaken with that of Jennifer Doyle in her work on the likes of Ron Athey and other performance artists and the "difficult" affect they produce. While we may share subtle overlaps, our uses of "difficulty" are largely divergent from one another.
[14] Forsythe, interview with the author, March 2, 2018.
[15] Diepeveen, xi.
[16] Moten, 255, n.1.

an infinitesimal and unbridgeable break."[17] What Moten refers to in turns as disruption and invagination, "the break" is the space of black performance, both the performance of *being* and the aestheticization and articulation of that performance through artistic practice. According to Moten, inherent to the break is its resistance to analysis. Just as a dancer would describe a choreographer's clarification of a movement phrase, Moten refers to clarifying analysis as a "breakdown," as in breaking movement down to expose its mechanics. In black radical performance, the break forecloses "breakdown," and what remains is "open analytic failure (the breakdown of the breakdown)."[18] Significantly, Moten suggests that the hegemony of the visual realm (in art and racism) can be rematerialized through a more expansive ensemble of the senses. Such ensemble is practiced and aestheticized in the black radical tradition: "the solo is an emanation of the ensemble."[19] At Ballett Frankfurt, the literal ensemble of dancers improvising together allows for the emergence of a soloist virtuoso, but, significantly for Richardson, it is the ensemble—of the group and, more profoundly, of the sense *and/as* the social—that allows for virtuosity's retreat into collective action. In his shift from the visually centered aesthetic of the soloist favored by the Ailey company to the collaborative, ensemble-based improvisation of Ballett Frankfurt, Richardson actively engages Moten's social-sensory "ensemble." While not part of the same project or era as the artists Moten refers to as composing the black radical tradition, Richardson's collaboration with Forsythe aligns him (and to an extent Forsythe as well) with black radical aesthetic traditions in surprising ways. Of course, a certain kind of modernist restraint is already embedded in an Africanist tradition, one to which Richardson had access before he met Forsythe. As Brenda Dixon Gottschild reminds us, the "Africanist aesthetic principle of the cool" in dance is such that "body parts might be working fast and furiously—or hot—in executing the steps, while in contrast

---

[17] Moten, 255, n.1.
[18] Moten, 140.
[19] "What I was trying to say in the book, and what I'm still trying to say, is that it's impossible to try and make a separation between what I was calling the 'ensemble of the sense' and the 'ensemble of the social'—and that notion of the ensemble of the social is directly out of early Marx, *Theses on Feuerbach*. I want to say that there's a sociality of the senses—which is a formulation Marx makes, *When the senses become theoreticians in their practice*—I was trying to talk about that, as something that is actually occurring in our encounters with art, and in particular with Black art. That goes against the grain of a whole lot of commonplace formulations people make about aesthetic experience, and about the place of aesthetic experience in the formation of the subject." "Fred Moten with Jarrett Earnest," *Brooklyn Rail*, November 2017.

the face exhibit[s] the detached, still life 'mask of the cool.'"[20] Forsythe's demand for improvisation onstage (within otherwise structured pieces) brings Forsythean fun and Africanist cool together, merging movement ideologies from Europeanist and Africanist veins.

Ballett Frankfurt's practices of improvisation depart somewhat from Gottschild's notion of Africanist aesthetics and refigure what Moten calls the "black radical tradition." Forsythe is an inheritor of the Africanist aesthetics of George Balanchine's neoclassical style of American ballet, which I elaborate upon in the coming pages. Africanist aesthetics also enter into Forsythe's work via musical influences of hip-hop and funk and, most importantly for the purposes of this chapter, via Richardson's hip-hop-informed improvisational style. Dance studies as a field has tended to maintain a barrier between studies of ballet and those of improvisation, and Richardson's work with Forsythe brings attention to a significant coalescence of ballet, improvisation, and the black radical tradition in and through dance. Richardson and Forsythe's collaboration is not without its racial politics. Racial authenticity and its related paradigms of accessibility and appropriation have continually haunted American culture. Due to its connotations of racial designation and ownership, authenticity is already a vexed subject. To rethink authenticity is to agitate complacent assumptions that certain artistic styles or techniques belong to certain racially determined groups. Germany provided Forsythe with the artistic space to subvert the racism and firmly held myth of authenticity informing ballet in America. In Ballett Frankfurt, ballet is not entirely the domain of white dancers, and hip-hop beats do not belong solely to Black choreographers. Nevertheless, one must resist equating the question of Forsythe's connection to black traditions with the question of what it means for Black dancers to do ballet. The historical power differential of oppression renders these formulations imbalanced. Deconstructing ballet technique from within with the use of postmodern improvisational practices, Forsythe's work allows us to think anew dance scholarship's habitual positing of dance improvisation in concert dance as either homogeneously white or inclusively democratic. Richardson's participation in—and influence on—Forsythe's work unsettles polarizing assumptions of contexts and participants of both ballet and improvisation.

---

[20] Gottschild, *Black Dancing Body*, 159. In the context of Forsythe's working environment, "fun" is most often used by dancers to describe a dual sense of collaboration and artistic agency in executing a challenge.

Richardson's collaboration with Forsythe reveals the complex relationship between improvisation as what Forsythe calls a "[staging] of disappearance," on the one hand, and what Moten refers to as the inevitably "improvisatory exteriority" of blackness, on the other. For Moten, blackness itself is defined by an ontology of improvisation. He sees this ontology reflected in the work of Black artists such as John Coltrane, Charles Mingus, Amiri Baraka, Samuel Delany, and Ralph Ellison and their improvisatory mobilization of "the break." In the context of Ballett Frankfurt, Richardson reveals how ontological improvisation in everyday life can coalesce with—or upset—assumptions and discourses of formal improvisation in contemporary dance. In Germany, Richardson's artistic experience is such that the improvisation of being meets the improvisation of being-in-the-studio and being-onstage. If Forsythe's improvisation is informed by the likes of Steve Paxton's experimental impulse of "surviving in a dance moment,"[21] not to mention his own invented modes, Moten helps us see how Richardson could make use of that improvisation differently. For Moten, the improvisation of blackness is an ongoing practice of improvising in and through the break, a rupture that can never be sutured: the "improvisatory exteriority" of blackness "can occasion something very much like sadness and something very much like devilish enjoyment."[22] Moten writes, "To refer to this exteriority, after, say, Artaud, simply as madness is no longer possible."[23] Moten's "exteriority," as opposed to an intentional externalizing of expression, refers more to the idea of blackness as being outside history yet involuntarily, transgressively public, no matter how reflective of the internality of the "break." In other words, the "break" is not a stage. The ontology and performance of blackness as working through the break are always defined by an irreducible surplus wherein irreducibility results in recognition for some and illegibility for others. This paradox—of externality as composed of internality and irreducibility—is mirrored by the paradox of Forsythe's imperative that improvisation "stage[s] disappearance." After all, Forsythe's concert dance works are made for the proscenium stage, the West's site of formalized *appearance*. Reconciling blackness's "irreducibly improvisatory exteriority" (after Moten) with Forsythe's mission of staging disappearance through improvisation, Richardson embodies and reinvents the crux of black radical improvisatory performance. The

---

[21] Paxton, http://vimeo.com/groups/contactimprovisation/videos/1731742.
[22] 255.
[23] Moten, *In the Break*, 35.

relationship between "sadness" and "devilish enjoyment" resonates with the relationship between difficulty and fun insomuch as both pairings indicate the emotional register of prevailing over challenge. Artists such as Mingus, Delany, Ellison, and (I would add) Richardson work in and through genres and/or instruments of the "master," appropriating forms canonized by Western civilization in the service of African American aesthetics and expressive practices. And even though Richardson's experience with Forsythe resonates with such transgressive reappropriation, this chapter focuses more closely on the apparatus concealed by the discursive function of "fun."

Exactitude: Deconstructing Ballet

In its title and execution, no piece makes more explicit Forsythe's sensation of fun than *The Vertiginous Thrill of Exactitude* (1996). Moreover, as an exploration of the dizzying "thrill" of precision in executing physically challenging dance, this piece undoes assumptions that choreographic fun is necessarily messy or haphazard. "*Vertiginous Thrill*," according to long-term Ballett Frankfurt dancer Stephen Galloway, is "one of [Forsythe's] most technically difficult classical pieces, and it was made on two African Americans—[Francesca] Harper and [Desmond] Richardson."[24] The fact that the *pas de deux* of *Vertiginous Thrill* was created on two Black dancers dispels biologically based discriminatory notions of the black body in ballet. Significantly, when Richardson and Harper look at each other while dancing this duet, they recognize each other as two black *selves*, entirely shifting the racially subjective relationship between dancer and choreography in ballet *pas de deux*. It is known as one of the most challenging pieces in all of ballet's repertoire. *Vertiginous Thrill* makes a point of utilizing a recognizable ballet vocabulary and is concerned more with order than distortion. Danced to Franz Schubert's Symphony no. 9 in C Major, third movement, the piece deconstructs classicism by placing steps out of their typically rendered sequence. If a *pas de bourrée* is usually followed by another similarly transitional step such as a *glissade*, *Vertiginous Thrill* asks its dancers to dispense

---

[24] Galloway, interview with the author. I interviewed Galloway at length about his career at Ballett Frankfurt with William Forsythe. I also had the privilege of speaking with Harper about her work and friendships with Richardson and Forsythe. Most of that interview material will be published elsewhere.

with ballet's familiar successions and launch into demanding pirouettes and jumps with very little preparation.

Stephen Galloway's groundbreaking work with Forsythe preceded Richardson's collaboration with the company, and Galloway describes Richardson's contributions as pivotal in shifting ballet's aesthetics and expectations. Galloway is an African American dancer who worked with Ballett Frankfurt for the entirety of the tenure of Forsythe's artistic direction. Besides mimicking *Soul Train* in his childhood living room (where he had to "make space where there was no space"), Galloway confirms that his only childhood dance experience consisted of rigorous ballet training from a very young age.[25] He grew up in Erie, Pennsylvania, studying with Kathleen Green and Sharon Battle (who had worked with Arthur Mitchell, New York City Ballet's first African American dancer) at Erie Bayfront Ballet before training with Jean-Luc Barre and Martha Rathaus. From France and Israel, respectively, Barre and Rathaus influenced Galloway's preference for contemporary European and non-American ballet aesthetics. Galloway was subsequently invited to study at American Ballet Theatre's highly selective summer program under Mikhail Baryshnikov. Nevertheless, when the possibility of dancing with American Ballet Theatre presented itself, Galloway feared tokenism: "They were preparing me to be this Black Prince Siegfried type of thing.... I'm six-foot-three-and-a-half." Thus, he decided instead to travel to Europe at age eighteen, preferring the work of European choreographers such as Maurice Bejart, Jiri Kylian, and Mats Ek. Within months, Galloway found himself in Forsythe's studio, learning a solo from *France Dance*, and was offered a contract the same day in 1985. Originally interested in dancing with the Stuttgart Ballet, Galloway explains, "Eventually I was going to go back to dance with Stuttgart and not stay with Bill [Forsythe], but it was *fun* and everything seemed to fit," recounts Galloway. "When I was there, there were eight people of color (five were American) with all different backgrounds."[26] As an exemplary Forsythean dancer, Galloway was chosen to appear in a film for Lufthansa Airlines welcoming passengers as they landed in Germany. At least in the eyes of the cultural tourist industry, Galloway was perceived as an ideal cultural representative, regardless of race.

Reflecting on Forsythe's comparatively radical casting choices, Galloway muses, "If [Harper and Richardson] had been in America, they never would

---

[25] Galloway, interview with the author.
[26] Galloway, interview with the author.

have been chosen to do those pieces because they wouldn't have been in [a ballet] company."[27] Paradoxically, the history of American ballet is forever changed via the employment of African American dancers in Germany. "I regard Desmond as one of the finest classical dancers," recounts Forsythe, "one of the most beautiful ballet dancers I have ever worked with. . . . He created that incredibly difficult role in *Vertiginous Thrill*."[28] Such highly kinetic choreography is made even more difficult by the exaggerated tutus (which look like flat, inflexible discs) created by Galloway. "That piece puts fear in every classical ballerina across Europe," says Galloway. "I've spoken to ballerinas who find it easier to do Balanchine's *Theme and Variations* than to do *Vertiginous Thrill*!"[29] Forsythe shares:

> I wasn't trying to make a statement like, "Look what Black people can do." It was because they could actually do the choreography which was incredibly demanding. I didn't even realize it was that hard until they weren't doing it anymore. . . . The rigor, the work ethic—that's why I love working with Desmond. The challenge of working with him was trying to find material that was adequate to his skillset. Desmond is perennially interested in everything. I don't think Desmond has ever experienced a molecule of boredom in his life. I asked myself, "what are the leadership positions I can put him in to pull my company further?"[30]

To grasp the racial significance of *Vertiginous Thrill*, it is important to understand the distinction between adopting Africanist aesthetics and casting African American dancers. While Forsythe inherits Balanchine's Africanist tendencies, he eventually exceeds them. According to Gottschild, American ballet (the tradition informing Forsythe's ballet background) is inherently Africanist and was inaugurated by Balanchine. She cites choreographer-anthropologist Katherine Dunham's view of how Balanchine became "the conduit for the (African) Americanizing of ballet": "'Balanchine liked the rhythm and percussion of our dances.'"[31] As Gottschild explains, "While the Africanist presence in modern art has received fluctuating attention over the course of the century, from the start the Africanist influence in American

---

[27] Galloway, interview with the author.
[28] Forsythe, interview with the author.
[29] Galloway, interview with the author.
[30] Forsythe, interview with the author.
[31] 63. Dunham was "referring to her own African American dance company and to their work with Balanchine on the musical, 'Cabin in the Sky' (1940)."

ballet has been tucked away in an interstice of history where it has been overlooked."[32] She writes:

> My purpose here is to retrieve the hidden legacy, the black text in Balanchine's Americanization of ballet. . . . It is clear that he was a ballet choreographer who worked in the ballet medium and subscribed to a ballet aesthetic. I hope to make equally clear that throughout his career, he introduced to the ballet canon Africanist aesthetic principles as well as Africanist-based steps from the social, modern, and so-called jazz dance vocabularies.[33]

Gottschild writes, "It's not the case that Balanchine was a choreographer of black dance," creating a distinction between "Africanist" and "black" dance. To Gottschild, black dance is that which works predominantly in diasporic dance forms and is performed mainly by Black dancers.

Research on Forsythe has tended to focus on formal issues (choreography, failure, improvisation technologies) and cognition.[34] Based on the lack of scholarship and criticism on sociocultural identity issues in his work of the 1990s, Forsythe is inadvertently framed as exceeding questions of race. This is likely due to the company's resistance to traditional narrative and literal casting choices. Forsythe's dancers are selected for their unique physical and technical attributes and their ability to improvise inventively, rarely asked to portray a character of a certain racial identity. Unlike the work of Bill T. Jones or Jawole Willa Jo Zollar, for example, the Ballett Frankfurt dancer is not asked to create discourse around her particular sociocultural position, rarely asked to comment onstage about her race, religion, sexuality, health, or other

---

[32] Gottschild, 59. Gottschild suggests four basic grounds upon which American ballet's Africanism should be assessed. The following are what she identifies as her "guiding principles . . . grounded in contemporary revisionist scholarship":
  1. Ballet is a form of ethnic dance (an observation made by dance anthropologist Joann Kealiinohomoku) and, like all (ethnic) dance, is subject to the influences and presences that are valued in its cultural context.
  2. Influences from past and present cultures are woven into, intermeshed with, and redistributed in any given cultural form (such as ballet, for example) at any given moment in time.
  3. The Americanization of ballet by a Russian immigrant, George Balanchine, shows both African American and European American influences.
  4. An Africanist perspective can be used to reveal the Africanist presence in American ballet. (Gottschild, 61)

[33] Gottschild, 60.
[34] See Gilpin, Hagendoorn, Vass-Rhee, Lambert-Beatty, Lehmann, and Siegmund.

markers of identity and subjectivity. Forsythe's works privilege movement-based as opposed to narrative or realist concerns. And when text or narrative enters, it does so in a fractured, fragmented manner.[35] It would be remiss, however, to assume that the absence of the self-conscious voice of the performer—one that tends to carry a documentary or pedagogical logic in, for example, Jones's work—signals an absence of conscious, complex thought on the part of the dancer. Quite the contrary: instead, the task of articulation falls on the dancer's ability to invent and deconstruct movement, during both rehearsals and performances. As Forsythe asserts, there is no hierarchy in his company; all Frankfurt dancers are charged with what we colloquially refer to in dance as "bringing it": "What you have to remember is that all these people dance as principals."[36] In addition to invention, a heightened degree of attention is required of the Ballett Frankfurt dancer.

Forsythe's relationship to ballet is such that he deconstructs the technique from within in addition to placing it in proximity with other dance forms.[37] As dance scholar and Forsythe dramaturge Heidi Gilpin explains:

> Rather than retrieving and reproducing classical balletic forms that are fixed entries in the roster of movement, Forsythe bursts open these forms so that previously hidden moments in balletic movements are made plainly visible. In doing so, not only are movement and form given a new life and a new set of possibilities, but so is ballet in general. Failure and falling, for example, are retrieved and revalorized as intrinsically necessary and equally valid structural components of classical dance. What Forsythe moves towards is an opening of the apparently immutable, because historically sanctioned, assumptions of his discipline.[38]

Like Rhoden's work for Complexions, such mutability from within ballet is augmented by the external influence of black vernacular dance vocabularies. Gilpin goes on to confirm that, in addition to making visible previously hidden elements of ballet, Forsythe indeed draws from vernacular styles such as breakdancing:

---

[35] In keeping with postdramatic theater and dance.
[36] Forsythe, interview with the author.
[37] Certainly, there are multiple styles of ballet—from (Italian) Checetti to (Russian) Vaganova—but for the purpose of this chapter, I will not engage in the subtle differences between ballet styles, with the understanding that the American style of ballet of the Joffrey Ballet (where Forsythe danced) is a mix of various styles.
[38] 122.

Although the Ballett Frankfurt dancers are trained in ballet (and other) techniques, and although the women frequently dance on pointe, it would be difficult to describe many of Forsythe's choreographies as ballet or simply dance... movement vocabulary ranges from classical ballet to breakdance.[39]

While Forsythe claims to have been influenced by Fred Astaire and participated in popular dance competitions in his youth, he becomes acquainted with African diasporic forms such as breaking, popping, and locking through dancers such as Richardson.[40] Such forms enter into Forsythe's vocabulary through the dancers' improvisation, and would likely not emerge without this space of experimentation.

A Sonic Break

Before embarking on a more detailed exploration of improvisational movement practices in Ballett Frankfurt, it is important to understand the role of musical and sonic appropriation and incorporation in Forsythe's rehearsal environment. To consider how Forsythe was specifically influenced by African American–derived rhythm and percussion, let us look at a detailed example of music functioning in his studio practice. To do so is to derive a sense of some of the Africanist presence in Forsythe's work. According to Galloway, "It all started with the music. [Forsythe's] working relationship with [composer] Thom Willems was amazing. They were creating scores (musically and choreographically) at the same time."[41] Richardson states that Forsythe "knows how to find the beat, and he would say, 'No guys, you have to find the beat,' and he would put on Funkadelic or something like that during *entreche trois*."[42] Galloway claims that Forsythe

> listens to rap; he listens to all of it because what he likes is that beat, that rawness.... I think he was opening up a dialogue. We [dancers of color]

---

[39] Gilpin, 117.
[40] Additionally, Freya Vass, who has been Forsythe's dramaturg, informs me (via research-based email exchange) that Forsythe often recounts a story about how he found acceptance in black clubs during his teen years, and that acceptance was based on his dancing skills (email to the author, April 1, 2011).
[41] Galloway, interview with the author.
[42] Richardson, interview with the author.

could have been offended, but not at all; I totally got what he was doing. . . . That music wasn't new to him. Billy [Forsythe] was always the soul brother number one.[43]

Forsythe explains to me that, during his childhood, he practiced black social dances of the time: "Whatever was happening was happening and we did it. . . . Balanchine is an influence. Tap on film was big. James Brown and Marvin Gaye were also great influences." As recounted throughout this book, several significant figures in Richardson's dance career have included dance artists of Jewish descent, namely, Penny Frank and Lar Lubovitch. In the US, Jewish Americans and African Americans have developed artistic and cultural kinship, often embarking on shared projects (and sometimes resulting in cultural theft or minstrelsy). While the music industry is full of examples of Jewish producers financially benefiting from Black musicians, Jewish-Black relationships in dance have been undertheorized, likely due to the field's relative financial weakness or mainstream ubiquity. Forsythe tells me, "I'm a secular Jew."[44] While he does not typically elaborate on his Jewish heritage in interviews, I find his background to be significant as it relates to both his childhood and his ensuing choreographic practices in the studio, as developed in this chapter. While Lubovitch found acceptance in black dance companies, Forsythe found refuge in an African American youth center in his hometown in Long Island, New York:

Back in the 1960s, I was being bullied and was called a "faggot." I was protected in high school . . . by the African American community. The African American community was small and not powerful. And I was also feeling not-so-powerful at the time. I was a short kid and as skinny as I am now. They took me into their youth center to dance with them, which no other white kid was being asked to do. I love funk, love Motown. I could dance and they realized I was being mistreated. There was some sort of solidarity and they said come on and dance with us. It was an afterschool program . . . in Manhasset, Long Island, in a space downstairs where you could dance like a club. I think it's different now. For men to dance now,

---
[43] Ibid.
[44] Forsythe, interview with the author, September 25, 2017 (different than other interview with the author).

there's almost a competitive edge because of competition culture and urban culture.[45]

Given the complex, lifelong influence of black culture on Forsythe, it is surprising that not more has been written on the topic. From a methodological standpoint, my hope is that this historical omission will encourage future dance and performance scholars to ask questions—to remain committed and connected to the sociocultural, intersectional realities of race, no matter how subtle or underexplored. Joining me in a conversation about Forsythe's black and Africanist influences and modalities and what we affectionately call "flavor," Richardson parallels Galloway's observation by stating, "Forsythe is a ridiculous mover—funky, musical."[46] In Figgis's *Just Dancing Around*, Forsythe appears in a staged rehearsal improvising to Public Enemy's rap song, "Fight the Power." In fact, it was Galloway who had brought in the song, and Forsythe used it to demonstrate the type of impulse he sought in a duet in *Invisible Film*.[47] According to Galloway, "That's how we used to do all the time."[48] "A lot of the vernacular influence was musical," says Richardson, "because [Forsythe] wasn't popping or locking." Hip-hop music, often abandoned for the actual performance score, was used in rehearsal to create a certain type of movement quality: "He took away the rap for the piece [*Invisible Film*]"—much of the score consisted of Handel—"but we kept the same intention, creating a great juxtaposition."[49] Africanist presence is there as activator of the movement if not explicitly there in the final performance.[50] Richardson claims that Forsythe "loves street dance; he rehearses to Outcast, hip-hop, then switches it up, but keeps the pops in the movement."[51] In its ghosting, Forsythe's use of rap is an *immaterial* example of Moten's *ensemble*. Later we will see that Forsythe's role in *Vertiginous Thrill* exemplifies Moten's ensemble in material terms.

---

[45] Forsythe, interview with the author. "Urban" can be a problematic term; it is the term Forsythe used at the time of our interview.
[46] Richardson, interview with the author.
[47] Galloway, interview with the author.
[48] Ibid.
[49] Richardson, interview with the author.
[50] Balanchine is said to have been influenced by the dance and music culture of Harlem (burlesque, jazz) and by composers such as Stravinsky who explored Africanist elements. In other words, he did not work with music in exactly the same way as Forsythe.
[51] Richardson, interview with the author, New York, February 2009.

By admitting that "We [dancers of color] could have been offended" by Forsythe's use of hip-hop, Galloway arrives at the crux of the question of authenticity defining the question of race in ballet. While his experimental compositional process affords his dances much spontaneity and his dancers much responsibility, in using rap as a generative source during rehearsal, only to remove it during performance, Forsythe risks effacing the cultural legacies maintained by hip-hop music. What happens when a foundational rehearsal influence remains but a trace in performance? On the one hand, Forsythe places radical trust in a dancer's physical memory, in their ability to retain a musical beat and transform it into corporeal terms no matter the sonic accompaniment in question; on the other hand, a diasporic cultural form becomes undetectable, relegated to ghostly status. Such a practice inadvertently reifies and reinforces the reliance on recognizable Western cultural genres and pieces, such as the Handel concerto that replaces Public Enemy in performance. Such a phenomenon might encourage us to question the political ramifications of theorizing the Africanist presence in the first place: What are the stakes of relegating unclaimed diasporic influences to the label of "Africanist" when such labeling risks encouraging effacement in the name of diversity, fluency, and versatility? At what point does the violence of "borrowing" overrun the supposed flattery of "influence"? Ultimately, Forsythe's practice of rehearsing to rap only to render it inaudible and undetectable during performance echoes his suggestion for dancers to leave their bodies behind, to make themselves disappear. These practices of removal, however, result in differing racial dynamics for different dancers and are not easily subsumed by a single discourse. Herein I explore how making one's body "disappear" through improvised movement contrasts with the process of removing music from a piece. While the audience is never privy to Public Enemy's rap in performance, they indeed witness the dancers' movement before it is left behind, left to disappear.

Improvisation

Although Forsythe employs virtuosic dancers, he challenges them further by identifying those qualities that made them exceptional and idiosyncratic in the first place, urging them to expand upon them more fully. In other words, he creates a practice of improvisation based on movements or flourishes that would merely be considered embellishment (or supplemental) in more traditional contexts of virtuosity.[52] Whether manifesting itself in a musical performance or a choreographic work, composition defines and embellishment supplements, and this supplementation betrays individuality in degrees only ever comparable to the entirety of the composition and its collection of fellow musicians or surrounding dancers. Improvisation, in contrast, places more emphasis on sustained inventiveness.[53] In the history of Western concert dance (especially ballet), virtuosity has been defined by distinguishing oneself from the collective, and improvisation has been defined by working within a collective. Ballett Frankfurt has not heretofore been included in what Susan Leigh Foster calls "genealogies of improvisation."[54] Forsythe's improvisational techniques have been theorized separately from genealogies that include contact improvisation figures such as Paxton and Richard Bull. To place Forsythe within a genealogy of contact improvisation is to complicate both the assumption of the practice's exclusionary whiteness and the assumption of its singular embrace of the pedestrian. By working at the intersection of classical ballet, vernacular dance and music, and improvisation, Forsythe's pieces create a space for virtuosity in the context of collective improvisation.[55]

Reflecting on the creative process at Ballett Frankfurt, Richardson explains that Forsythe encourages dancers to improvise according to "Laban's kinesphere and [Forsythe's] own alphabet and matching methods. I was there

---

[52] Virtuosity is often defined through the discernment of a certain excess, an embellishment of form that exceeds the call of a composition. In the case of classical musical works such as concertos, the virtuoso tends to be a soloist who sets himself apart from the orchestra by embellishing an existing composition. Such embellishment, while improvisatory to varying degrees, operates in the service of a predominantly scripted aesthetic: the virtuoso is an individual, an embellishment himself who stands apart from (yet must answer back to) the collective. Such embellishments might have taken shape in movements such as the flick of a wrist in a piano concerto or the insertion of an extra ankle beat (battu) or fouetté turn within an otherwise set choreographic composition.

[53] Thus, if embellishment is transgressive, improvisation is creative. Embellishment's transgressions are only made possible in relation to an otherwise bounded composition; improvisation is a continual act of creating anew. Nevertheless, with improvisation's unending creation comes its own disappearance and destruction. Therefore, the embellishment found in traditionally virtuosic performance exemplifies allowable transgression's function as that which ultimately maintains the norm. Improvisation, while subsuming the role of both transgression and norm in a studio full of its practitioners, is only transgressive to the extent that it is set apart from mainstream concert dance genres and practices.

[54] Throughout Richard Bull text.

[55] Nevertheless, I find it important to point out that improvisation in contact improvisation is quite different from improvisation in jazz music. Perhaps Foster makes too easy a connection between the two.

for the inception of the alphabet."[56] The kinesphere refers to Rudolph Laban's notion of the space surrounding the body and one's awareness of moving through that space. Forsythe's "alphabet" is a process in which words and their order correspond to certain movements and the phrases they comprise. In other words, a movement "was given a name such as book, ball, beard, brick, bottle, oyster, pizza, chest, crack, wallet, lion, atlas, faint, zebra. The dancers could then jump from one word to another, in the sense that 'honey' could give way to 'pizza,' because they are both food items, but also because they are both five-letter words."[57] According to Richardson, "[Forsythe] would say, don't only use your classicism, use different styles of movement, and orient it different ways. . . . 'Shift the room: the floor is up there, and you have two long pencils in your ear; you are writing your name with your ear.'"[58] While Forsythe tells me that Paxton was one of many influences (and not the sole influence) on his methodologies, their mutual embrace of reorientation is notable. According to Paxton, "Contact Improvisation constantly challenges one's orientation: visual, directional, balance, and where in the body and consciousness is positioned. . . . Contact Improvisation treats the space spherically, so you do not have the horizontal with sky above and floor below reality."[59] "My attention went more toward other dancers onstage," recalls Richardson. "With contact improv, you're not necessarily having to look. You have to listen, and you have to listen with your body. . . . Bill would talk about Paxton and say, 'This was my background in New York City.'"[60] By combining ideas from contact improvisation, Laban's kinesphere, and his own alphabet method, Forsythe creates a hybrid type of improvisation that

---

[56] Richardson, interview with the author. Cognitive dance scholar Hagendoorn describes the alphabet system as motor schema: "A motor schema is an abstract representation of a prototypical movement sequence such as a tennis serve or an arabesque. It refers to the pattern or the structure of a movement sequence rather than giving a full description of its dynamics. . . . This approach is one of the cornerstones of William Forsythe's *Self Meant to Govern* (1994) and *Eidos: Telos* (1995), of which *Self Meant to Govern* is now the first part. *Self Meant to Govern* is based on a collection of some 130 movements and a number of associative rules for combining them. First, every one of the 130 movements was given a name such as book, ball, beard, brick, bottle, oyster, pizza, chest, crack, wallet, lion, atlas, faint, zebra. The dancers could then jump from one word to another, in the sense that 'honey' could give way to 'pizza,' because they are both food items, but also because they are both five-letter words. The dancers could also take the last letter of one word as a cue for a movement starting with that letter: 'wash' could then be connected with 'honey.'" Hagendoorn, 225.
[57] Hagendoorn, 225.
[58] Richardson, interview with the author.
[59] Paxton, 178; http://www.youtube.com/watch?v=XrUeYbUmhQA&feature=related.
[60] Richardson, interview with the author. Paxton was "previously a dancer in the Merce Cunningham Dance Company and an active participant in the Judson Dance Theater" (Goldman, 95).

invites the chance occurrences that come of spatial reorientation and unconventional movement phrasing.

Dance scholar Danielle Goldman refers to improvisation as a "vital technology of the self... primarily concerned with *practice*."[61] Because improvisation is primarily a mining of one's individually generated movement, the self in this case is not conceived as a static entity, but in constant motion, inevitably subjected to—and subjecting—change. Richardson recalls the need to remain in a heightened state of awareness during such improvisatory rehearsals and performances, a space that allowed for one's individual emotions to enter the creative process.[62] According to Galloway, "I was always able to be me in the repertoire.... As far as improv, if I was pissed off, I could be pissed off.... [It would not result in] a pissed off section; it would inform movement choices." Thus, emotions enter into the choreography not through dramatic expression but through formal choices made under conditions that allow for emotionally charged experimentation. While improvisation might benefit from emotional experimentation from its practitioners, the viewer of Ballett Frankfurt's improvisatory methods registers its effects on a formal level.

Richardson engaged an already multidimensional improvisatory method, one invested in breaking, popping, and locking that reflected his childhood dance experiences. When Forsythe encouraged him to improvise, Richardson drew from these vernacular forms, popping with the same ease he approached ballet and modern dance movements. In addition to his committed interest in musical beats from hip-hop and rock,[63] Forsythe was interested in the way the dynamics of popping and locking informed contemporary ballet. As Richardson recounts of his hybridization of popping and ballet:

> The initiation behind popping and ... ballet is ... extremely similar and exacting. In popping, your hand must be specific, coming from a place and coming down from it. Transitions are the connectors, especially in street dance and ballet. There is air in the transitions. Bill said the good ballet dancers dance the transitions.[64]

---

[61] Goldman, 88.
[62] Galloway echoes such description of (and delight in) Forsythe's improvisatory working methods.
[63] Rock is a genre with African American foundations, however effaced or frequently forgotten those foundations may be.
[64] Richardson, interview with the author.

Richardson points to the complexity of Forsythe's improvisatory process and how combining multiple modes of improvisation invites both fracture and flow. If the imperative to connect otherwise disparate movements (based on words from the alphabet method) creates a somewhat jerky passage, paying heed to the smooth transitions afforded by ballet and popping inserts what a B-boy would refer to as a "liquid" dynamic. According to Forsythe, "For the art form (ballet) to survive, we need an entirely new environment with competing forms that are very open and require tremendous amounts of skill and rigor—like street dance."[65] Recounting his experience rehearsing *Invisible Film*, Richardson explains:

> [Forsythe] wanted us to have ferocious velocity, yet return to softness. My partner Stephie is extremely feminine, but I can be extremely masculine with force and power. He liked the dichotomy of that but didn't want us to . . . growl. He wanted us to . . . hit and melt, hit and melt. I stop, she goes down, I pull her up. That's the tension in between (Interview with the author).

On the performance of gender and sexuality, which can often be read through movement quality, no matter how subtle, Forsythe says, "I wasn't interested if the dancers were gay, straight, or something in between. It was just simply, 'can you dance, will we be compatible?'"[66] Richardson suggests that Forsythe's unique hybridity of movement modes results in nuanced gendered relationships in which men are given license to be "soft," to "melt" when partnering with speedy women who forcefully "hit" their movement. In fact, Forsythe echoes Richardson's observation: "I didn't care if you were masculine or feminine, effeminate or sinuous. Alan Barnes for example— what a phenomenal classical dancer with a completely unique take on ballet coordinations."[67] Barnes is also African American and studied with Richardson and Harper in New York as a teenager. The use of multiple improvisatory methods is what lends Ballett Frankfurt its ability to fold ballet in on itself, to deconstruct itself, leaving behind only a trace of recognition.

Gerald Siegmund refers to this formal "folding" of the body and technique as a process of rendering the choreographed body illegible. He writes:

---

[65] Forsythe, interview with the author.
[66] Forsythe, interview with the author.
[67] Forsythe, interview with the author.

The result of this turning in on oneself, of folding the body over, is an overriding of its historical text, which cannot be written anymore, an effacement which makes the body illegible. You cannot read these bodies anymore because they refuse to become signs in an economy of exchange.[68]

Much of the illegibility (if ballet is the "historical text" to which legibility refers) is due to the introduction of African diasporic dance vocabularies like popping and locking. Siegmund suggests that after *Vertiginous Thrill*, Forsythe's work tended more toward an "internalizing of space":

> They refer to ballet's vocabulary as a trace in their bodily memories, but they do not stand in for it. The dancers have absorbed the historical language of ballet into their bodies only to make it implode by undoing its coded relations. The moving body here does not so much create kinaesthetic space but rather internalises space, thereby imploding both visible space and body in the process.[69]

Siegmund is astute in recognizing the use of a classical "text" (ballet) to efface its own legibility through "undoing its coded relations." The idea of internalization would seem to complicate Moten's discussion of the black body's externalization, its hypervisibility, except that what Moten refers to as externalizing is a making-public in the face of exclusion or what Krista Thompson (after Saidiya Hartman) calls "blinding" hypervisibility. "Between looking and being looked at, spectacle and spectatorship, enjoyment and being enjoyed," writes Moten, "lies and moves the economy of what Hartman calls hypervisibility."[70] Richardson's career exemplifies such hypervisibility, that despite the prevalence of his image circulating in an economy of visual culture, audiences do not necessarily recognize his formal contribution to the work of choreographers such as Forsythe. This lack of recognition can be attributed to two phenomena, namely, the naturalization of normative images of blackness in the public's imagination and the way improvisation can render the visible illegible. While the former exemplifies the way visual culture operates in relationship to AAADT, the latter epitomizes Forsythe's work.

---

[68] Siegmund.
[69] Siegmund.
[70] 1–2. It is, of course, Hartman's concept of hypervisibility that Thompson elaborates on and I discuss in Chapter 2.

By performing with Ballett Frankfurt, Richardson subverts habituated modes of viewership in a global cultural economy of visibility dominated by easy correlations between skin color and performance style. In contrast to his earlier career, Richardson's work with Forsythe "refus[es] to become signs in an economy of exchange," foreclosing the possibility of reading his movement according to surface or technique that characterized previous readings. Richardson exercises a praxis of Moten's "Blackness," which "is always a disruptive surprise moving in the rich nonfullness of every term it modifies." "Such mediation," according to Moten, "suspends neither the question of identity nor the question of essence."[71] The external folds into the internal, the visible into the invisible. In other words, the presentational quality favored by the Ailey company is abandoned in favor of Forsythe's insistence on the demonstrative, movement that highlights itself as opposed to showing off a character, a narrative, or a canon of recognizable feats. Richardson describes the demands of performance quality such that "in America it's a little more in-your-face; in Europe it's very internal."[72] In Ballett Frankfurt, he explains,

> if you're going to perform something you have to be absolutely demonstrative [with movement]. You have to tell the audience ... how it goes so they're with you. They're looking at your exchange, how you are in and out of the movement, the articulation of the steps.[73]

The shift from the presentational to the demonstrative is a shift from showing *off* to showing *how*. By "presentational," I mean something like "I offer myself (or a character) to you," and by "demonstrative," I mean "here are the mechanics of movement—and their effacement—revealed for you."

---

[71] Moten, 255, n.1. Moten is astute in pointing out that "nonfullness" and improvisatory modes of art and everyday life do not necessarily mean a loss of identity. I include here Gilpin's claim that Forsythe's working methods could indeed force a "loss of identity." While I agree with her explanation of Forsythe's motion toward the idea of "disappearance," I disagree with her claim that identity could ever be lost, especially as we turn to questions of race in Ballett Frankfurt's repertoire and rehearsals. Gilpin writes, "Forsythe's strategies of composition and performance differ significantly from those of other contemporary movement performance director/choreographers. He is extremely committed to working within already existing paradigms of dance, even if he attempts to transgress, augment, and explode them in the process. Forsythe celebrates dance to such an extent that, at least in some of his productions, the body disappears. Although an ambivalence about the dancing body still exists for Forsythe, he plays it out in other ways: he displays the dancing body's dizzying beauty while at the same time forcing its loss of identity."
[72] Richardson, interview with the author.
[73] Ibid.

(no matter how complex or illegible the resulting aesthetic may seem). Thus, Richardson undergoes a shift in subjectivity from a "look at me" presentation of self or character to an idea of the self as creator/executor of movement. Paradoxically, such an eschewing of self-identity within the work in favor of the identity of the work itself results in—and is produced by—a more autonomous (and responsible) dancer than that required by traditionally look-at-me presentational choreography. Instead of steadfastly adhering to a prescribed (normative, legible) identity, Richardson is instead exercising his artistic agency. Within these frames, it is thus possible to see how an apparently restrained collaboration with a Frankfurt-based white male formalist choreographer could be experienced by Richardson as an exercise of agency. Agency, as it turns out, has been an important aspect of artistry to Forsythe for years; as it pertains to his recent University of Southern California college students, he tells me, "I'm working with them on self-reliance."[74]

To view Richardson dancing in Forsythe's work is to witness an "implosion" of both racial and choreographic signifiers, as Richardson disrupts both expectations of the black masculine body and those of ballet technique. Herein lies Richardson's unexpected contribution to a particular black radical tradition. If, as Moten posits, "Blackness—the extended movement of a specific upheaval, an ongoing irruption that anarranges every line—is a strain that pressures the assumption of the equivalence of personhood and subjectivity,"[75] it is, paradoxically, through nonrepresentational choreographic action that Richardson sutures the rupture between "personhood and subjectivity" that has historically defined blackness. To observe Richardson in Ballett Frankfurt is to observe a person (not merely a personality) making decisions—kinesthetically, spatially, rhythmically. As Forsythe explains, "The tensions of the piece come from literally watching people having to make drastic decisions."[76]

Forsythe explains the company's process as such:

We used the improvisation technologies that we'd been developing over many pieces, which involve minute arithmetic, or geometric physical analysis that keeps iterating. It's like a fractal: you solve the situation and you

---

[74] Forsythe, interview with the author.
[75] Moten, 1.
[76] Burrows, Forsythe, 1998. Casperson provides some genealogical background for Ballett Frankfurt's impulse to encourage decision-making in dance: "Balletic training itself is great, but I find often the ballet institutions instill a strong sense of shame in the dancers and weaken their belief in their own ability to make decisions about art" (Burrows, Casperson, 1998).

feed the result back into the situation again. Any given state produces another movement.[77]

According to Galloway, Forsythe's pieces lack strictly bounded finish: "A piece wouldn't have an identity. It was constantly evolving. You would always go back and work on a piece."[78] Gilpin mirrors Galloway's observation by writing:

> Forsythe is not interested in the survival of his work as an object; that would fetishize the work as a finished, categorizable, reproducible object. He is similarly adamant about the fact that his choreographies, unlike classical ballets, cannot be recorded using Labanotation.[79]

Thus, Forsythe's works inadvertently personify Moten's resistance of the object. Moreover, it is Richardson's intentional engagement with black performance (popping, breaking) within the context of Ballett Frankfurt that highlights the dispossessive force of the object, the cycle of formation and deformation defining the relationship between subject and object. As Moten asserts:

> The history of blackness is testament to the fact that objects can and do resist. . . . While subjectivity is defined by the subject's possession of itself and its objects, it is troubled by a dispossessive force objects exert such that the subject seems to be possessed—infused, deformed—by the object it possesses.[80]

We can think of Forsythe's pieces (especially their reliance on ballet technique) as objects and Richardson as the (Black) subject who is "deformed—by the object [he] possesses." We can also invert this formulation to ascertain the slipperiness between the status of subject and object in the context of ever-evolving improvisatory choreography. In other words, in pieces such as *Invisible Film*, Richardson both takes part in and is at the mercy of the unpredictable status of the product. According to Galloway, much of Forsythe's

---

[77] Forsythe in Burrows.
[78] Galloway, interview with the author.
[79] Gilpin, 123.
[80] Moten, "Resistance of the Object," *In the Break*, 1–2.

resistance to finish and categorization is realized through the dancers' improvisation onstage as well as off:

> We also improvised onstage. Studio improv would change onstage because I would have forgotten about studio movement, even during partnering. Pieces like *In the Middle Somewhat Elevated* or *The Second Detail* . . . were more set, but as far as our work was concerned . . . we would never do a *pas de deux* the same way each time.[81]

Regarding the piece *ALIE/NA(C)TION*, choreographer and dancer Dana Casperson reveals, "We don't do the same thing every time. We have this established structure and then we're composing with it."[82] Despite his own resistance to the idea that his pieces are objects, Forsythe's works are sold to dance companies internationally, even in their ever-changing states. Like Richardson's virtuosity, it is that which is most precarious about Forsythe's choreography that affords it its sellable aspect. If audiences flock to witness Richardson's exceptional movement quality—to see if he can reproduce the same phenomenal feats of yesterday's performance—they are similarly attracted to the kineticism and surprise of Forsythe's deconstructive pieces. The work's fetishizability as a finished product is up for debate: it can certainly be sold and reproduced; yet, this reproduction embraces its refusal of identical duplication.[83] Thus, its very resistance to objecthood is precisely that which generates its fetishizable auratic sheen. Ultimately, by remaining open to the unpredictability of improvisation, Richardson and Forsythe's pieces are implicated in the continuous possession and dispossession of the subject/object's relationship to blackness.

The further Forsythe moves from pieces like *Vertiginous Thrill* that rely on ballet vocabulary, the more he approaches a working in and through the "break" as vocabularies from popping and hip-hop enter into his movement palette through Richardson. Although this lingering in the rupture of the break may exceed the racial identity of the dancer, it relies on African diasporic movement. Pieces such as *Vertiginous Thrill* are more Balanchinian in their adherence to recognizable ballet vocabulary and are therefore more easily categorized as Africanist, as subtly inviting a hip thrust or polyrhythm.

---

[81] Galloway, interview with the author.
[82] Burrows, Casperson.
[83] Lizzie Leopold writes about financial aspects of Forsythe's works in *The Futures of Dance Studies*.

As Forsythe demands more and more improvisation and dancers such as Richardson lend Forsythe's movement more breaking and popping, the choreographic heteroglossia of Gottschild's notion of Africanism becomes less relevant, and the work begins to resonate more closely with Moten's "Blackness." The concept of Africanist aesthetics still asks of us to recognize and acknowledge diasporic elements and movements. As psychosocial modes, blackness and moving through the break, however, embrace the impossibility of resolution, of authenticity or originary movement. To theorize within an Africanist framework is a positive exercise of attribution and identification, whereas theorizing blackness in Moten's mode is a melancholic act, a commitment to remaining active within a cycle of loss. Moten's "difficult" blackness rather than Africanism turns out to be a more productive lens to think through this phase of Richardson's career. Not only is he literally "breaking" (inserting break dance into ballet), but also, by improvising in Forsythe's work, he is actively dancing through the "break." Melancholia suggests a compulsive return, and Forsythe's choreography intervenes to recognize and reverse such return with a compulsive "leaving behind," a "disappearance." He claims that his dancers are repeatedly "leaving behind" their bodies, and their actions are a kind of "letting go." As the body folds over on itself, it approaches something like "transparency" and "disappearance":

> The more you let go of your control, and give it over to a kind of transparency of the body, a feeling of disappearance, the more you will be able to capture differentiated form, and differentiated dynamics. You can move very fast in this state, and it will not give the same impression—it won't give the impression of violence. You can also move with tremendous acceleration provided you know where you leave the movement—not where you put the movement, but where you leave it. You try to divest your body of movement, as opposed to thinking you are producing movement. So it would not be like pushing forward into space and invading space—it would be like leaving your body in space. Dissolution, letting yourself evaporate. Movement is a factor of the fact that you are actually evaporating.[84]

---

[84] Forsythe in Siegmund, 136–37. Gilpin refers to such practice as "disappearance." I might hesitate in rehearsing this trope, especially in regard to race. "The movement composition research of the Ballett Frankfurt attempts to expose and examine precisely these disturbing moments of lost attention. In such choreography, the double-edged tension of disequilibrium is a state that emerges from the infinite operations that dismantle historically established bodily configurations. This state reveals what is always in the process of disappearing; the dancing thereby highlights the continuous vanishing moments of movement, and offers a redefinition of dance as we have come to know it."

More a sensorial guide for the dancer than a critical assessment of the body's actual relationship to space and time, Forsythe's discussion of "leaving" the movement as opposed to creating an "impression of violence" is a choreo-philosophical embrace of the trace, one that dispenses with production and offense. Forsythe recognizes that such kinetic, forceful dancing typically gives the impression of violence. He stages movement that could otherwise be read as violent in a manner that is in fact an active refusal of violence, transforming the function and legibility of velocity in contemporary dance. By both experimenting with the break and maintaining a degree of expression carried over from the mainstream work of Ailey, Richardson thus informs and makes more explicit in Forsythe's work the bridge between popular dance and an aesthetics of difficulty.

Difficulty and the Socked Foot

The complexity of influences informing Forsythe's improvisational process and the velocity of his style results in an aesthetic that can be challenging for the audience to experience and interpret. A concept that deserves translation from the realm of the literary to the realm of the choreographic is that of "difficulty" as put forth by Leonard Diepeveen, who frames difficulty "in terms of a reading process," central to "high culture." He refers to difficulty as a "form of attention,"[85] writing:

> Modernism's difficulty . . . is not merely a classifiable set of techniques. To discuss difficulty solely as the property of texts is to impoverish it and miss how difficulty became an integral part of high culture. Difficulty must be understood in terms of a reading process, and it manifests itself socially; modernism begins with a typical interaction between art and its audience.[86]

Dance, as Forsythe's work suggests, is a process of embodied disappearance.... This work embodies a process that can only be witnessed in the act of its disappearance" (Gilpin, 121).

[85] 244.
[86] Diepeveen, xi. A a reminder, he writes, "Difficulty . . . is that recurring *relationship* that came into being between modernist works and their audiences." Despite its reference to the literary in his work, Diepeveen imbues difficulty with a sense of the bodily and the affective. He writes, "Difficulty is an odd aesthetic experience; using their whole bodies, people react viscerally to difficulty, often with anxiety, anger, and ridicule. The public debate about difficulty and its scandalousness, then, was much more than a story of elitism and middle-class anti-intellectualism. It was also a story of anger, of pleasure, and of the body. Moreover, those affective responses are enmeshed in the standard ways of conceptualizing difficulty and profoundly influence how difficulty shaped modern culture" (xiv).

According to Diepeveen, high modernist poetry (such as that of T. S. Eliot, Ezra Pound, and Gertrude Stein), while certainly difficult to write, ultimately places the demands of difficulty onto the reader, withholding or delaying pleasure until the reader's labor of interpretation reaps its intellectual rewards. For high modernist critics, intellectual pleasure comes from the reader's fulfillment of the difficult task of interpretation. As such, a certain degree of intellectual virtuosity is attributed to the astute reader of a "difficult" text.[87] What we see in Ballett Frankfurt is that Richardson transitions from a company (Ailey) in which difficult movement is called upon to satisfy an easily "read" aesthetic to a company (Frankfurt) in which difficult movement works in the service of an aesthetic that is challenging for the viewer. Unlike that of Diepeveen, performance scholar Jennifer Doyle's discussion of difficulty refers less to experiments of *form* (that can cause intellectual difficulty for the audience) and more to extreme *content* (that may cause affective difficulty for the audience), as in cutting, penetration, and self-harm. The performance art examples Doyle raises are outside dance and literature and include artists such as Ron Athey and Aliza Shvarts. By eschewing abstraction and embracing individual, personal action in the moment, such performance can have the effect of repelling instead of inviting and more fully rejects canonical texts and techniques. In other words, whether intended or not, "difficult" performance art can generate shock value, whereas "difficult" contemporary dance generates something more like a sense of formal opacity and an overabundance of virtuosity.

Modernism in American dance does not share an easily grafted chronology with literary or visual art modernism. Martha Graham is considered the quintessential modern dance choreographer. According to dance scholar Mark Franko, Graham is aligned with early modernism,[88] but not the late modernist aesthetics and modes we may recognize in, say, the writing of Gertrude Stein. Unlike Stein's goals of abstraction and absurdity, Graham instead emphasizes a synthesis of expression and form.[89] While Balanchine is often referred to as a "neoclassical" ballet choreographer, Susan Manning and other dance scholars note that his frequent rejection of characterization and narrative aligns him more securely with the modernist project. Franko refers to neoclassicism in dance as "ballet modernism."[90] As an inheritor of

[87] I elaborate on "spectatorial virtuosity" in the Chapter 3.
[88] Mark Franko, *Martha Graham in Love and War*.
[89] Dance scholars who have elaborated on the modernism/postmodernism debate in dance history include Sally Banes, Susan Manning, Susan Foster, and Ramsey Burt.
[90] See Mark Franko's *The Fascist Turn in the Dance of Serge Lifar*.

Balanchine's proto-modernist tendencies, Forsythe further abandons theatrical conventions, more fully satisfying a modernist preoccupation with difficulty.[91] It is this stylistic inheritance that makes Gottschild's discussion of Africanist aesthetics applicable to Forsythe's work, but the departure from Balanchine lends Forsythe's work its difficult abstraction, aligning him more closely with Moten's own modernist commitments and strategic modernist "breaks." Choreographic aesthetics of choreographers such as Forsythe and Rhoden linger more in abundance than lack. Such abundance parallels what Diepeveen refers to as modernist poetics' "too-muchness." Difficulty in postdramatic theater and dance can arise, however, not only from "too-muchness" but also from its opposite (which we could call "not-enoughness").[92] Forsythe is the rare choreographer whose aesthetic of abundance has satisfied critical demands for intellectual/receptive difficulty.

By way of conclusion, perhaps no piece's creative process better exemplifies Richardson's participation in Forsythe's aesthetic of difficulty than *Eidos: Telos*. In 1994, Richardson and Forsythe launched their collaboration with *Eidos: Telos*, a piece whose title translates from Latin to "final form" (after the death of Forsythe's wife, Tracey-Kai Meier).[93] Pieces such

[91] The tension between intellectualism and its opponents in dance reception is put forward by Franko, who writes, "The journalistic response to Forsythe, and Forsythe's critical reaction to that response, reveal the dirty little secret of 'anti-intellectualism' in American dance criticism" (Franko, 42). "Forsythe's relationship with the American critical establishment during the 1980s was, indeed, complex, if not vexed. I attribute it to the rejection of intellect in dance, and most particularly to the rejection of intellect in ballet" (Franko, 40). The 1990s, however, signal a shift in Forsythe's journalistic response, for as he became more established and his work entered the repertoire of more ballet companies, his work no longer represented the occasion to reject the intellect in dance and instead became the gauge of a sought-after ingeniousness. As of late, the perception of a certain brand of intellectualism has become imperative in contemporary ballet and dance, which is precisely why much dance by Black artists (such as that of Rhoden) working in a vein similar to, but decidedly more continuously kinetic than, Forsythe is admonished by critics as too physical and muscular, and not intellectual enough. This is due partially to a privileging of kineticism in the work of Rhoden (and others influenced by Forsythe), but also due to racial biases about the relationship between intellectualism and kineticism. Explicit engagement with the discursive has much to do with such bias. Forsythe himself is known for "[speaking] back to the critics" (Franko 41). By speaking back to critics in their own language, referencing their use of critical theory and hiring resident philosophers and dramaturges, Forsythe creates a forum for himself to engage intellectually with critics on their own terrain, as opposed to relying solely on the "genius" of his choreography to speak for him. Forsythe's verbal discourse works in conjunction with the difficulty of and in his choreography in that the discourse buttresses any difficulty the viewer might encounter in the work. More in keeping with the visual arts domain, the artist who speaks creates a foundation for the acceptance of difficulty and intellectualism in the work.

[92] Diepeveen mentions "too-muchness" in reference to high moderns such as Gertrude Stein.

[93] It should be noted that, due to his resistance to finish in his improvisation-driven pieces, the only finality Forsythe locates is in death itself. Also, Tracey-Kai Meier was a principal dancer with San Francisco Ballet (SFB) when I was a student in the school. She was always my favorite dancer and had an appetite for the contemporary. As a student I had the great privilege of peeking into Forsythe's rehearsals with Meier and SFB as he was developing the piece *New Sleep* and of attending the premiere performance. Meier was a daring dancer with a kind, generous spirit. We would gift each other

as *Eidos: Telos* in the 1990s inaugurated the now-pervasive European aesthetic of sock-footed dancers, evoking the warming and cocooning of the foot and ankle that typically takes place at the very beginning of dance class. According to Galloway, socks first made a formal appearance in Forsythe's works when Galloway costumed the piece *Quintet*.[94] The costuming of *Eidos: Telos*—socks and relaxed warmup pants—effaces the masculine, raced muscularity for which Richardson is known in the US.[95] That Richardson could slip and fall at any moment distances him from the star status he attained at Ailey, which relied on the traction of the bare foot. The sock represents the nexus of difficulty and fun, spectacle and responsibility in Ballet Frankfurt. If the bare foot offers contemporary dancers a certain level of stability and traction and the pointe shoe creates an unnatural sense of tapering height, the sock creates a slippery surface that completely alters the relationship of the foot to the ground, thus the frequency of flat-footed slides in Forsythe's work. Between the bare foot's grip and the pointe shoe or ballet slipper's rosin-assisted stability, the slipperiness of the socked foot is charged with sliding back and forth within a liminal zone of risk. Sock-footed choreography relishes in the swoosh and the near fall, the teeter and the freewheel. The sock dismantles the single stardom of the virtuoso, creating a collective of vulnerable virtuosos (idiosyncratic still) who achieve a sense of fun in the face of difficulty. It also brings the playful experimentation of the studio onto the stage. The precariousness of dancing in socks ultimately magnifies Richardson's virtuosity, but it does so by reminding us of the imminent threat of failure. Gilpin writes:

> Forsythe explores . . . the extrakinespheric moments when the boundaries of equilibrium are transgressed, when falling is imminent because something has failed. That something is balance. . . . Failure contains within it notions of absence, of lack, as well as very distinct elements of movement and performance.[96]

roses backstage (when I had the chance to perform in children's roles with SFB) and she signed her pointe shoes for me to keep.

[94] Galloway, interview with the author.
[95] Forsythe's ruminations on the relationship between economy and authorship resonate with my discussion of agency and blackness later in the chapter. "The cost of time is so drastic. . . . How is this economic context within which we all work shifting the future of work and the future of authorship? . . . There [are] different levels of authorship. If I've made the material and you're realigning it . . . you don't get paid for it, but if you're developing the material yourself and I need to use it, then . . . you get paid for that section." Burrows, Forsythe, 1998.
[96] Gilpin, 120, 114.

The "absence" and "lack" Gilpin points to returns us to Moten's melancholic blackness, the continual working in and through a rupture that can never be sutured.

But more interestingly, Forsythe insists that the body's constant absenting of itself—its intentional failure—stages the dancers' accomplishment. Dance critic Roslyn Sulcas (who has written extensively on Forsythe) observes, "There is no exhibition of prowess in *Eidos: Telos*. Every movement is full of understated, elaborated detail as different body parts appear to initiate their own small dance simultaneously; no step ever serves as a transition to another, more important visual effect."[97] Forsythe tells Sulcas, "'What I wanted to show in *'Eidos* . . . is the extent of the dancers' accomplishment.'"[98] Forsythe does not necessarily link a dancer's accomplishment to high-flying, breakneck kinetics, despite his frequent embrace of such physical fireworks. Rather, understated intricacy and compositional skill become the marks of accomplishment. In fact, Richardson had to adapt himself to a more understated presence at Ballett Frankfurt. As Galloway recounts, "Sometimes [Richardson's] charisma (and presentational quality) fit in our company and sometimes Bill [Forsythe] had to tone it down."[99] By refusing to call upon one movement to transition to the next in a manner that is habitual to ballet, Forsythe further locates himself in the nonnarrative, fractured aesthetics of modernist difficulty. In *Just Dancing Around*, Forsythe warns in rehearsal, "We're running the risk of a kind of disconcerned modernity, whereas I think it needs far more economy. I think everyone should get to the point." The "economy" to which Richardson was accustomed functioned according to the logic of giving the audience what they paid for. In other words, as Galloway reflects, "Bill [Forsythe] and I used to joke: Desmond [Richardson] is not going to waste your time when he's on stage."[100] "Getting to the point" in Forsythe's work, however, is more about sustaining attention within demanding and highly kinetic choreography as opposed to dancing dramatically or traveling from point A to point B in as short a line as possible.

While his audience experiences an aesthetics of difficulty, in soliciting an economical practice, Forsythe is actually asking for quick decision-making, and thus a more efficient process of continually "disappearing" the body.

---

[97] Roslyn Sulcas, "DANCE; Transcendental Meditations on the Possibilities of Form," *New York Times*, November 29, 1998, https://www.nytimes.com/1998/11/29/arts/dance-transcendental-meditations-on-the-possibilities-of-form.html.
[98] ibid.
[99] Galloway, interview with the author.
[100] Galloway, interview with the author.

Figure 4.1 Desmond Richardson, Francesca Harper, Francesca Caroti, Jone San Martin, and Maurice Causey in *Eidos: Telos* by William Forsythe, Ballett Frankfurt, Opernhaus Frankfurt am Main, 1995 (See color plates).
Copyright Dominik Mentzos.

Figure 4.2 Desmond Richardson, Francesca Harper, Francesca Caroti, Jone San Martin, and Maurice Causey in *Eidos: Telos* by William Forsythe, Ballett Frankfurt, Opernhaus Frankfurt am Main, 1995 (See color plates).
Copyright Dominik Mentzos.

Figure 4.3 Desmond Richardson and Francesca Harper in *The Vertiginous Thrill of Exactitude* by William Forsythe, Ballett Frankfurt, Opernhaus Frankfurt am Main, 1996 (See color plates).
Copyright Dominik Mentzos.

Figure 4.4 Desmond Richardson in *The Vertiginous Thrill of Exactitude* by William Forsythe, Ballett Frankfurt, Opernhaus Frankfurt am Main, 1996 (See color plates).
Copyright Dominik Mentzos.

Significantly, Forsythe cites a kind of "muscle memory" in recounting the body's continuous acts of disappearance. Sulcas notes:

> Forsythe . . . likes to think of the dancers' responsibilities in [*Eidos: Telos*] as similar to those of virtuoso musicians who make choices about order and timing when performing sequences in a cadenza. "It's not a question of memorizing intellectually," he says. "It's about the body being a form of memory; the physical patterns in your body are listening to the music and recalling themselves."[101]

In other words, Forsythe's concept of "disappearance" relies not on forgetting, but on memory. Similarly, Richardson is not meant to forget the diasporic traditions of his past in working in Forsythe's experimental studio. It is not a matter of "unlearning" the techniques of his past, a logic driving much contemporary dance training. Rather, he relies on his body as "a form of memory," and as a dancer in this context, he makes choices, embracing both a loss of control and a sense of agency and authorship. By rejecting a combination of movements that could be identified as one style or another, Richardson in Ballett Frankfurt relinquishes the relative legibility of Africanism (and classical ballet), choosing to work in the break, in the illegible space of blackness. It is, paradoxically, through nonrepresentational choreographic action that Richardson sutures the rupture between "personhood" and "subjectivity" that has historically defined blackness. With Forsythe in Ballett Frankfurt, Richardson engages his virtuosity to "stage disappearance" and reduce the publicity and visibility of what Moten refers to as blackness's "improvisatory exteriority": given over to difficult fun, the ensemble of dancers (functioning here also as the "ensemble of the senses and the social") provides virtuosity with a rare space of refuge within the opacity of its own production.

---

[101] Citation.

5

Otherwise in Blackface

American Ballet Theatre and San Francisco Ballet's *Othello*

[*Othello*] is pure melodrama. There is not a touch of character in it that goes below the skin. [1, 2]

—George Bernard Shaw, 1897[3]

Lar Lubovitch choreographed American Ballet Theatre (ABT) and San Francisco Ballet's (SFB) coproduction of *Othello: A Dance in Three Acts* in 1997, the year Desmond Richardson returned to New York after dancing with William Forsythe's Ballett Frankfurt.[4] Having set his choreography on Richardson at Alvin Ailey American Dance Theater (AAADT) in the early 1990s and noting an absence of Black male dancers at ABT (where the production was created), Lubovitch requested Richardson from outside the ranks of the company for the title role.[5] When Richardson was not dancing the role of Othello, alternate casts were painted in bronze face and body makeup. Richardson's presence—and absence—in the role of Othello compels a consideration of the haunted and heretofore unexamined relationship between blackface, virtuosity, and racial melodrama in ballet.

---

[1] The *New York Times* refers to it as "shimmering bronze makeup" and I link such descriptions of surface to Chapter 2 (on surface and photography).

[2] Louis Chude-Sokei, *The Last Darky: Bert Williams, Black-on-Black Minstrelsy and the African Diaspora* (Durham, NC: Duke University Press, 2005), 36.

[3] Bernard Shaw, "Othello: Pure Melodrama," 1907.

[4] Richardson continued to co-direct and dance with Complexions during his time working with ABT and SFB. The Othello collaboration should not to be mistaken for Kate Elswit's "coproductions" as they relate to Pina Bausch.

[5] Lubovitch's production of *Othello* was initially created on ABT in 1996–1997; it was subsequently set on SFB.

Lubovitch's *Othello* is steeped in melodrama, both in the story's original plot and in the racial melodrama of Richardson's casting in (and subsequent absence from) the role. To account for the melodrama intrinsic and extrinsic to Lubovitch's *Othello*, this chapter will engage film scholar Linda Williams's studies of melodrama in film and racial melodrama in televised media. After Peter Brooks, melodrama is defined by Williams as a mode that starts and ends in a space of innocence, focuses on virtue, oscillates between too late and just in time (the temporality of pathos and action), borrows from realism, and is consumed with good and evil.[6] And racial melodrama, according to Williams, concerns itself most with virtue ("of racially beset victims") and villainy ("of racially motivated villains").[7] Because Lubovitch constructs the already melodramatic narrative of his production through filmic storyboarding, Williams's treatment of melodrama will prove to be especially fitting. Of course, the choice to present Othello in blackface is a long-held tradition in opera. In Lubovitch's production, when casts other than Richardson are dancing, Othello's bronze makeup signals immorality: blackface lends itself to melodrama's fixation with virtue and its deterioration. "Virtue," bear in mind, shares the Latin root "vir" with "virtuosity" and "*virtus*"; "vir" translates to "man" and is most often associated with courage and strength. As we come to find later in the chapter, *virtus* is that which lends the virtuoso their credibility: virtuosity's pathos is buttressed by the virtuoso's ethos (*virtus*).[8] Richardson's participation in the melodrama of Lubovitch's *Othello* enlivens the intersection of "vir's" range of affixed meanings.

That Lubovitch's creative methodologies borrow from American film and European opera lends his production a unique sense of melodrama, on the one hand, and an archaic treatment of race, on the other. What of the coexistence of regressive artistic practices (like blackface) and progressive political gestures (such as the hiring of a Black principal dancer)? By focusing my attention on Lubovitch's production of *Othello*, I interrogate the function of the nonspeaking, dancing body in the context of blackface and melodramatic ballet, developing the term "corporeal blackface." Focusing on embodied aspects of performance that blackface makeup accompanies, this chapter explores how *choreographic leitmotif* arises alongside corporeal blackface in Lubovitch's *Othello* as a tool to indicate racial otherness in the plot, no matter

---

[6] Linda Williams, 28–40, to be discussed in more detail later in the chapter.
[7] Ibid., 6. This will be discussed in full later in the chapter.
[8] Brandstetter, "Virtuoso's Stage," 181.

how essayistic or nonnarrative. Lubovitch's style brings together ballet and modern dance, creating a type of "contemporary ballet" within companies (ABT and SFB) that have historically considered themselves "classical ballet" companies (but now indeed invite choreography that exceeds classicism).[9] This chapter theorizes *Othello* through virtuosity and melodrama's shared relationships to temporality, excess, and virtue. As such, blackface, as it interfaces with—and compulsively tries to recover—Richardson's distinct virtuosity, becomes the site upon which racial melodrama takes place on and off the balletic stage.

Displacements: Casting Race

The story of *Othello* is a story of displaced characters and desired relationships; Lubovitch intentionally foregrounds Iago's homoerotic, racial, and political triangulations, as revealed in my discussion with the choreographer.[10] Homoerotic displacement (inherently entangled with racial displacement) within the ballet mirrors the racial displacement that occurs when one dancer cast in *Othello* replaces another. The sense of desire for the Other within *Othello*—as Black, as politically more powerful, as virile—is uncannily reproduced extrinsically in the ballet through incomplete racial fulfillment: blackface makeup signals yearning for authenticity. We thus locate the potential violence of approximation. In Richardson's absence, surrogate casts are painted in blackface on their faces and bodies, not only to approximate black skin, but also to supplement an attempt to affectively recover Richardson's virtuosity. In doing so, stylistic approximation translates into incomplete racial mimesis. Nevertheless, it would be limited to suggest "authenticity" as a counterpoint to the warped, racial approximation of "blacking up." Directors of Europeanist *Othello* productions in theater, opera, film, and dance have actually relied on obtuse arguments of "authenticity" (that blackface is "authentic" to the theatrical needs of the story) to rationalize the use of blackface. Adding to the multiple displacements taking place in Lubovitch's *Othello*, the ballet dancer tries to embody the modern

---

[9] Nevertheless, I would not equate Lubovitch's style of "contemporary ballet" with that of William Forsythe, who is more intentionally deconstructive and postdramatic in his aesthetic. Nor would I equate it with that of Complexions, despite some similarities. He calls his style "dance" (and not "ballet," "modern," or "contemporary").

[10] Interview material (author with Lubovitch) appears throughout this chapter.

dancer's technique; the white man plays black. And in the process, contemporary dance becomes equated with the racial Other.

ABT artistic director Kevin McKenzie and Lubovitch's decision to hire Richardson for the production also serves as a glaring reminder of the history—and continued practice—of exclusionary hiring practices in ballet, where ability has been correlated with whiteness. In the words of Richardson:

> My involvement with ABT [and SFB] probably reinforced the idea that non-white dancers do and can be leads in story ballets and can hold the stage through artistry, technique, and ... thought-provoking performances. For me it was not a conscious decision, yet I believe my involvement [shows] ... that someone of color can carry a three-act ballet.... I did not realize that I was the first principal dancer of color since the inception of ABT, but I gladly wear that title if it draws inspiration to others.[11]

Richardson's reaction to his casting betrays an awareness of his contribution to American dance history yet reveals the fact that his decision to take on the role was motivated by factors other than political. Such a perspective allows him to inadvertently dismiss the troubling aspects of the production. On the one hand, Richardson is hired to accommodate the fact that Black dancers of his caliber exist but are not hired by classical ballet companies; on the other hand, to hire Richardson to carry a full-length ballet is to announce an inclusionary impulse, no matter how belatedly. Traditionally racially prejudiced hiring practices in ballet have much to do with the desire for the appearance of homogeneous casting, but also with the assumption that Black dancers lack the degree of technique and ability found among white ballet dancers.[12] Attempts at the already impossible category of technical authenticity are subsequently grafted onto the racial appearance of characters in narrative ballets that call for the ethnic Other: the conundrum of white dancers having to play non-white roles is incompletely resolved through the use of makeup,

---

[11] Richardson, interview with the author, 2010. And according to Lubovitch: "He is physically capable of all of those classical requirements. I think he rightfully saw himself as a major player. I thought it was a missed opportunity for Desmond and for American Ballet Theatre, but Desmond didn't want that. He is a free artist who can choose what he wants. He didn't want to have to be part of a cause, I don't believe. I think he wanted to be regarded as the key artist that he is, and treated that way. He didn't want to be set up as an example of a tall Black man being accepted into a white company."

[12] Certainly, the sociocultural and economic makeup of the board of directors of a ballet company (responsible for funding much of the company's budget) is often reflected in racially biased hiring practices.

costuming, musical motifs, even exoticist choreographic allusions. As such, blackface functions as one of several intertwined elements in the attempt to embody the Other.

As far as casting is concerned, Lubovitch explains that when ABT's McKenzie approached him to create an evening-length ballet, he immediately thought of the Othello story with Richardson as the lead. According to Lubovitch, artistry was at the center of his choice of Richardson, but his use of "authenticity" blurs artistry and race:

> When I brought the project to Kevin McKenzie, I said, "This is a project for Desmond Richardson." Desmond didn't know that. I am very comfortable that anybody could dance the role. But I thought to *create* the role, to give it the real authenticity, Othello should be danced by Desmond—not because of his color, which is something we should talk about, but because of his superb artistry, and that it's a story about a universally famous black character.[13]

Lubovitch goes on to say that Richardson's artistic nuance came to his attention during the staging of *North Star*, most notably performed by Richardson and Sarita Allen in 1990. Lubovitch tells me, "I met Desmond at the Alvin Ailey American Dance Theater when I set *North Star*. Ailey was the only company that did it besides my own company. Desmond did the lead male role; Sarita Allen was the female lead."[14] Having danced in Lubovitch's works at AAADT, Richardson explains that he was honored to accept an invitation to star in *Othello*, as he had always been "drawn to [Lubovitch's] movement."[15] The artistic compatibility between Lubovitch and Richardson is apparent not only onstage but also in my interviews with both. Central to Lubovitch's choreographic vision is an insistence on the appropriate dancer for a part. When deciding on a production for ABT, he conceived of storytelling and embodiment together, explaining:

> I was looking for a story that could be told in pictures. *Othello*, out of all the great tragedies, is one I felt could be told in pictures, especially because it involved such a universally understood emotion: jealousy. It didn't need to

---

[13] Lubovitch, interview with the author.
[14] Lubovitch, interview with the author.
[15] Richardson, interview with the author.

be spelled out since the audience could bring their knowledge of the story. I was interested in the embodiment of emotions and a psychological approach to dance.[16]

Lubovitch elaborates, "There are particular things that I respond to in dancers: mobility, technique—physical mobility applied toward movement poetry." He seeks an embodied poetry: "I look for people who speak poetry and recite it with their bodies, and that is not as definable in words as it is to the eye. I understand when I see it." Richardson "inherently [exudes] both of those things: he is physically extraordinary and inherently poetic. He is extremely musical—fast with music. Dancers I look for embody one whole physical gift; they are related—the musicality, the movement, and the physical ability."[17] The style of movement in question, while informed by ballet, is decidedly contemporary in its circularity, weighted stance, and seemingly unending fluidity.

In fact, the ballet opens with Richardson crouched over in a ball, emerging with arm movements that alternate between circular and straight, symmetrical and asymmetrical, dramatically framing his face as if to indicate psychic tension. This arm and torso pattern becomes a leitmotif of sorts throughout the piece to signal pain, confusion, and waning trust. Richardson's movement style, born of a mastery and rigorous hybridizing of classical ballet, modern dance techniques, popping, and his own individual approach, is in keeping with Lubovitch's choreography.[18] Both artists have been trained to the highest degree in ballet and modern dance but have worked predominantly in modern and contemporary dance settings.[19] Richardson states, "Othello was an ideal role for me (having danced non-narrative roles at Ballett Frankfurt and Complexions Contemporary Ballet), and allowed me

---

[16] Lubovitch, interview with the author.
[17] Lubovitch, interview with the author.
[18] In Chapter 3 (on virtuosity), I go into detail about the vernacular influences in Richardson's movement style (which include breakdancing, popping, and locking).
[19] For the purposes of this chapter, I use "modern dance" to denote techniques that emerged during the first half of the twentieth century (including those of Martha Graham, José Limón, Katherine Dunham, Lester Horton, and the like) and "contemporary dance" to refer to contemporary (in the sense of recent or current) concert dance that draws mainly from the individual style of the choreographer in question. For example, even though Lubovitch has trained in ballet and modern dance, I call his choreography "contemporary" because he is still alive and working, but also because he exceeds the demands of classical or neo-classical ballet yet remains in a realm that emerges from ballet and modern dance without delving into, for example, decidedly vernacular or regional dance forms (such as breakdancing, flamenco, or Bharatanatyam). While I would be comfortable calling some "postmodern" dance "contemporary," such a discussion is only peripherally relevant to this chapter. See Ramsey Burt's book on the Judson Dance Theater.

to explore that side of me that loves to tell a story through dance (in fact it is where I feel I soar)."[20] Richardson relished the opportunity to engage in a narrative, story ballet; what emerges from this artistic partnership between Lubovitch and Richardson founded in an appreciation for drama is an embrace of melodrama, much of which is inherent to the original story of Othello and would be difficult to temper, no matter how movement-driven a treatment it received.

Black in White Company, White in Black Company

Lubovitch began his formal training quite late by concert dance standards, and despite the normativity and privilege afforded by his cis white male identity, he embarked on a nontraditional path marked by his delayed training, Jewish background, and participation as the only white member in black dance companies. He shares:

> My parents weren't okay with it. I had no validity, no funding, not even close. I was, entirely in charge of myself. But my parents were not restrictive at all. Nor did they pay much attention to me. I grew up a wild child and I did anything that I wanted knowing that they never said no to me. I kind of invented myself at a very early age. I invented myself as an artist. I was painting and drawing by the time I was about five years old. . . . I use drawing in the studio sometimes when I am struggling. . . . I started dance quite late and my formal training began at the Juilliard School. I went to Juilliard for less than two years because I had opportunities right away to be a professional dancer. I didn't see the point in continuing. I wasn't interested in the degree. I was interested in dance.[21]

Lubovitch's teachers at Juilliard included the renowned José Limón, Martha Graham, Anna Sokolow, Anthony Tudor, and Margaret Craske. Classes

---

[20] Richardson, interview with the author. "I have also taken this approach with my Broadway endeavors, as it is similar in nature—having to understand the ins and outs of a character and deliver an honest performance to the audience so that they are fully invested in the character and story."

[21] "I grew up in Chicago, but I went to Iowa as a visual art major. I went to college at the University of Iowa and there was a woman there who found me and had me dance with her. Her name was Marsha Thayer. There was no training per say. She was looking for someone to dance with, and she came to the gymnastics team and I was working at gymnastics (I was a very minor gymnast). I was at Juilliard in 1963 I think, maybe 1962" (Lubovitch, interview with the author).

included ballet, modern dance, jazz, choreography, and composition. Even though he was readily being hired as a dancer, Lubovitch immediately felt his calling in choreography:

> When I discovered dance, I said, "I am a choreographer." And then I made the choice that I would have to dance for a number of years in order to understand being a dancer. I was learning from Anthony Tudor, who gave the choreography classes. He had a very particular relationship to music. It was about embodying a physical sensation that captured the inherent emotional condition described by the music. There was a connective tissue. I think that is primarily true about my own work, and also true about Tudor's; there are no important steps.[22]

The "connective tissue" of Lubovitch's ensuing choreography became his signature quality, mesmerizing in its circularity and flow. Professional opportunities were especially ripe for men in American concert dance during Lubovitch's dancing years. He confirms, "If you were a man dancing in New York, you danced with just about everybody because there were only a few of you." Nevertheless, such demand did not amount to a livable salary: "At this time there was no such thing as a full-time dance job or a full-time dancer." In fact, Lubovitch supplemented his career with various odd jobs, such as "waiter, office temp, but mostly professional go-go dancing," explaining that his "major job was at a famous disco club called Trudy Hellers and also at the Twist Club in Greenwich Village."[23] Often, professional modern dancers, while closer to a sense of renegade movement cultures of change, sacrificed the relative financial security a ballet career could offer. To that end, a modern dancer could be said to have more of a sense of what we colloquially refer to as "hustle" than ballet dancers. The hustle and experimentation of patching together jobs to pay rent and jobs in "pickup" dance companies tended to bring together dancers working across ethnic and racial divides. Dancing in clubs, as explored in Chapter 3, also introduces stylistic dialogism to otherwise codified ballet and modern dance techniques—a queer edge or subtly shifted orientation.

Lubovitch's family background is "Russian Jewish and completely secular."[24] As evidenced by Penny Frank's work with Black students at

---

[22] Ibid.
[23] Lubovitch, interview with author.
[24] Ibid.

LaGuardia, not to mention the Jewish support on the board of directors of the Ailey company (mentioned in Chapter 1), American artists with Jewish and black heritage often engaged in relationships of mutual support, having undergone discrimination (albeit differently) from the mainstream. Since the early twentieth century, the modern dance community in New York, more than that of ballet, used dance as a platform to express cultural struggle. Lubovitch found himself dancing during a time of increased visibility for Black choreographers in America, and some of those choreographers took great interest in Lubovitch's dancing. He danced with Donald McKayle and Pearl Primus and says he was "the only white person" in both companies at the time. "I was taking Afro-Haitian classes with Pearl's husband, Percival Borde, and he invited me to come to rehearsal with him."[25] This chapter finds itself in dialogue with Chapter 2 insomuch as Lubovitch shares with me that he "performed McKayle's *Rainbow 'Round My Shoulder*, and at the time, Carmen de Lavallade or Mary Hinkson played the role of the woman. And I was in the company with Gus Solomon."[26] Lubovitch certainly received an education in black dance and culture while working with Primus and McKayle, presumably preparing him to be more aware of African American issues, including racism, than the average white dancer in New York. Nevertheless, it would be remiss to equate being white in a black company with being Black in a white company. While difference is a commonality between the two formulations, uneven power dynamics in relation to sociocultural aspects of race, class, oppression, and minoritarianism preclude any ethical claim of sameness. This section has introduced the heretofore undocumented history of Lubovitch's involvement in black dance companies, and the remaining portions of this chapter will focus largely on Richardson's work in *Othello* with what could be described as culturally and racially white dance companies, namely ABT and SFB.

The Moor's Balletic Past and Melodrama

In comparison to theater, film, and opera, the history of concert dance productions of *Othello* is limited. As a story originating in sixteenth-century Italy, blacking up in *Othello* has become accepted practice in theater

---

[25] Ibid. He also danced with Pearl Lang, Glen Tetley, and Donna Butler at the time.
[26] Lubovitch, interview with author.

and opera, and is less common in the history of ballet. In the early twentieth century, we find blacking up in ballets such as Mikhail Fokine's 1911 *Petrushka* with music by Igor Stravinsky, starring Vaslav Nijinsky. Restaged most recently by the Joffrey Ballet, the Moor in *Petrushka* continues to be played in blackface. The practice of blacking up is often seen as central to Othello's racially ambivalent character, and this ambivalence is reflected in the ambivalence between ballet and modern dance (brought about by their hybridizing) in many concert dance versions of *Othello*. In ballet contexts, productions of the tale have been the occasion for modern and contemporary ballet choreographers to introduce modern dance to the classical story ballet format.[27] Previous choreographers of *Othello* have included Jacques d'Amboise, who created a production for New York City Ballet (NYCB) in 1967, and John Butler, who made a twenty-minute trio to Dvořák for the La Scala Ballet in 1976. Ex-NYCB dancer Jean-Pierre Bonnefous choreographed a full-length version for the Louisville Ballet in 1981. After retiring from NYCB, Bonnefous had been "taking classes at the Martha Graham School, and originally thought he might perform *Othello* modern-dance style: 'I thought I might do it barefoot, like Laurence Olivier in his wonderful movie version. Olivier said at the time that he needed to feel the floor for the role. Isn't that a typical modern dance remark?'"[28] In 1985, John Neumeier, known for infusing ballet with modern dance, choreographed a version to the genre-crossing sacred music of Arvo Pärt (and others) for the company he has directed for decades, the Hamburg Ballet. The last version of the ballet performed by ABT was by Mexican modern dance choreographer José Limón, who set his well-known 1949 quartet *Moor's Pavane* on the company. Unlike Lubovitch's version, Limón's was never danced in blackface. Most recently in 2009, Dwight Rhoden (the codirector of Complexions Contemporary Ballet and subject of Chapter 3) choreographed a contemporary ballet version of *Othello* for the North Carolina Dance Theatre, with music composed by David Rozenblatt.[29] Rhoden's version eschewed blackface and employed a racially inclusive and diverse cast.

While common in opera, the model of the coproduced evening-length work has occurred in ballet only more recently. Lubovitch had previously staged

---

[27] Even in 1911, *Petrushka* is also a ballet that departs from classicism.
[28] http://www.nytimes.com/1981/02/15/arts/a-full-length-othello-by-bonnefous.html.
[29] He explains, "My version of *Othello* is loosely based on the music industry. . . . The story of *Othello* is the same, but I wanted it to be modern. I think people will be able to relate to the story because it could be ripped from the headlines of today." https://clclt.com/theclog/archives/2009/05/11/longtime-dancer-to-leave-nc-dance-theatre.

several of his shorter ballets on ABT, and ABT and SFB's shared *Othello* came about when McKenzie approached Lubovitch to create a proposal for a new work under the executive directorship of Michael Kaiser (renowned in the dance world for his financial savvy, including a period with AAADT). It was Lubovitch's idea to embark on a version of *Othello*, and McKenzie appreciated the "tale of envy" and the way, through "tone, color [and specificity]," Lubovitch built a heightened level of "suspense."[30] Because the production called for an original evening-length musical score, costumes, and sets, McKenzie sought the financial and artistic partnership of SFB, directed by Helgi Tommason, who had danced with Lubovitch in Harkness Ballet in the 1960s.

According to Lubovitch, his initial impulse was to choreograph a full-length ballet, which led him to explore *Othello* "because, of all the classical stories, it was the one that could be done best in pictures."[31] Based on the original Giovanni Battista Giraldi (often referred to as "Cinthio")[32] version of the Othello story (*Un Capitano Moro*) published in Venice in 1565, Shakespeare adapted the text into the play *Othello, the Moor of Venice* around 1602. Lubovitch was compelled more by "the psychology of [the] story, not so much by the precise series of events."[33] The tension between authenticity and intentional imprecision permeates the production: as a moor, Othello is meant to evoke the Other without adhering to a specified racial appearance, Lubovitch favors "pictures" to a "precise series of events," and the set designer chooses to allude to general exoticism as opposed to pinpointing an exact locale. Designed by George Tsypin, the set evokes large slabs and broken fragments of glass, serving as French doors, hanging scrims, or transparent glacier-like furniture.

> The composer Elliot Goldenthal needed some sort of visual image to work with, so he and I came to the idea that Iago had a shattered personality. It was like a broken mirror wherein the shards reflect jagged angles and there are pieces of yourself all over but you never see your whole self. In Iago's big solo, the music is about this shattered glass. The set designer picked up on that idea; he made those large panels with broken glass coming through them.[34]

---

[30] Kevin McKenzie (with Lar Lubovitch and Wes Chapman), "American Ballet Theatre, a Shakespeare festival," video-recording, Works and process at the Guggenheim, January 29, 2007, NYPL.
[31] Lubovitch, interview with the author.
[32] Also known as Cintio.
[33] Lubovitch, interview with the author.
[34] Lubovitch, interview with the author.

In this *Othello* production, music composition, set design, and choreography were all motivated by image. Lubovitch's interest in a pictorial depiction of *Othello* resulted in his use of storyboarding. "This was... idea driven as opposed to music driven," explains Lubovitch. "I wrote out a score... storyboarding. I wrote the whole dance out like a movie, and I described the music and length."[35] Richardson states, "Working with [Lubovitch] on this project was very much like working on a film project—the conception, the communication of his ideas, the costumes, the sets and overall staging."[36] The aspects of Lubovitch's production borrowed from film—namely, storyboarding, episodic scenes, Goldenthal's cinematic score, and an emphasis on bodily action—further augment the inherently melodramatic aspects of the Othello story. Of importance here is the pairing of virtuosity and theatrical characterization, as other instantiations of Richardson's virtuosity appear in contexts that call for an abstract aesthetic, as opposed to one in which Richardson is asked to play a theatrical role. In other words, historically speaking, the virtuoso soloist in music and dance tends to perform as him or her "self," as opposed to satisfying the demands of a character. The fact that Richardson must play a role in *Othello* affords further opportunity to theorize the ballet in terms of melodrama, a term that emerges in theater and film studies in the context of theatrical conventions such as character and plot.

According to Williams, who builds upon Peter Brooks's seminal text on melodrama, the five main features of melodrama can be described thusly:

1. "Home: Melodrama begins, and wants to end, in a 'space of innocence.'"
2. "Melodrama focuses on victim-heroes and on recognizing their virtue. Recognition of virtue orchestrates the moral legibility that is key to melodrama's function."
3. "Melodrama's recognition of virtue involves a dialectic of pathos and action—a give and take of 'too late' and 'in the nick of time.'"
4. "Melodrama borrows from realism but realism serves the melodrama of pathos and action."
5. "The final key feature of melodrama is the presentation of characters who embody primary psychic roles organized in Manichean conflicts between good and evil."[37]

---

[35] Ibid.
[36] Richardson, email interview with the author, October 2010.
[37] Linda Williams, 28–40.

Furthermore, Williams describes racial melodrama as engaging "melos pointing sometimes to the virtue of racially beset victims and sometimes to the villainy of racially motivated villains."[38] Adapting the tale into the structure of a three-act ballet heightens *Othello*'s melodrama by relying more on the action of the body than narrative plot. While formally structured as a tragedy, the original Othello tale has also been described as proto-melodrama due to its European origins and predating of American melodrama's emergence on the nineteenth-century stage. Lubovitch's production falls between proto-melodrama and American melodrama to the extent we can use the term to describe dance. Three aspects of Lubovitch's production situate his *Othello* within what Williams calls the "melodramatic mode."[39] First, by hiring Richardson, an itinerant star whose offstage persona lends a dimension of "drama" to staged performance, Lubovitch borrows a system of (co)production from opera that relies on the circulation and fetishizing of fame. Second, the use of filmic storyboarding techniques melodramatically emphasizes action over literal narrative or text. Finally, the use of the dancing body itself as the embodiment and motivator of action, such that action is the most emphasized element of the production, encapsulates melodrama's requisite "dialectic of pathos and *action*."[40] That Lubovitch's *Othello* is danced (not spoken) and described in storyboarded "pictures" is essential to its melodrama. According to Williams:

> Brooks's central thesis is that the quest for a hidden moral legibility is crucial to all melodrama.... The theatrical function of melodrama's big sensation scenes was to be able to put forth a moral truth in gesture and picture that could not be fully spoken in words.[41]

The central elements of *Othello*'s plot rest on the structure of the "recognition of virtue"; it is "too late" that Othello recognizes the virtue of his wife (Desdemona) and the deceitful acts of Iago. Surprisingly, to support his commitment to dance's unique capacity as an art of emotion, Lubovitch

---

[38] Ibid., 6.
[39] I believe the melodramatic *mode* can exist within tragedy.
[40] Williams, 28–40, my emphasis.
[41] Ibid., 18. "Brooks interestingly shows, in fact, that the rise of melodrama was linked to the ban on speech in unlicensed French theaters, which originally turned to pantomime as a more powerful and direct form of communication.... Music, gesture, pantomime, and, I would add, most forms of sustained physical action are the elements of these sensational effects most familiar to us today in film, television, and musical theater."

borrows structuring frameworks from opera and film. "I wanted to make it a dance," explains Lubovitch. "A dance is not a play. A dance is best served by capturing a synthesis of emotional conditions. I wanted to capture the story in a nonnarrative way so that a great deal of dancing took place."[42] Nevertheless, because audiences tend to be aware of the plot, no production of *Othello* can be wholly devoid of narrative. Heightened emotion is a critical element of melodrama, and in Lubovitch's dance, movement itself takes the place of spoken text. As such, the body, even more so than the face, becomes the important site of racialized attention. Thus, the way the blackened body figures into melodramatic dancing invites a choreographic reading of melodrama. In the case of Richardson—and the body-painted counterpoints in his absence—blackface and virtuosity contribute to the aforementioned conditions necessary for melodrama to emerge in this balletic context.

Choreographing Leitmotif and the Homoerotics of Iago

In the absence of spoken text in *Othello: A Dance in Three Acts*, Lubovitch develops a sophisticated approach to movement wherein choreographic tropes throughout the ballet function as leitmotifs would in opera. We will discover that Lubovitch's choreographic leitmotifs lend themselves to the production's racial melodrama. Lubovitch's arcing movement in *Othello*'s *pas de deux* carries action (in the service of plot) to the forefront, and this emphasis on such symbolic action contributes to the work's melodramatic mode. For example, in Othello and Desdemona's first duet, Othello lifts Desdemona's entire body in an upward arc, onto his shoulder, around to the back, circling downward again. Their love and commitment to each other tend to be symbolized with the circular, and when such curvilinear flow is interrupted, we are to believe that trust has been broken. When Iago has convinced Othello that Desdemona has betrayed him, Othello breaks the circular flow of a subsequent duet with Desdemona by throwing her to the ground or pushing her aside. Later, toward the end of the ballet, when Desdemona is begging for Othello's trust, she creates a closed circle with her arms and tries to envelope Othello, who escapes her embrace out of spite. The trope of the white handkerchief acts as a supplement to the circular movement, and we trace the drama of the tale through the location of the

[42] Lubovitch, interview with the author.

scarf, which was originally given to Desdemona by Othello. As Iago moves the handkerchief from character to character, suspense builds. In the end, Othello kills Desdemona with the very handkerchief. That Lubovitch calls upon undulating, curvilinear movement to communicate emotion continues to foreground action.

Placing importance on the idea of dance as "motion-sound," Lubovitch explains:

> All of my dances are the story of the music, and it is a story with a beginning, a middle and an end. So, I became intrigued with the idea of a story ballet, and I rarely used the term "ballet" to refer to my work; I just called them "dances."... I think of dance as motion-sound. In this case I was interested in taking ballet and extending it to a contemporary understanding.[43]

He extends his "motion"-driven style to include allusions to the visual in addition to the sonic: "Sometimes I call my dances motion drawings.... I am concerned with the entire space—the front, back, side to side, top to bottom.... I am bending the space around them by moving them through it." The designation of "leitmotif" is my own and, while not identical, relates to Lubovitch's commitment to the framework of the "essay." He tells me:

> Like essays, these characters came into being.... The first essay is Cassio. He does a solo concerned with kindness, generosity, spirit, and youth. Then there's the essay of Desdemona, then an essay of their relationship, which is regret; it ends with an essay of Iago, and an essay of his relationship with his wife Emilia—five essays. The first act is concerned with these essays.[44]

Calling for "very little pantomime" (which I consider to be in the linguistic, communicative realm), it was important for Lubovitch to rely on the "language of dance" instead of the more literal storytelling gestures of pantomime.[45] Richardson suggests that choreography—not psyche—allows him to further access his character in *Othello*: "To get to the dramatic narrative of the role it was imperative for me to allow it to come through the choreography; never did I want to impose myself on it."[46] Richardson's privileging

---

[43] Lubovitch, interview with the author.
[44] Lubovitch, interview with the author.
[45] Ibid.
[46] Richardson, email interview with the author, October 2010.

of movement over acting technique resonates with Lubovitch's insistence on the importance of "the language of dance" over pantomime.[47] While it might seem at first that dance movements could take us further away from melodrama, Lubovitch's choreographic leitmotifs (nonliteral but highly symbolic movements created to be thematically recognizable) actually heighten *Othello*'s melodrama.

Lubovitch's choreographic leitmotifs are short thematic movement phrases or gestures repeated during points in the ballet when one is to be reminded of a certain dramatic theme.[48] For example, the *port de bras* (arm movements) of Richardson's opening crouching sequence are repeated throughout to indicate Othello's psychic strife, the melodramatic trope of "too late." A movement style that is repeated in leitmotif fashion is that of the corps de ballet, which engages in numerous unison group sections and divertissements (often to entertain Othello and Desdemona, of an upper class) composed of folksy flex-footed legwork and two-dimensional geometric arm movements that might otherwise seem to strive toward a general notion of the "ethnic." Lubovitch has discussed his interest in the tarantella in *Othello*, that he wanted to include a once-forbidden dance that had been subjected to legal bans:

> The ensemble is part of this vast tarantella. The tarantella was an earthy dance that swept Europe in the fourteenth century and it was accused of causing insanity and leading to forbidden love. It was terrifying to god-fearing catholic churches. The name came from "tarantula" because it looked to them as if they had been bitten by a tarantula. . . . I used it to indicate Iago's insanity.[49]

For the *Moor's Pavane*, Limon called upon the Pavane, a court dance. Lubovitch explains to me that the tarantella is a Southern Italian dance known for its increasing speed. In 6/8 time, legend has it that it could cure one of a poisonous tarantula bite.[50] Lubovitch uses the tarantella for Bianca

---

[47] I should note that I do not believe dance is a "language" in the strict sense of the term, as dance does not point to subjects in the same way as a signifying system of language. I only wish to emphasize Lubovitch's privileging of dance and choreography that does not use gesture or pantomime in a way that is recognizable and signifying in the same way as, say, sign language.

[48] Adorno cites Wagner's repeated use of leitmotif in opera as a weakness of ego, and Nietzsche sees it as an appeal to the masses. Both correlate leitmotif with virtuosity, a category that makes them wary.

[49] Lubovitch, interview with the author.

[50] Lubovitch, interview with the author.

and villagers associated with her character, and to emphasize contact with the earth, most of the women in the ballet wear ballet slippers instead of poine shoes. Just as a jazzy saxophone enters Goldenthal's cinematic score as a leitmotif for sultry villagers or a sense of psychic strife, the tarantella is employed as a general indicator of sexual excess. These leitmotifs tread dangerously toward stereotypical uses of minoritarian sounds and movement to suggest the "ethnic," the "sexual," or danger.[51] In light of Lubovitch and Goldenthal's leitmotifs, it is no great surprise that a production comfortable with exoticizing uses of tarantella and saxophone would go on to make use of blackface makeup, no matter how well intentioned. In *Othello*, both music and makeup are used to sexualize ethnicity and evoke ethnicity as danger: tarantella is meant to portray the "insanity" of excess "earthy" feminine sexuality, and blackface is designed to characterize Othello as a moor with threatening, masculine virility.

Much of Lubovitch's essayistic approach was dedicated to his treatment of Iago as a character tangled in homoerotic desire. "There is a very specific spin I took on the character of Iago," explains Lubovitch. "The strongest part of Iago's attachment to Othello is homoerotic. One of his major motivations in my story for destroying Othello is because he has to destroy the object of his forbidden desire."[52] This psychosexual angle on the Othello story is echoed by Shakespeare scholars such as Robert Matz, whose queer reading of Shakespeare's version suggests that

> *Othello* projects same-sex desire within English culture onto racial and cultural others, but this is not because the play functions as a return of the repressed. Rather, *Othello* is written in the terms of a discourse of sodomy that in the increasing encounters between Europe and racial or cultural others would be used to demarcate difference between the foreign and familiar.[53]

---

[51] Exemplifying his later work, *The Case of Wagner* serves as a platform for Nietzsche to express his disdain for what he sees as performance—specifically Wagnerian opera—generated for the masses. If we think of mainstream film, the genre most influential to Lubovitch's production, as the potential endpoint to Nietzsche's logic, it would not be remiss to assume that Nietzsche would interpret ABT/SFB's *Othello* as diluted for conservative (if not mainstream) consumption.
[52] Lubovitch, interview with the author.
[53] Robert Matz, "Slander, Renaissance Discourses of Sodomy, and Othello," *ELH* 66, no. 2 (Summer, 1999): 261–76 (16 pages).

That homoeroticism stands in for colonial anxieties of miscegenation comes through in the visual depictions of race throughout the ballet. Despite the primacy of visual and sonic elements in his production, Lubovitch was most compelled by having at his disposal a personal understanding of the Othello tale as homoerotically charged, even if not verbalized for the performers or the audience. He notes:

> Of all the theories that attracted my attention and had the most authenticity was the Freudian theory. I never told the dancers; it's in the choreography. In the last act, in the duet Iago does with Othello, Iago becomes Desdemona—he acts out sexual scenes that he is describing between Cassio and Desdemona, but he is becoming Desdemona in those scenes. But only I need to know that. In the play, there is a scene where Iago is trying to convince Othello of Cassio's attachment to Desdemona. He tells Othello that he was in the barrack sleeping with Cassio in the same bed, and that he was awake but Cassio was asleep and was murmuring and talking in his sleep. And as he was murmuring he threw his body over Iago and felt his tights and mumbled, "Desdemona, Desdemona" as he groped and grappled my thighs. It's deeply homoerotic.[54]

There is an uneasiness to Iago's physicality—full of jolts, angularity, and darting pivots. Lubovitch states, "To express Iago's 'jagged' emotions, I made the specific choice to go in a very angular and percussive direction—the physicalization of certain emotions were not smooth, lyrical, curvaceous, or fluid," even though he otherwise believes, "To me, dancing is all transitional. There are no destinations. The destination is the overall curve, the arc that is being spoken of."[55] Iago is queered through both characterization and ensuing movement style—a jaggedness that interrupts a dominant flow.

As far as choreographic leitmotif goes, *Othello*'s handkerchief is rife with symbolic value. A cloth that "changes hands many times," we notice that it travels from character to character, defining, even ending, relations, as it is used in the eventual murder of Desdemona at the hands of Othello. Lubovitch states, "The handkerchief is integral to the story of Othello, and Shakespeare went to great lengths to weigh it down with symbolism and meaning. Shakespeare claims it was woven from the gauze of mummies—virgins who

---

[54] Lubovitch, interview with the author.
[55] Ibid.

were put to death." Lubovitch believes that "when Othello's mother gave him the handkerchief, she told him that to beware: if the handkerchief was given to the wrong woman, it would end up in the deceit of the person who gave it to them."[56] As an extension of Iago's "social illegitimacy" within Venetian society, the handkerchief functions as an object with agency—always in motion—moving and, when at one's disposal, moved, personifying a range between a liminal state and a performative act(or). "In *Othello*," according to Matz, "Iago's accusations of adultery always focus on ambiguous signs (most famously, the handkerchief)."[57] Lubovitch frames death as freedom for religious Desdemona:

> Othello eventually kills her in my version because he loves her so deeply. The only way to preserve the purity of their love was to prevent her from being impure by taking her life. In my version, she accepts it, and in the very last moment at the end, when he wraps the scarf around her neck, she reaches her hands to him in an act of thanks for delivering her to a better world, a place where her purity would be undeniable. Desdemona is deeply religious.[58]

This murder via handkerchief prevents the possibility of concluding the story with miscegenation, as if to suggest murder is more socially acceptable than interracial love. Of course, homoeroticism is also left unresolved. In this ballet, both interracial love and homoeroticism are left unfulfilled, the expression of which is made clear through Lubovitch's choreographic leitmotifs.

Othello's Racial Melodrama

The racial tensions present in *Othello* are, to an extent, mirrored in Richardson's life and career as far as issues of blackness and classicism are concerned. Richardson's career trajectory as a modern and contemporary dancer has made certain critics wary of his ballet classicism. Such wariness is misguided, as Richardson's versatility is in fact more suitable to Lubovitch's

---

[56] Lubovitch, interview with the author.
[57] Robert, "Slander, Renaissance Discourses of Sodomy, and Othello," 261–76.
[58] Lubovitch, interview with the author.

contemporary ballet style, a style challenging for ABT dancers trained solely in classical ballet. Despite his widely recognized skill, Richardson finds himself in tension with certain accepted racial hierarchies. This tension bears an uncanny resemblance to the character of Othello himself, a moor who ascends military ranks in a society dominated by white people. Because Richardson has not spent time on the roster of a classical ballet company, critics have sometimes found it difficult to trust his ability in a leading role with a major ballet company, despite his serious training in classical ballet. Allan Ulrich writes:

> [Lubovitch] created Othello for Desmond Richardson, who trained as a modern dancer and who will perform in the telecast. Even with an experienced ballerino in the role (Cyril Pierre), the opportunities for profound exchanges between the protagonist and Desdemona are limited because they do not dance in the same language.[59]

Ulrich's ill-informed assumption that Richardson's modern dance training eclipses his ballet training even contaminates his perception of other dancers in the title role. Anxieties about competence and dance techniques serve as placeholders for managing larger anxieties about excess and race. Revealed in Ulrich's anxious reaction is a nervous correlation between race and inability. He doubly interpellates Richardson as modern dancer and Black man. By conflating these already binding identities, Ulrich generates a certain kind of racialized anxiety that permeates his view of the demands of the role itself, as if the role has been essentially "dumbed down" to accommodate Richardson and his alternates. Such bias is demonstrative of a history of dance criticism that has all too easily equated race with style, more specifically with inability.[60] Certainly all the performers in *Othello* are dancing in a uniform style, the contemporary ballet idiom called for by Lubovitch. Finally, Ulrich has mistaken Lubovitch's style for classical (as opposed to contemporary) ballet.[61]

---

[59] Allan Ulrich, "Lubovitch's 'Othello' a Tragedy in More Ways Than One," SFGate.com (*San Francisco Chronicle*), February 28, 2002, https://www.sfgate.com/entertainment/article/lubovitch-s-othello-a-tragedy-in-more-ways-than-2868847.php

[60] While Ulrich's opinion may be common, it is not universal, as other critics (such as those mentioned in Chapter 3 on virtuosity) hail Richardson for being one of the greatest virtuosos to grace the stage.

[61] Ironically, the type of movement that Richardson is known for in Complexions and Ballett Frankfurt—sharp and fragmented but also liquid, hyperflexible, and gender ambiguous—is given to the role of Iago, not Othello. The only time Richardson approximates such sinewy movement is

That Richardson undergoes racially biased criticism while working in the service of an already racially melodramatic ballet places Lubovitch's *Othello* squarely in the realm of what Williams calls racial melodrama. Having recently emerged from the media frenzy that was the 1995 O. J. Simpson trial, the 1997 public was well poised (though perhaps too exhausted) to engage with a story featuring the racial melodrama of a Black man murdering his white wife. Williams extends her discussion of melodrama in film to the racial melodrama of events in the media. Referring to the racial melodrama of "playing the race card,"[62] Williams writes:

> The melodramatic playings of the race card will be best understood, then, as a story cycle brought to life by a circulating set of transmuting icons and melos pointing sometimes to the virtue of racially beset victims and sometimes to the villainy of racially motivated villains.[63]

While Williams points to the real-life drama that was the O. J. Simpson trial, we could consider any production of *Othello* as implicated in the logic of playing the race card, as the title character's actions will inevitably be read according to visual cues provided by performances themselves as well as racially charged current events defining any given cultural moment. Moreover, in his mistrust of Richardson's integrity to ballet technique, Ulrich's review creates a kind of villain out of Richardson himself, playing into what Williams identifies as racial melodrama's "circulating set of transmuting icons and melos."

The way that Richardson's personhood intersects with the unique conditions of his performance in *Othello* resonates with Gabriele Brandstetter's observation of the virtuoso's conflation of pathos and ethos:

> The credibility of the speaker's performance—beyond its use of staging and argumentation—was ultimately conveyed via his person: the pathos of

---

during a heartbroken solo in which he portrays a sense of betrayal after assuming that Desdemona has been adulterous. He jumps and falls to the floor in rapid succession and shows angst through terse, contracting movements.

[62] Keep in mind that there are various differing uses of the phrase "playing the race card" in everyday vernacular, and for the purposes of this chapter, I am working with the way Williams uses the phrase in her argument.

[63] Ibid., 6.

the performance was added to by the ethos of his person, his status, his honour—his *virtus*.[64]

In this case, we can alter Brandstetter's remarks to account for the "credibility of the [*dancer's*] performance" and take into consideration Richardson's individuality and public persona alongside his performance and characterization (his *virtus* and virtue in addition to his virtuosity). Richardson's "celebrity" status relative to the dance world has the potential to ease in the viewers' imagination the severity of the fact that alternate casts perform the role in bronze makeup—in blackface. In other words, due to the proliferation of posters, the PBS telecast, and its subsequent DVD sale, the ABT/SFB role of Othello is equated with Richardson—a Black man—and ensuing casts are thought to work in the service of the larger production, ever dominated by Richardson's presence. Perhaps most surprising is Richardson's own outlook on his blackfaced counterparts:

> Dancers playing the title role ... painted in bronzed makeup did not disturb me as much as one would think simply because the role is indicative of a Moor of African descent, and seeing that American Ballet Theatre did not have any other Principal male dancers of color beside myself and Jose Carreño, it was necessary to draw a distinction between the characters. I did not consider this blackface, as blackface performances had a very real and negative connotation toward African Americans. Othello being the title role and the character being of royalty would be an honor for any performer to play. I do know that the other dancers playing the role felt slightly uncomfortable ... but quickly let it go to envelop the role. ... I believe [Lubovitch's] interpretation of *Othello* on ABT was a progressive move.[65]

Because he does not detect blatant racism in Lubovitch's production (and even calls it "progressive"), Richardson is able to accept it in positive terms. While he chooses to view the ballet as an opportunity to explore a character-driven role (or does so as a form of disavowal), his acceptance of the practice of blackface in *Othello* reminds us of the importance of his presence on ABT and SFB's historically homogeneous stages. And, in the trajectory of African American performance, it is of the utmost importance that Richardson has

---

[64] Brandstetter, "Virtuoso's Stage," 181.
[65] Richardson, interview with the author.

enjoyed so much success and recognition in all arenas of dance. He has a great deal more agency and control over his career than most professional dancers. Nevertheless, we find him negating the possibility of *Othello's* makeup as "blackface" (which he regards negatively), and this negation inadvertently betrays a compulsion to protect one of the few starring roles available to Black ballet dancers.

Facing the Surrogate and Corporeal Blackface

Numerous studies have squabbled over interpretations of the Moor's appearance; some have claimed the importance of place and faith over race; all have bickered over the exact tone of his complexion. Richardson enters into historically fraught responses to *Othello*. Ironically, an older review of a 1970 play of *Othello* by theater and dance critic Clive Barnes finds blackface to be a necessary component of the telling of *Othello* and disapproves of a Black actor in the role: Barnes, referring to Moses Gunn in a 1970 production of the play, does "not approve of black actors playing Othello—it is too obvious.... Othello was written for a white actor in blackface. Mr. Gunn plays him black—plays him from the deliberate position of black consciousness."[66] Of course, this statement is problematic on multiple levels, not the least of which is the assumption of a white actor's access to "black consciousness," especially in a theatrical context. Nevertheless, it points to a widely accepted perspective that Othello should be played in blackface as to appear explicitly mutable, ambivalent. Thus, the aesthetic of ambivalence is met with ambivalent criticism.

For all the ambivalence surrounding Othello, however, the role still comes with a decided sense of the monstrous, and this monstrosity is attached to race and rage. According to Richardson's surrogate, Marcelo Gomes, "I literally wasn't performing in my own skin; I was painted to appear darker than I actually am. Each act you get more and more paint on your body because you have less and less clothing on.... Othello is such a beast." Noted as recently as 2007 without an inkling of disapproval, a *New York Times* critic writes, "Mr. Gomes, painted a striking bronze with body makeup, cuts a fervent figure as the general betrayed by the conniving Iago.... As Desdemona

---

[66] Clive Barnes, "Stage: Kahn Stages 'Othello' with Gunn as Moor," *New York Times*, June 22, 1970.

Ms. Kent is gentle and pure; her dewy innocence is radiant."[67] Not only is Gomes's bronze makeup described as "striking," but also it is placed in contrast to Kent's "pure," "dewy" complexion. Thus, the bronze tone is implicitly equated with impure morality, further aligning blackface with melodrama's preoccupation with virtue and morality.

In addition to blackface makeup and brown tights, dancers playing Othello are subjected to armorlike costuming evoking six-pack abdominals and large pectoral muscles, and later the metallic covering is removed to expose the dancer's actual musculature. Lubovitch states

> The kid leather is painted to look like chest plates and abs because we wanted Othello to have a kind of a nakedness. The costume designer, Ann Hould-Ward, wanted him to be very vulnerable even when he was in armor.[68]

Nevertheless, there is something hypersexualized as masculine in the actual appearance of the armor and "naked" torso, as if to equate black masculinity with virility, strength, and the potential for violence. The increased shedding of costuming and exposure of the dancer's body corresponds with the breakdown of Othello's morality and virtue. Pointing to the level of ambivalence surrounding the production is the following description of the makeup as decreasing in amount throughout an SFB performance in which Cyril Pierre played Othello in blackface: "Pierre's bushy hair and minstrel show makeup, which grew progressively lighter through the evening, was disconcerting, if not downright offensive."[69] For some, blackface is essential to Othello; to others, it offends. Seemingly unapparent to the production's creators, however, is the parallel between Othello's moral breakdown and the morally questionable practice of blacking up used to portray such collapse.

Whereas most studies of blackface and minstrelsy have addressed minstrel shows or contemporary popular performance such as hip-hop music, dance scholars Susan Manning, Juliet McMains, and Hanna Jarvinen have more recently theorized the practices specifically in dance. Manning and McMains apply the terms to dance traditions not immediately associated with minstrelsy, complicating the assumption that any practice resembling blackface or minstrelsy should be perceived as necessarily offensive. In doing

---

[67] Gia Kourlas, "With the Handkerchief, a Hint of Ice Capades," *New York Times*, May 24, 2007, http://www.nytimes.com/2007/05/24/arts/dance/24othe.html>.
[68] Lubovitch, interview with the author.
[69] Ulrich, "Lubovitch's 'Othello' a Tragedy in More Ways Than One."

so, do they ostensibly pardon otherwise culturally problematic performance practices? Manning develops the term "metaphorical minstrelsy" to account for 1930s modern dance in America in which white dancers took on nonwhite subjectivity. According to Manning:

> *Metaphorical minstrelsy* [is] a convention whereby white dancers' bodies made reference to nonwhite subjects. In contrast to blackface performers, modern dancers did not engage in impersonation. Rather, their bodies became the vehicles for the tenors of nonwhite subjects. Modern dancers did not mimic others but presented an abstraction or personification of others—Oriental, Indian, Negro. During the 1940s metaphorical minstrelsy disappeared as a convention within modern dance, and thus it is difficult to fathom the historical moment of the 1930s, when it was a dominant convention in American theater dance.[70]

The unspoken crux of Manning's concept, however, is visuality. She seems to suggest that because racial mimesis operates in early modern dance such that it does not rely on visible surface cues on the face or body (namely, makeup), practitioners of "metaphorical minstrelsy" should be absolved of accusations of "impersonation." Such a statement assumes that impersonation, firstly, is related to the visuality of surface and skin, and secondly, is the more violent practice. It seems that the absence of the reliability of visual cues is what compels Manning to label this practice "metaphorical." Therefore, we might question the validity of bringing in the term "minstrelsy" at all to refer to practices that eschew blacking up in favor of corporeal and choreographic appropriations of subjectivity, of haphazardly embodying the Other. If minstrelsy refers more to genre, blackface refers more to formal signifiers of the minstrelsy genre that may or may not work in the service of a minstrel show proper. Manning suggests that choreographic embodiment assuages the potential violence of otherwise imitative, minstrel performances. In other words, modern dance's supposed investment in the dancing body's ability to manifest subjectivity sets it apart from the "mask" of minstrelsy.

McMains's example comes from contemporary ballroom dance competitors who paint their faces and bodies brown to satisfy "Latin" categories. Unlike Manning, McMains focuses on surface more than style. She writes:

[70] Manning, 10.

Although competitive ballroom dancers are not the only consumers of self-tanning products, the prevalence of artificially darkened white skin in DanceSport Latin competitions invites examination into the relationship between ballroom "Latin" dances and their ethnic referents. I introduce the term brownface, not a word used in the DanceSport industry, in order to call attention to the racial and potentially racist consequences of this practice.... Eastern European DanceSport competitors may ... be solidifying their own white status by performing distance from Latinos in brownface.[71]

Like numerous theorists of blackface before her, McMains associates blackface (and "brownface") with the reification of whiteness even more than the impersonation of blackness. Because blackface and blackness already signal ambivalence within a predominantly negative framework, we might do without a distinction between blackface and brownface. "Brownness" has been positively reappropriated in studies of Latinidad by the likes of José Muñoz to signal affective or empathetic kinship and affinity, as in "feeling brown." Brownface (as opposed to feeling brown) carries a negative connotation and functions similarly to blackface in its reliance on visuality and approximating the Other. Brownness as a category does not exclude blackness as a category of othering; thus, brownface would best be thought of as a form of blackface. It is important to note that the body carries style in Lubovitch's *Othello* differently than the "Latin" dancer in DanceSport: if the ballroom dancer tries to approximate a foreign style, *Othello*'s demands are in the realm of Western ballet and contemporary dance, styles that are only legible to the extent the audience is versed in Africanist influences inherent to American dance and those contributed by Richardson's individual versatility.

Although blackface practices initially invite theorizations of the face and the mask, Eric Lott reminds us that

> we are justified in seeing early blackface performance as one of the very first constitutive discourses of the body in American culture. Certainly minstrelsy's commercial production of the Black male body was a fundamental source of its threat and its fascination for white men.... The minstrel show as an institution may be profitably understood as a major effort

---

[71] McMains, 109, 147.

of corporeal containment—which is to say that it necessarily trained a rather constant regard on the body.[72]

By referring to blackface performance as a masculinist "discourse of the body," Lott suggests that the "face" in blackface is a placeholder for larger racially mimetic concerns regarding the growing dominance of the "production" of the black body in American entertainment culture. While early minstrelsy produced the black male body through repeated performances of acting, song, and dance representing caricatures such as Jim Crow and Zip Coon, Lubovitch's contemporary *Othello* does not "produce" the black male body insofar as it compulsively tries to recuperate a corporeal authenticity of blackness *through* bodily performance. Furthermore, ballet operates in a nonprofit framework, and its images are not proliferated and reiterated in the commercial realm to the same degree as those of historical minstrel shows. While black corporeal authenticity is already an impossibility, the idea that Richardson has the capacity to lend the role of Othello a degree of racial believability is essential to the logic behind blackening the bodies of subsequent dancers in the role. I refer to the bronzed body as the "blackened body" in order to draw parallel conclusions between the function of blackface in minstrelsy and the darkened body in contemporary ballet. In other words, I refrain from suggesting that bronze—as opposed to black—makeup somehow alleviates the severity of the practice; thus, tone is not correlative with degree of racism. In this way, I point to a practice that may appear similar to that of McMains's "brownface" while theorizing its results differently. Non-Black Othellos blackening their faces and bodies is less a reification of whiteness and more a striving for virtuosity and authenticity of blackness.

Lubovitch's *Othello* shifts the attention from the face and mask toward the body and its dancing, allowing for a consideration of how the blackened body supplements and exacerbates elements that have already been theorized around blackface. For one, the relationship between performer and penis as

---

[72] Lott, *Love and Theft*, 117, 118. The foregrounding of action and appearance of the body in this ballet are critical to broadening the discussion of blackface in performance, as most studies of the form have lingered on the "face" in blackface as an opportunity to theorize the mask. It is important that the body—and not just the face—becomes covered in makeup in this production. Blackface is another element of Lubovitch's production adopted (or inherited) from film and opera. I am interested in what occurs when we shift our discussion to the painted and costumed body. To depict blackness through associations with the masked or the sculptural recalls modernist fetishizations of "Africa," for example, Picasso's 1907 *Les Demoiselles d'Avignon*.

illustrated by Lott's discussion of blackface's racialized masculinity is altered. Lott writes:

> As [Ralph] Ellison puts it, "The mask was the thing (the 'thing' in more ways than one)." . . . Bold swagger, irrepressible desire, sheer bodily display: in a real sense the minstrel man *was* the penis, that organ returning in a variety of contexts, at times ludicrous, at others rather less so.[73]

While we might assume that the blackface mask operates as a phallic prosthesis, Lott equates blackface (as performed by whites) with the penis itself, suggesting a violent amputation and resuturing (or "re-membering," as it were) of the organ, as opposed to remaining in the realm of the symbolic. By not donning blackface, Richardson is at once emasculated and already in possession of the sexually suggestive "penis" of blackness sought after by whites in blackface. In terms of costuming, noticeably adorning Richardson's legs are brown Lycra tights. Moreover, his is the only pelvic area that remains relatively exposed, for all the other male characters have an extra flap of fabric covering the region. As such, the actual anatomical bulge serves as a reminder of Othello's ever-brewing anger, conflating sexuality, race, and rage.[74] When Richardson embodies the role, masculinity seems to be returned to the Black performer, only to find that his is the penis being stolen and apportioned in the name of authenticity when others play the role. Thus, virtuosity takes on the role of phallus, as it is ultimately Richardson's virtuosic movement quality that is coveted by Othellos in black makeup.

The blackening of Richardson's surrogates further reveals the role's messy harnessing of masculinity. It is less during Richardson's performance itself and only retroactively—after learning that other casts are blackened up—that we would be compelled to consider the provocation that Richardson may be performing black-on-black minstrelsy. Upon the realization that Lubovitch's *Othello* is otherwise performed in blackface, Richardson's participation in the ballet attains the problematics of what Chude-Sokei refers to as Burt Williams's black-on-black minstrelsy. Chude-Sokei offers nuance to the difficult task of having to reconcile the face and the body in blackface:

---

[73] Lott, 25. "Racial defensiveness was imaged in this period in more disguised ways as well. Minstrelsy's obsession with the penis and with the world's mother seems to have given rise to an inordinate amount of anxiety and fantasy regarding the threat of castration" (Lott, 151).

[74] "The fact is that minstrel songs and dances conjured up not only the black body but its labor, not only its sexuality but its place and function in a particular economy" (Lott, 117).

Figure 5.1 Desmond Richardson and Sandra Brown in American Ballet Theatre's *Othello* by Lar Lubovitch (See color plates).
Photograph by Roy Round.

Given that traditional minstrelsy was based on the absence of actual Negroes, the mask signified what Wilson Harris calls the "absent body" of the represented. Bert Williams's presence onstage was thus rendered through a hyperbolic absence, and his performance danced in and around that "zone of non-being" that Fanon locates behind the mask that overdetermined black flesh.[75]

[75] Chude-Sokei, 35.

According to Chude-Sokei, Richardson's presence in the role does not necessarily reverse the "absent body"; instead, it is more akin to a doubling of absence. As the black body is hyperbolically emphasized in *Othello*, it is simultaneously removed, mirroring what Lott refers to as "cultural strategies ... devised to occlude [the] recognition" of exploited human labor at the foundation of America's economy.[76] Blackface practices are always haunted by the specters of slavery, and the blackened dancing body both effaces and reveals the physical labor of the slave. It would be simplistic to assume that the historical distance of Lubovitch's *Othello* from chattel slavery and early minstrelsy absolves his production of participation in what Chude-Sokei (after Fanon) cites as blackface's capacity to "overdetermine black flesh." If we recall Hortense Spillers concept (from Chapter 3) that flesh is both the site of the slave's wound and the site of the dancer's labor, it would seem that the blackened dancing body would desire nothing more than to match that overdetermination of flesh with an overdetermination of dance technique, namely, virtuosity.

In refusing to determine a stable "racially beset victim" or a "racially motivated villain," Lubovitch's *Othello* ultimately satisfies Williams's concept of racial melodrama, both within the production's performances and through surrounding practices of hiring—and replacing—Richardson. Like virtuosity's mode of revealing and concealing the body's labor, leading to a hyperbolic aesthetic, *Othello*'s melodrama lies in its appropriation of blackface to hyperbolically present and absent the black dancing body.[77]

---

[76] "In reality... it is *human labor* that must reproduce itself as well as create surplus value. In these societies the body is a potentially subversive site because to recognize it fully is to recognize the exploitative organization of labor that structures their economies. Cultural strategies must be devised to occlude such a recognition: reducing the body purely to sexuality is one strategy; colonizing it with a medical discourse in which the body is dispersed into discrete parts or organs is another. Shackling the body to a discourse of racial biology is still another, and in western societies the black body in particular has, in [Richard] Dyer's words, served as the site of both '*remembering and denying* the inescapability of the body in the economy,' a figuration of the world's body and its labor, easily called up and just as easily denied. In antebellum America it was minstrelsy that performed this crucial hegemonic function, involving the black male body as a powerful cultural sign of sexuality as well as a sign of the dangerous, guilt-inducing physical reality of slavery but relying on the derided category of race finally to dismiss both" (Lott, 118).

[77] Lubovitch in an interview with the author: "I want the audience to know that Shakespeare didn't invent the story of Othello and that I was drawing from original sources just as Shakespeare had. I don't want them to assume that they are going to see the play without words onstage." "It took us a while to find a makeup that was acceptable—that didn't look like blackface, but suggested a person of color. It didn't have to be black particularly but someone other than white Venetian society. We were really attempting to look at the various colors of North Africa." "I personally don't think that the companies have an attitude towards color, I think that with the advent of black dance, most talented Black dancers are more interested in an expression that comes from their history and their background and are less interested in making white statements and having white feelings about movement." "I call it dance. I don't give it an appellation any more definitive than that because I draw on any dance that I have ever felt or seen, from any vocabulary. It's a series of interlaced physical sensations that I call dance."

6
Bad

Freakery, Iconicity, and Michael Jackson's Ghost

> It is important to recognize how the oft-told history of Michael Jackson's rise to stardom resembles the institutional history of the freak show.... Jackson gave his manager a copy of a book about P.T. Barnum's "theories and philosophies," telling him "[t]his is going to be my bible and I want it to be yours" and adding "I want my whole career to be the greatest show on earth."... It is intriguing that many of Barnum's hoaxes played with a similar dialectic between static and plastic freakishness.... These hoaxes played with the distinction between the animate and inanimate, the organic and the inorganic, much as Jackson's music videos and hoaxes do.
> —David D. Yuan[1]

Just after earning the Presidential Scholar in the Arts award and before dancing with the Alvin Ailey American Dance Theater (AAADT), teenaged Desmond Richardson danced in Michael Jackson's music video, "Bad." The dancers chosen to perform in "Bad" were meant to evoke heteronormative machismo, a quality Richardson was accustomed to fulfilling. Jackson himself stated (in his autobiography, *Moonwalk*):

> "Bad" is a song about the street. It's about this kid from a bad neighborhood who gets to go away to a private school. He comes back to the old neighborhood when he's on a break from school and the kids from the neighborhood

---

[1] David Yuan, "The Celebrity Freak: Michael Jackson's 'Grotesque Glory,'" in *Freakery: Cultural Spectacles of the Extraordinary Body*, ed. Rosemarie Garland Thomson (New York: New York University Press, 1996), 372–73.

start giving him trouble. He sings, "I'm bad, you're bad, who's bad, who's the best?" He's saying when you're strong and good, then you're bad.[2]

Needless to say, Richardson's appearance and dance ability were "strong and good," and thus "bad." The kind of masculinity he called upon and evoked in "Bad" was also attractive to the Ailey company (as we saw in Chapter 2). Both the song and video premiered in 1987, the same year Jackson disassociated himself from the Jehovah's Witnesses.[3] In addition to leaving the Jehovah's Witnesses, Jackson was distancing himself from the do-gooder image he incurred in 1984 by lending his hit, "Beat It," to Reagan's anti-drunk driving campaign, through which he procured the Presidential Public Safety Commendation. A number one single, "Bad" lent Jackson's image a harder edge. Although Jackson wanted Richardson to continue working with him and join him on tour, Richardson made the difficult decision to remain in Ailey II, the feeder company for AAADT. He maintained his initial goal of dancing for Ailey but later carved out time to dance with Jackson numerous times over the course of his career. Richardson tells me:

> "Bad" was the first time I worked with Michael [Jackson]; the second time was the *21st Annual American Music Awards* (choreographed by LaVelle Smith and Travis Payne, organized by Frank Gatson). Then was the *History* promo tour in Budapest, then [*Michael Jackson: 30th Anniversary Celebration* at] Madison Square Garden on 9/9 and 9/10 (choreographed by Glenn Packard and Brian Thomas), the days leading up to the 9/11 tragedy.[4]

In addition to these four staged and televised appearances with Jackson, Richardson was part of a rehearsal development team that Jackson would gather regularly over a number of years to workshop and generate material. According to Richardson, "Michael liked to work with a certain group of

---

[2] Michael Jackson, *Moonwalk* (New York: Doubleday, 1988), Kindle Edition, 264 of 301.
[3] "The New Pop Cinema, however, transformed the visual space by placing African Americans, women, and queer artists at the forefront, including dynamic pop superstars like Michael Jackson, Madonna, Prince, and George Michael. As important as were their identities, the alternative idea(l)s they communicated and the alternative methods they used to communicate them were just as meaningful. Among the most crucial features of the New Pop Cinema was dance. Dance was the antithesis of rigidity, machismo, and conservatism. Interestingly, the identity group most averse to dance as a legitimate element of film or videos comprised heteronormative white men.... Dance music, it was argued, lacked substance and authenticity. It was emotional, not cerebral. It appealed to blacks, gays, women, and other minorities" (from Vogel chapter on *Freaks in Reagan Era*).
[4] Richardson, interview with the author, 2010.

people [and was] very loyal." Rehearsal was a crucial part of Jackson's career. Richardson states:

> Although [Jackson] wasn't a trained dancer . . . it was clear that he was a natural. He could pick up and remember steps like nobody's business and I think it's all a part of how he was trained at Motown—to rehearse, be on time, know the music, all those things. He had no issue as a "non-dancer."[5]

But Richardson's account of Jackson as a "natural" is combined with his observation of Jackson's unwavering work ethic, born of the disciplinary training of Motown. Recounting a conversation he had with Michael's sister, Janet, also known for regimented studio sessions, about the Jackson siblings' ability to "pick up" choreography and movement, Richardson says, "Janet knows how to rehearse and she knows how to take a rehearsal. She [and Michael] know how to be active in rehearsal." Richardson elaborates that Michael Jackson wasted no time in rehearsal and possessed the utmost commitment to process. Just as Richardson told Jackson he finds dancing to be his "calling," Jackson told Richardson, "I'm just a performer. I love to perform. I know my calling. I received my calling early."[6] Dance, for Jackson, composed an integral part of the whole, of being a performer.

The making of the video for "Bad" exemplifies the ways in which artists and celebrities mobilize and manage ambivalence in order to exert a degree of control over their success: by posturing with a gang of guys in the "Bad" video to assert any street cred his character may have lost by attending prep school, Jackson wants to harden his own feminized image. He effectively borrows the performed, hard masculinity oozing from his dancers. Later in this chapter we find that Jackson's contemporary, Prince, felt that appearing opposite Jackson, who sings, "Your butt is mine," would have sent his masculinity (and thus his career) too far in the direction of homosexuality and submissiveness, and therefore he backed out of an offer to perform in the video. And, although Richardson found consistency in the masculinity he put forth in "Bad" and the gender type he fulfilled on the Ailey stage, he chose to continue on his originally intended path of dancing with Ailey. While the media

[5] Ibid.
[6] Ibid.

can sway public perception, all three artists often exert control over their careers by making calculated decisions about gendered appearance, performance, and embodiment. At the crux of this chapter is the dialectic between agency and objectification in the formation of iconicity, and ultimately how the ambivalence of *freakery* unfolds and is managed through Jackson's and Richardson's careers.

As Richardson's career catapulted in the 1990s and he went on to co-found Complexions Contemporary Ballet, he became a dance icon, while Jackson's iconic status was becoming tainted by negative perceptions of his surgical bodily alterations, vitiligo, and accusations of child molestation. This chapter considers together Richardson and Jackson's iconicity and broad-ranging associations of the trope of the "freak" in their parallel, and sometimes overlapping, careers.[7] As such, it is as much a study of discourse as it is a study of dance in American culture; we find that the histories of populist vernacular language and popular performance run parallel to each other, especially in regard to meanings of the word "freak." Like "virtuosity," "freak" is also a term characterized by a "you know it when you see it" quality and ambivalence: it oscillates between derogatory and celebratory. Its vernacular roots are not unlike those of "Bad" in Jackson's song title ("bad" means good, and "freak," at least sometimes, means virtuoso). Central to the range of meaning of both "virtuosity" and "freak" is excess. Both words are used colloquially and otherwise to point to excessive traits and performances that lie beyond the grasp of normativity. Especially because the term has been deployed in black vernacular that has permeated mainstream banter, the multiple connotations of the "freak" are relevant to Richardson's and Jackson's work and lives. To scrutinize these connotations is to reveal the complex dynamics at work in the formation of a cultural icon, a figure who exists at a distance but is felt intimately, exalted only to become vulnerable to the threat of disparagement. In thinking through virtuosity and freakery together in terms of Richardson's and Jackson's careers, I theorize both discourse and performance, specifically at the intersection of ability, disability, race, sexuality, dance, fandom, and agency.

---

[7] Connecting to the book's introduction, my discussion of the freak raises a point by Joseph Roach, namely, that there is a social "apartness" to those who possess the "it" quality.

The five categories of the term "freak" mobilized by Jackson are virtuosity, disability, hypersexuality, fandom, and control. In regard to the first category, virtuosity, a performer (most often a dancer) is colloquially called a "freak" when her performance seems inhuman, replete with feats beyond the reach of everyday mastery. Such a formation communicates a sense of excellence as exceptionalism. The second category of freakery as disability is rooted in historical British and American freak shows, ethnological freak shows, and sideshows. The idea of the freak as Other, as an oddity to be gawked at by the general public, was most popular in the US in the nineteenth century, and its residues are still palpable today. Minstrel shows mimic the cultural violence of the freak show's objectifying mode of spectatorship. Ethnological freak shows and minstrel shows emerged from the logic of colonialism and slavery, which rendered humans exploitable commodities and possessions. The phrase "freak of nature" bridges the first and second connotations of freakery, and we ascertain how freak in the sense of the abject Other was reappropriated to suggest otherness born of excess excellence, a pivot from disgust to applause. The third category of freak, In popular culture and music, can be someone who exudes sexual excess, one who appears to desire or engage in sexual activity beyond that which is deemed socially acceptable. Think of Rick James's 1981 song "Super Freak": "That girl is pretty wild now / The girl's a super freak / The kind of girl you read about / In the new wave magazines / That girl is pretty kinky / The girl's a super freak." A fourth meaning of freak circulating is the freak as fan. When someone encounters their favorite celebrity, they are said to "freak out"; groups of fans of someone or something are often referred to as freaks (Michael Jackson freaks, dance freaks, etc.). Freakery as fandom points to the excessive reaction of audiences and fans, that their demeanor is almost crazed. The first and fourth categories are often inextricable from one another, as a fan will "freak out" when they are in the presence of a performer who is so virtuosic in their estimation that they are a freak. Richardson shares with Jackson, to varying degrees and meanings, the freak designations of virtuosity, hypersexuality, and fandom (but not disability). In gauging different types of freakery attached to Jackson's and Richardson's work and personhood, we find how, in the face of seemingly objectifying attributions, both artists have tried to modulate their perceived freak status to control audiences and gain agency over the outcome of their careers. Thus, a fifth type of freak, the control freak, enters the scene.

Virtuosity—"Freak of Nature" and Disability—"Freak Show"

> Part of the horror of being a Black American is being trapped into being an imitation of an imitation.
>
> —James Baldwin[8]

It is, perhaps, no accident that one of the world's greatest dancers would work with the "king of pop," at one time the world's most recognizable (and unrecognizable) celebrity. Both performers have been labeled "freaks." This term seems to connote, on the one hand, innate physical features (or at least appearances that are not part of formal staged performances), and extreme skill and effortlessness, on the other: freak as physical outcast and freak as virtuoso. If we think of virtuosity as the endpoint of ability, then disability is assumed to be its opposite. Of course, disability cannot be equated with freakery; while freakery is explored in disability studies, their distinctions are such that freakery points to the way societies *label* (and often put on *display*) those considered abnormal, and disability describes how societies *disable* those with physical or mental differences (by refusing to provide accessible spaces or discriminating based on perceived deviations).

In the introduction to *Freakery: Cultural Spectacles of the Extraordinary Body*, Rosemarie Garland Thomson traces a genealogy of the term "freak" and its uses in culture and performance. She dates its initial appearance in English to Milton's 1637 usage, "fleck of color."[9] If a lack of color (or something like whiteness) denotes normalcy, then a fleck of color hints at a difference, evoking discussions of racial difference that factor centrally in texts on minstrelsy (and diaspora). Later in the seventeenth century, "freak" goes on to mean "whim," "fancy," and "wonder," only to evolve into the 1847 use of the term as "human corporeal anomaly." Leslie Fiedler points to a late nineteenth-century protest staged by freak show performers who demanded an abandonment of the term "freak" for their preferred term "prodigy." While this term may not have taken hold in the public imagination, it points to the crucial—yet underexplored—relationship between ability and anomaly in the careers of freak show performers and performers in other

---

[8] James Baldwin, *Essence Magazine*, 1984.
[9] Rosemarie Garland Thomson, ed., *Freakery: Cultural Spectacles of the Extraordinary Body* (New York: New York University Press, 1996), 1–22.

realms who become labeled "freaks." Thomson explains that by 1903, after the performers' protest, Barnum and Bailey replaced the stigmatized term "freaks" with "human curiosities."[10]

If the "freak" of freak shows and side shows of yesteryear are "anomalies," "different," and inducers of "horror" and "terror," then Louis Chude-Sokei reminds us that minstrelsy is a "constant erasure of the black subject through the hyperbolic presence of blackface."[11] Paradoxically, what appears to the contemporary eye to be the most "freakish" aspect of minstrelsy—namely, blacking up with burnt cork—is, according to Chude-Sokei, its most assimilationist, conservative aspect. This tension between visibility and invisibility (not to be mistaken with absence, in the case of Bert Williams) lies at the core of blackface, especially when engaging with the topic of Black people in blackface, exemplified by Williams.[12] What, then, of Michael Jackson's performance of whiteface, Desmond Richardson's extraordinary physical ability, and the connection between minstrelsy and freak shows? Chapter 5 on *Othello* detailed how blackface practices persist even today. In the violent history of ethnological freak shows, "Africans" were put on display in museums and the like. Jackson was labeled by the press as "Wacko Jacko." Jacko was a nineteenth-century derogatory term to mean monkey. In histories of spectatorship, the ethnological lies troublingly close to the zoological.[13] The freak factor lay in simply existing—as different, without any expectation of the freakery of virtuosity. Jackson and Richardson represent expectations of blackness-as-animatedness (as elaborated on by Siane Ngai in *Ugly Feelings*).[14] Freakery as virtuosity lies in stark contrast to the expectation of merely existing of ethnological freak shows. But we find that minstrel shows are a vehicle for highlighting expectations for animatedness and, as relevant to Jackson's dance vocabulary, birthed the moonwalk.[15] During minstrel shows, certain dance moves become fetishized and then sedimented into an American logic of objectifying a gimmick. To that end, simply "being," as was the "performance" of ethnological freak shows (and museological human

---

[10] Ibid.
[11] Louis Chude-Sokei, *The Last Darky: Bert Williams, Black-on-Black Minstrelsy and the African Diaspora* (Durham, NC: Duke University Press, 2005), 36.
[12] Ibid., 45.
[13] Joseph Vogel, "How Michael Jackson Made 'Bad,'" *The Atlantic*, September 10, 2012, 2.
[14] And discussed in Chapter 3.
[15] Meghan Pugh has researched the minstrel show origins of the moonwalk in *America Dancing: From the Cakewalk to the Moonwalk* (New Haven, CT: Yale University Press, 2015).

displays), relied on the same kind of gawk-and-awe fetishization as minstrel shows and their delivery of astonishing dance steps.

Although "freak" has mainly been a colloquial term (despite its mingling with science, taxonomy, and performance), it goes in and out of fashion, depending on the political inclinations of its era. But like many stigmatized terms, it has enjoyed reappropriations in various contexts, often signaling something like a beautiful outcast. In the realm of celebrity and popular culture, someone like Jackson is labeled a freak for eschewing a stable, normative identity—both on- and offstage; in the concert dance world, Richardson is labeled a "freak" for his extraordinary ability, compelling presence and stature, and the ease with which he travels through the world and across stage. In pornography—or in everyday youth culture when referring to one's perceived sexual practices—one is labeled a "freak" if he or she is not only promiscuous but also impressively tolerant of multiple activities and "risky" behaviors. "Freakery" defines a tension between attraction and repulsion. If Thomson frames this tension in terms of one's relationship to the self at the precipice of modernity, films like Tod Browning's 1932 *Freaks* and texts such as Fiedler's *Freaks* posit the idea that "all freaks are perceived as erotic."[16] In fact, Browning's film lingers on romantic relationships between characters ranging in normalcy and freakishness, and Fiedler insists that "the pornographic is implicit in all freak shows."[17] Thomson periodizes both Browning and Fiedler, moving beyond their arguments to mine the relationship between modernity, freakery, and subjectivity. For example, she points out that the mechanical concept of "efficiency became a measurement of bodily value."[18]

Modernity's preoccupation with efficiency has direct consequences on dance and vocal performance. Part of what makes Richardson such a compelling performer is his efficiency—that the slightest of leg propulsions can result in a 180-degree leg extension in the blink of an eye. Similarly, Michael Jackson's minute, yet highly precise, movement vocabulary and vocal style make him an incredibly efficient performer. Yet in both cases, efficiency is utilized in the service of expressive arts, which are practiced outside a system of industrial commerce. Thus, what defines the freak during modernity is a body with "boundless liberty and appalling disorder . . . the promise and

---

[16] Leslie Fiedler, *Freaks: Myths and Images of the Secret Self* (New York: Anchor, 1993), 137.
[17] Ibid., 18.
[18] Thompson, 11.

threat of democracy."[19] Thomson extends her discussion to include the increase of "unstructured leisure time" afforded by "wage labor and urbanization," which brings the social practices of the spectator into the discussion of freak shows and their offshoots. Both Jackson and Richardson embrace the tension between human and machine that defines late capitalist movement aesthetics. According to Joseph Vogel, the meeting of machine and human (as soulful) in Jackson's dancing is matched by the aesthetics of the musical pursuits of the *Bad* album: "What makes the *Bad* album so timeless, however, is the way Jackson was able to compliment this technological innovation with more organic, soulful qualities."[20] Judith Hamera has suggested a correlation between modernity and machinelike dance vocabularies throughout various eras, including the unison moves of chorus girls and Jackson's oft-robotic performances.[21] And Mark Franko has researched labor movements and their representation in modern dance. My particular focus on Jackson and Richardson's shared interest in the human as machine takes into consideration the productive friction between machinelike movement and the display of black soul (and post-soul) aesthetics. As discussed in Chapter 3, Brenda Dixon Gottschild describes soul as a spiritual reaching toward heaven from a grounded, earthly stance. Thus, Jackson and Richardson's human-machine preoccupation deftly brings together the earthly, the fleshly, the machinic (as "cool"), and the spiritual, precipitating a defining shift in black American performance that would become globally revered and imitated but never surpassed.

As for the relationship between freakery and ability, I find it crucial to explore Richardson's and Jackson's technical skill and what their collaborations offer to a study of contemporary performance and the genealogy of the freak. If Jackson's innate physical characteristics (skin color, plastic surgery) are freakish precisely due to their un-innateness—their ever-changing quality— then Richardson's body is not so much freakish as it is the epitome of an ideal, that of mainstream black masculine beauty. It is not Richardson's body but his virtuosity that is freakish. With a handsome face and enviable muscularity, Richardson embodies that which Jackson's audience might have expected, given his childhood features. In Thomson's *Freakery*, Yuan's chapter on Michael Jackson lingers on Jackson's use of skin-whitening techniques in

---

[19] Ibid., 12.
[20] Vogel, "How Michael Jackson Made 'Bad,'" 5.
[21] Judith Hamera, *Unfinished Business: Michael Jackson, Detroit, and the Figural Economy of American Deindustrialization* (New York: Oxford University Press, 2017).

his grappling with vitiligo as a performance of whiteface (and masking of blackness) and his obsession with the Elephant Man's skeletal remains. Yuan is astute in pointing to Jackson's self-conscious, knowing deployment of freakery to further his fame—his "deliberate indeterminacy." As Richardson points out after having spent much time working with Jackson:

> I don't think he sorted his "freakdom," if you will. The whole lightening of his skin—a lot of people just don't realize that the Jacksons have vitiligo in the family.... Maybe he would have opted for another choice at this point in the game, but he probably felt the best way to go was to get the melanin out of his skin [to avoid] splotchiness.... That's why he wore the cuff on his forearm.

In other words, Jackson's deployment of freakery, when intentional, was sometimes an example of one kind of freakery used to conceal another. Over the years, Jackson ended up overcompensating, and his bodily metamorphosis far exceeded societal norms. Richardson's indeterminacy lies only in his unchanging charm and politeness offstage and his consistently high level of skill onstage. In Jackson's and Richardson's careers, labor is concealed during performances of virtuosic wizardry, and the body as commodity is both absolutely unbounded, on the one hand, and caught in the spectator's grasp, on the other.

While virtuosity and disability both indicate excess, they also indicate lack. Virtuosity often points to excess ability (technique), and it also seemingly betrays a lack of restraint, normalcy, or the sense of a collective. As for assumptions of disability, it signals for many an excess of abnormality and a lack of ability. Freakery is not often discussed in terms of degrees, but in thinking about how Jackson and Richardson harness certain kinds of freakery to certain ends in overlapping and distinct career "moves," as it were, the deployment of freakery in doses is a way of controlling one's own career. That control is not always within one's hold, and Yuan theorizes how the dreaded stasis of enfreakment can result when control over one's freakery and image slips away. He writes:

> Jackson's goal is to be freakish enough to arouse a restless public's interest, but not so freakish that fans are shocked or repulsed by him. But Jackson feels he must avoid static enfreakment above all; he must always be moving, evolving, transforming himself. In the world of pop entertainment, stasis

means a weakening of one's grip on the public; entertainers not on the cutting edge soon become irrelevant. Stasis means allowing the mystery that is vital to celebrity to be dissolved under the fixed gaze of a public intent on knowing all there is to know. The theme running through Jackson's music videos, for example, is escape metamorphosis: Jackson metamorphoses from man to zombie, from man to animal, from man to cyborg in an attempt to escape fans, reporters, or cartoon-like villains.[22]

In Yuan's formulation, stasis represents the inability to move with the times. Plasticity, then, would encompass an ability to transform one's image to produce a sense of surprise for audiences and fans. In the case of Jackson, attempts to change in the hyperbolically literal sense of undergoing plastic surgery resulted in a kind of artistic stasis, as in altering his facial and epidermal features took him into such a zone of freakery as to render him too freaky to be seen any longer as an "authentic" artist. The more plastic surgery and skin whitening Jackson underwent, the more artistic "stasis" set in. Where Jackson did, however, engage a productive mode of plasticity was in his actual dance rehearsals and choreography—physical practice as plasticity. Two kinds of alteration take place, surgical and technical: the body is transformed by knife and rehearsal. Furthermore, the question of the mechanical comes to the fore in regard to surgery, on the one hand, and dance technique (as technology), on the other. As discussed in Chapter 2, Richardson's versatility was born of a deeply explored practice of mutability; he donned and shed numerous techniques and styles and developed his choreographic identity through a consistency of rigor and virtuosity across many contexts of artistic production. Unlike Jackson, Richardson trained for years in hip-hop, ballet, and modern and contemporary dance; thus, he had at his disposal a rich cache of techniques to lend virtuosity to any role, no matter how dramatic or abstract. Jackson, alternatively, did not see himself as solely a dancer and altered—or rendered plastic and mobile—other aspects of his cluster of skills and persona. This included musical production styles, facial features, skin tone, costuming, red carpet outfits, interview material, and even the display or concealment of homes, romantic relationships, children, and exotic animals. Given Jackson's celebrity status, almost anything was up for grabs. Richardson, on the other hand, was exercising mutability in the service of compositions, maneuvering plasticity precisely in the same

---

[22] Yuan, 371.

terrain as his virtuosity. In doing so, it seems that his mobilizing of plasticity over many years approached something closer to *elasticity*. Whereas plasticity evokes change without return, elasticity conjures the flexible back and forth of stretch and retraction. If plasticity risks suicidal finitude, elasticity desires infinite resilience. For Richardson, freakery (as virtuosity and mutability) operates in the same vein as his artistic performances: there is no freakery outside of repertory. He elastically stretches himself within the work instead of plastically altering himself at the level of surface; in Richardson's domain, the flesh work of labor takes precedence over the tweaking of surface. As for Jackson, sometimes psychological scarring exposes itself on the outermost epidermal canvases.

While virtuosos are often touted for their originality, they are always inevitably influenced by their predecessors, for virtuosity is only ever noticed within a framework of recognition. To that end, what would it mean to contemplate Jackson's and Richardson's plasticity and stasis in relationship to influential figures from musical theater? Taking a detour from expected designations of "appropriation" to describe Jackson's and Richardson's emulation of Broadway stars allows for a reading of influence that avoids distilling similitude to theft.[23] We have witnessed that histories of appropriations of blackness (and even imitations of whiteness by Black performers) and concepts of "mastering the master" are meant to insert a redemptive gesture in this violent history. Of rather unexpected fascination is Jackson and Richardson's shared adoration of the choreographic nuances of idiosyncratic movers Bob Fosse, Fred Astaire, Gene Kelly, and Jack Cole, all of whom were white (and were inevitably influenced by earlier Black dancers themselves). I move away from the concept of "mutability" and toward that of "plasticity" here to make a distinction between taking *up* codified techniques and taking *on* individual styles; it is the difference between learning ballet, jazz, and tap, on the one hand, and dancing like Fosse or Astaire, on the other—form versus flare.

In a now-classic article, "Dancin' in the Rain," film scholar Carol Clover astutely points to the issue of credit in the troubling racial dynamics of Gene Kelly's choreographic "influences." She distills the crux of her argument

---

[23] Here I shall avoid a full elaboration on the Beyoncé/Fosse issue, no matter how rich a topic for dance studies at the level of copyright, appropriation, and ownership (in fact, JaQuel Knight, Beyoncé's choreographer, once instructed by her to replicate Fosse, is currently exploring the option of copyrighting his own choreography). As an aside, Fosse, similar to Lubovitch, performed in burlesque clubs.

about race and dance in the Hollywood musical such that "too many of the unseen artists whose moves have been put to such brilliant and lucrative use in the 'white dancer's field' of the film musical are black."[24] Referring specifically to the work and omission of credit by Gene Kelly, Clover writes:

> That *Singin' in the Rain* is not uninterested in progenitors is clear from the extended preface to the Broadway number, which takes us from the burlesque stage to vaudeville to the Ziegfeld Follies to the musical of the film's present, all clearly seen and clearly labelled under the urgent lyric "gotta dance." This spelling out of genealogical "credit" reminds us of the film's larger concern with individual credit, which in turn invites us to ponder the completeness of this particular evolutionary account. Which in its turn leads us to the thought that, although this may be a correct enumeration of the institutional categories that precede the cinematic dance musical, it is history with something missing. The omission is all the more striking in light of what some might consider outright "quotations" from the routines of, for example, Bojangles Robinson, John Bubbles, the Berry and Nicholas Brothers (especially backflips off the wall), Peg Leg Bates (one-legged dancing), and other tap artists of the forties.[25]

Clover's mention of the likes of the Nicholas Brothers and Peg Leg Bates further illustrates the meeting point of virtuosic dance moves and disability performance as similarly embraced through a logic of the fetishized gimmick. Fetishized virtuosity, whether performed in Clover's examples by Black ablebodied or Black disabled dancers, is at once quoted and ghosted by Kelly and *Singin' in the Rain*. Despite such historical erasures, Jackson was known to have publicly expressed his deep admiration for Kelly, and Kelly famously stated that Jackson was one of his favorite performers of all time. Similarly, Astaire was also impressed with Jackson:

> In 1983, Fred Astaire, impressed by Jackson's galvanizing performance during a Motown television special, telephones to congratulate him, praising him for being "an angry dancer" and "a *hell* of a mover." . . . After Michael left the Jackson 5 to develop himself as a solo star, he was finally able to exercise complete control over his career.[26]

[24] Carol Clover, "Dancin' in the Rain," *Critical Inquiry* 21, no. 4 (Summer 1995): 722–47, 729.
[25] Ibid., 728.
[26] Yuan, 371–72.

Control over one's pop stardom is linked in these cases to soloism and the slick execution of dance moves of black origin. One of Clover's most significant observations is that "black men's dancing bodies haunt even the film's title number."[27] Not only is Kelly's *Singin' in the Rain* haunted by Black men's dancing bodies, but also it is haunted by histories of performances of white men in blackface. Is this to say that Jackson and Richardson are reclaiming black performance by emulating and inviting Kelly's (and Fosse's, Astaire's, and Cole's) style into their own dance styles? Africanist aesthetics, as Gottschild might suggest, no matter how ubiquitous in American culture, circulate in complex ways and represent a layered history of appropriation, omission, and racial politics. It is no accident, then, that current copyright issues and debates in dance center around more lucrative commercial work such as that of JaQuel Knight (who works with Beyoncé, who has lifted choreographies of Fosse and Anne Teresa De Keersmaeker in her music videos). Debates on copyright in dance (as thoroughly explored by Anthea Kraut) tend to emerge more robustly when financial profit is in question, and the topic cannot be thought outside considerations of race and power. Without question, Jackson was maneuvering his career through, above, and around the "influences" of white Hollywood film stars who were, in turn, "influenced" by the Black performers mentioned above. Jackson's interest in white entertainers who emulated Black performers extended to his romantic choices, which is where some have cited a touch of freakery, if not the excessive visibility of celebrity "odd couples": Jackson, as some may recall, was briefly married to Lisa Marie Presley, the daughter of Elvis Presley. If Elvis doesn't encapsulate the appropriation of black sound in the service of white rock and roll, then no one does. We can speculate about Jackson's choices, but it is clear that he revered—and intended to surpass—white performers who revered Black performers, and made a spectacle of it. Richardson, as a dancer who traversed both Broadway and concert dance, took control of his career differently, by entering into the work of white Broadway creators a generation or two after their initial appearances on the scene.

Dare I call upon the all-too-apt saying of "following in the footsteps of," Richardson indeed traveled a path similar to predecessors Alvin Ailey and Judith Jamison, both of whom found success on Broadway in addition to concert dance. In 1999, Richardson was nominated for a Tony Award for

[27] Ibid., 738.

Outstanding Featured Actor for his role in the Broadway production of *Fosse*. Like Ailey and Jamison, Richardson did not discriminate between concert dance and Broadway dance. The fluidity—and relative financial success—Richardson, Ailey, and Jamison find between their concert dance and Broadway work recalls Chapter 1's discussion of Lincoln Center dance training's preparation for a variety of professional dance contexts. It also reignites the question of who is scripting the black experience (as discussed in Chapter 1). Richardson and Jackson also have in common the Hollywood musical (Broadway musicals adapted for film), including *Cabaret* (Richardson) and *The Wiz* (Jackson). Richardson reflects:

> When *Fosse* began, I was in rehearsal with American Ballet Theatre [ABT]. We had a break for lunch, so I went upstairs. I used to go up through the building at 890 Broadway. Two minutes later, Chet Walker said to me, "You have a little bit of time? Why don't you learn some material?" . . . because I had my dance clothes on. . . . Then he asked, "Do you sing?" . . . So I came back singing a Duke Ellington song, "Don't You Know I Care," because I love jazz and my voice lends itself to that. . . . At ABT I was on a set contract for the whole year, and this was in the middle. Then [Gwen] Verdon came into the room, saw me dancing, heard me singing, and said, "We need to have you." I responded, "Well, no, I am with American Ballet Theatre" to which she responded, "Oh, Honey, no, we gotta have you." . . . I said, "Well, at this moment at ABT I think that I have done all I can." I felt like I was hitting a ceiling there [due to racialized casting]. The story unfolds that they bought me out of my contract. I finished out with ABT, and started with *Fosse* in Toronto, then LA for three months, and then came to Broadway. . . . And we got a Tony nomination! My role was Mr. Bojangles and Percussion 4, for which I was nominated [for a Tony Award] in 1999. I was in it for two years. . . . I was running back and forth to Complexions rehearsals. It was a hard schedule but it was invigorating. I loved having the opportunity to work with Ann Reinking. . . . That was one of those moments that you say, "We don't turn this down."[28]

This anecdote defines a moment in Richardson's trajectory in which he made a choice to call the shots of his career. He was disappointed that ABT was placing him in sixth and seventh casts of lead roles within his wheelhouse

---

[28] Richardson, interview with the author.

presumably due to race: Romeo of ABT's *Romeo and Juliet* was not, at the time, performed by any Black dancers. The creative team at *Fosse* insisted on hiring Richardson and paying him appropriately. In order to be treated with respect while fulfilling a long-held artistic aspiration, Richardson made the professional choice to engage in the minor transgression of severing a contract to sign another. He continues:

> I had taken musical theater classes back in the day because I always loved Bob Fosse's work. From the moment that my mother took me to Radio City Music Hall to see *The Little Prince* when I was young, I fell in love with his performance of the "Snake in the Grass." I didn't realize until later that what that man did is what inspired Michael to do his *Motown 25* number. All the movements and steps—the kick, the hand crossing—is all Bob Fosse. We were doing the show and Verdon said, "Well you know Michael [Jackson] loved Bob Fosse!" . . . I realized it's exactly what Michael was doing, that he was influenced by that. A lot of people don't even realize it, and I wanted to work like that. I knew that Fosse liked line, though he wasn't a classically trained dancer; he was a tapper and a hoofer. Michael put his own spin on it. He's always been a chameleon in the sense that he gets influenced but he adopts it to himself. . . . As a young person growing up in the Motown era, watching folks like James Brown, Smokey Robinson, and Stevie Wonder perform and all those other folks that performed in groups—he took that in and figured out a way to work that in with Bob Fosse and Jack Cole and Fred Astaire. He loved the elegance of Fred Astaire.[29]

In pointing to Fosse's and Jackson's compelling dance styles, Richardson reflects on his desire to try a different mode of dance, a mode whose impetus didn't reside in formal technique. Richardson clarifies that Fosse "wasn't a classically trained dancer" but that he, like Jackson, had created an amalgamation of influences in order to arrive at an acutely captivating style. Whereas it would be almost impossible for an untrained person to replicate Richardson's movement from Complexions' choreography, such a person could more easily pick up Fosse's or Jackson's moves. Their popularity had much to do with the accessibility of their movement. In the case of Jackson, his moves (although not necessarily his delivery) could be mimicked by many, and that accessibility worked to downplay some of the freakish inaccessibility of his

[29] Ibid.

otherwise schizophrenically cagey yet overexposed persona. Conversely, Richardson (albeit far less in the public eye) is accessible in terms of his personality but his moves are unreachable by most. For Broadway, Richardson tones down his virtuosity but plays up his charisma. Jackson's dancing, when in the presence of Richardson, moves closer to virtuosity. One dimension completing an intersectional study of Jackson's and Richardson's identities as affecting and affected by control is the performance of gender and sexuality in their work and lives.

Sexuality—"Super Freak" and Agency—"Control Freak"

The Michael Jackson cacophony is fascinating in that it is not about Jackson at all. I hope he has the good sense to know it and the good fortune to snatch his life out of the jaws of a carnivorous success. He will not swiftly be forgiven for having turned so many tables, for he damn sure grabbed the brass ring, and the man who broke the bank at Monte Carlo has nothing on Michael. All that noise is about America, as the dishonest custodian of black life and wealth; the blacks, especially males, in America; and the burning, buried American guilt; and sex and sexual roles and sexual panic; money, success and despair—to all of which may now be added the bitter need to find a head on which to place the crown of Miss America. Freaks are called freaks and are treated as they are treated—in the main, abominably—because they are human beings who cause to echo, deep within us, our most profound terrors and desires. Most of us, however, do not appear to be freaks—though we are rarely what we appear to be. We are, for the most part, visibly male or female, our social roles defined by our sexual equipment. But we are all androgynous, not only because we are all born of a woman impregnated by the seed of a man but because each of us, helplessly and forever, contains the other—male in female, female in male, white in black and black in white. We are a part of each other. Many of my countrymen appear to find this fact exceedingly inconvenient and even unfair, and so, very often, do I. But none of us can do anything about it.

—James Baldwin[30]

---

[30] "Here Be Dragons," in *Price of the Ticket* (New York: St. Martin's Press, 1985).

In musing on homosexuality, blackness, and the trope of the "freak" in his seminal 1985 essay "Freaks and the American Ideal of Manhood," James Baldwin likens the "cacophony" surrounding Michael Jackson to America's fears and latent desires around black success coupled with androgyny. The essay (often referred to as "Here Be Dragons") was published in *Playboy* after Hugh Hefner intentionally sought out an African American editor, Walter Lowe Jr.[31] While some feminists take issue with *Playboy* and there is much room to critique the idea of a magazine composed of photographed nude women designed to titillate men, Hefner was a proponent of civil rights. Through the public stage of *Playboy*, Baldwin had the opportunity to indirectly confront mainstream American men about the ambivalent push and pull of attraction and repulsion at the core of the idea of "freaks." As someone who embodies gendered, racial, and financial excess, Jackson became Baldwin's example of the rare person whose gendered freakery is actually visible, suggesting that most people perform determined gender roles. In doing so, Baldwin avoids, however, putting forward a theory of that which Jackson is keeping invisible. For Baldwin, most freaks do not appear to be freaks; through his logic, Jackson is publicly visible as a freak, as opposed to publicly hiding (what some have insinuated as the possibility of his) homosexuality. Today, one wonders if Baldwin's discourse would replace "androgynous" with "queer" or if he would move further away from binaristic gender vocabulary. No matter what, Jackson left much of his life up to the imagination, and fans were left with the choice to either fixate on trying to "solve" the problem of androgyny or ignore or accept it in favor of an appreciation for the music. While Jackson's sound embodied the complexity of post-soul falsetto's high notes and expressions of desire, such sonic indulgence, unlike androgynous, ambivalent, or ambiguous visual gender presentation, was already widely accepted by mainstream America as suitable for heterosexual singers and heterosexual listeners alike.

Jackson's post-soul falsetto might recall another pop icon of his generation discussed earlier in this book, namely, Prince.[32] Prince, in fact, was approached to appear in Jackson's "Bad" video (alongside Richardson) in the role ultimately belonging to Wesley Snipes. In a VH1 interview with Chris Rock, Prince stated he declined the offer to appear in the Martin Scorsese–directed video when considering the song's first line:

---

[31] https://lithub.com/on-james-baldwins-radical-writing-for-playboy-magazine/.
[32] "Post-soul" is a term elaborated on by Francesca Royster and is discussed at length in Chapter 3 of this book.

That Wesley Snipes character? That would have been me. Now, you run that video in your mind. The first line in that song is, "Your butt is mine." Now, who's gonna sing that to who? Cuz you sure aint singin it to me, and I sure aint singin it to you. Right there we got a problem.[33]

In a peculiar twist, Prince declined the role of rival in a video of an artist rumored to be his real-life rival and arrived at his decision through homophobic reasoning (or a performance of it therein). While both Jackson and Prince put forward queer aesthetics in their artistry and appearance, one will never know if Prince's homophobia in that moment was born of a fear of public perception or wholly internalized by the artist himself. Both artists were relatively diminutive men who presented themselves with a certain degree of gender ambivalence such that audiences could interpret them variously.[34]

The irony of Prince's expression of queasiness at the thought of another man declaring "your butt is mine" is that that line is meant to butch up a heretofore feminized image of Jackson—that only an antagonistic straight guy would signal dominance over another by posing such a dare. Precisely in the moment Jackson is constructing an overdetermined straight masculinity, Prince feels threatened by the effects of his perceived homosexual overtones. Richardson, even though openly gay, was hired along with the other dancers to lend the video an overtone of heterosexual masculinity. The choreographies of black male sexuality in the careers of Jackson, Prince, and Richardson are complex and numerous. All three artists are, to varying degrees, inherently ambiguous in terms of gender, depending on performance context; but, more importantly, each of them is calculating in how they deploy images of their own gender and sexuality. Rick James's "Super Freak"[35] is a compelling document of the circulation of "freak" vernacular in that a woman who is a "super freak" is presumably in control of her own sexuality—she feels free to take risks and surely indulges in kink and fetish. In James's funk imaginary, "freak" referred to feminine sexual agency. In reference to Jackson and Prince, are designations of freakery inherently feminized and feminizing? Slippery in its connotations, a "super freak" can

---

[33] Prince and Chris Rock, VH1 interview, https://www.youtube.com/watch?v=nd97mAsvR0g.
[34] Regardless of Michael Jackson's, Prince's, or Richardson's precise intentions, their gender presentations (no matter how differently) offer young viewers images of gender flexibility, freedom, and survival.
[35] Considered by him to be a crossover song.

be just as easily fetishized as she is fetishizing. She is at once in and out of control. Whether referring to a "super freak" woman, a "super freak" man, or anyone beyond the binary, "super freak" indicates sexual excess or deviation, to be sure. "Super Freak," despite James's hope that it would function as his "crossover" song, was not permitted on MTV, but Jackson is often cited as breaking the color barrier with videos from his *Thriller* album, followed by the *Bad* era. Scholars such as Faedra Chatard Carpenter have suggested that Jackson's play with whiteness fed into his acceptance as a "crossover artist" who, while freakish in some ways, was able to gain acceptance by white audiences.[36] Likely because dance does not operate within the same kind of market-driven system, the term "crossover artist" is rarely applied to dancers. Jackson's freakery rarely centered on the perception of excess blackness. Rather, Jackson's fans (and "haters") pointed to freakish displays of skin alteration, offstage behavior, gender, and sexuality. While Richardson exudes sexual confidence along with his virtuosity onstage, his performances do not spill over into "super freak" territory. At Ailey, he tended to portray heterosexually masculinist roles, but his style and presence in Complexions were (and still are) more decidedly queer. Richardson's embodiment of queer aesthetics should not be mistaken, however, with the expression of "super freak" mannerisms. In contrast, Jackson inaugurated his crotch grabbing in the *Bad* era as a hyperbolic announcement of severing ties with the Jehovah's Witnesses, and Prince oozed sex in songs like "Cream" or "Come." Richardson, despite working in a sweaty, bodily artistic medium, withheld performances of overt sexual freakiness.

All in the public eye, Jackson and Prince try to control performances of their sexuality to control the successes of their careers. Their conscious gender modulations occur at the level of vocal style, lyrics, costume, choreography, gestural flourish, and, needless to say, public displays of affection or lack thereof. Jackson and Prince play with the allowable transgression of falsetto-as-soulfully-heterosexual—a display of masculine yearning for feminine love and sex. In other words, as discussed in Chapter 3, post-soul falsetto, despite its embrace of high notes (just like Richardson's high leg extensions), doesn't necessarily signal femininity or homosexuality. The play with the high range does, however, leave room for ambiguity, if not ambivalence. Of importance is the fact that Richardson was openly gay. A critical

---

[36] Faedra Chatard Carpenter, "Whiteness as 'Becoming': The Corporeal Crossovers of Daniel Tisdale and Michael Jackson," in *Coloring Whiteness: Acts of Critique in Black Performance* (Ann Arbor: University of Michigan Press, 2014).

difference is that he did not travel in the realm of pop icon celebrity; dancers, unlike pop stars, do not experience the same high degree of financial stakes every time they state something publicly, nor are they often asked to speak publicly. Dancers, for better or worse (especially in the 1980s and 1990s), are able to enjoy a greater degree of anonymity. While Ailey's company was not actively sharing the sexual preferences of its director or dancers (and was, in effect, operating as a "closet"), one could be openly gay in the studio and amid the company's internal culture. Thus, Richardson was not pretending to be a straight man onstage; rather, he happened to embody a type of black masculinity that was embraced by American culture as attractive and ideal for straight Black men (but also, as discussed in Chapter 1, assumed to be violent by racists). The inversion we find is that, at least during his Ailey career before Complexions, Richardson's modulation of sexuality occurred in his performances, in that he continued to dance with a certain muscular strength that didn't announce homosexuality and instead leaned into expectations of heterosexuality; Jackson and Prince, on the other hand, were freely exploiting the high range of falsetto singing (high, feminine) while trying to put across an overall image of heterosexuality in their career choices. I do not assume Jackson and Prince enjoyed queer private lives, and something like "proof" lies beyond the scope or interest of this project, but what is important is that a seeming overcompensation was taking place in the way they controlled their careers, as in, "I'm a little freaky and want to draw you in with my virtuosic excess, but I promise I'm not gay." If Richardson embodies virility, Jackson and Prince (albeit not identically) embody frailty, with a sexual edge. All three artists work against stereotypes, as Richardson's virility is in the service of a queer aesthetic, and Jackson's and Prince's frailty is tempered by an outpouring of heterosexual lyrics and gesturing.

Examining the question of modulating the image of one's sexual freakery in the performing arts reaches heightened urgency when the issue of survival enters the scene. By this point, both Jackson and Prince have passed away, but before that, talk of drug use and overuse circulated in regard to both figures. Medication is commonly used to mask pain, whether physical or psychological. There was a sense that Jackson and Prince, despite their hugely public careers, had something to hide. Were we witnessing sublimated sexual identities? By the mid-1990s, in contrast, Richardson was openly in an artistic and romantic relationship with Complexions co-founder Dwight Rhoden, and the company's content and marketing photographs featured them together in subtly erotic union. Richardson, by this time, was comfortably "out" and "proud," and this coincided with his continued physical health and fitness, as he is still dancing today. One wonders if a key to Richardson's survival was his chameleon-like artistic mutability (he fulfilled "dancer," not a particular pop iconic character), his relatively calm public life (paparazzi do not tend to follow dancers), or his commitment to mentorship and teaching of youth. Sometimes living one's queerness invites danger, but the other side of that is self-acceptance and a healthy conscience of knowing oneself and finding queer community. Pop icons, often to tragic end, are forced by the industry to construct a persona and to risk career "death" if found to deviate from an already successful image.

Michael's sister, Janet, also born into a family of paternal abuse and maternal religion (two insidious forms of control), famously sang "Control" during an effort to find independence:

> When I was 17 I did what people told me
> Did what my father said,
> And let my mother mold me
> But that was a long ago
> I'm in control, never gonna stop
> Control, to get what I want
> Control, I like to have a lot
> Control, now I'm all grown up
> First time I fell in love, I didn't know what hit me
> So young and so naive, I thought it would be easy
> Now I know I got to take
> Control, now I've got a lot
> Control, to get what I want
> Control, never gonna stop
> Control, now I'm all grown up
> Jam, woo woo
> Rebel, that's right
> I'm on my own
> I'll call my own shots
> Thank you
> Got my own mind
> I want to make my own decisions
> When it has to do with my life, my life

> I wanna be the one in control
> So let me take you by the hand,
> And lead you on this dance[37]

Richardson knew both Michael and Janet Jackson. What he shared in common with the sibling entertainers was a commitment to polish, artistry, and discipline. But Richardson was, from a young age, consistently encouraged to pursue his artistic career in his own way, unfettered by the binding expectations of controlling parents. The trope of the "control freak" in this chapter is manifold: it refers to the desire to control one's own artistic career in the wake of abusive parental (and/as career) control, as well as modulating the "freak factor" of one's image in order to control popular and financial success. In attempting to do so, are the Jacksons replacing the "freak show" of their childhood with the "freak show" of their adult pop stardom? Michael was known to disguise his own children in public, purchase rare animals, and build the juvenile fantasy Neverland, and much more troublingly, he was accused of molesting children and engaging in criminal sexual behavior (the rape of minors) one would struggle to even imagine as the endpoint of the logic of the "super freak." Tragically, Michael (according to his victims) exercised control over young boys and placed them in a compromised position of lacking control. Some ask if the artistry of someone accused of such acts is redeemable. I am not here to answer that question; instead, I question the choices made when taking on or obscuring performances of the "super freak" and the "control freak" in the service of one's career. In conceiving of virtuosity as something to be cultivated then attained, childhood would seem to be the site of aspiration for virtuosity in music or dance. What does one make, then, of the fact that Jackson is said to have abused children while Richardson has taken the time to teach youth, especially preprofessional teenagers? Ever since the "freakish" death of his baby, Prince was rarely documented interacting with children. But we find that Jackson and Richardson occupy opposing poles of involvement with youth. While dance is the entire focus of Richardson's career, it functions as but a portion of Jackson's and Prince's performances. To that end, dance for Jackson and Prince is both a conduit of sexual freakery and a site of liberatory self-expression that invites mass imitation. In other words, along with the songs themselves, dance in their cases has a global democratizing

---

[37] Excerpt of Janet Jackson's "Control."

effect as it becomes part of the pop cultural fabric of choreographic commerce. Richardson's dance, no matter how inviting, circulates in more limited networks of live (and sometimes onscreen) performance. The paradox I am pointing to is that children are more easily able to mimic the dances of Jackson and Prince, no matter how "unrelatable" their personas may be beyond the content of their songs and accompanying dances. Richardson, thusly, spends more time *with* children, teaching them for hours on end in studios across the globe, for it takes time to acquire the skills needed to dance in his style. Teaching allows for a certain degree of control of one's carefully honed style, and that kind of control operates on an entirely different scale than the controlling of one's image and career through the calculated doling out of one's own freakery. Any kind of control is sure to result in effect, and the effects of Jackson's and Richardson's control lead to very different kinds of outcomes, though similarly entangled with the libidinal desire of fandom.

Fandom—"Freak Out"

> In our own time, this lust by fans to mingle the life of a star with that of a character is exacerbated to the point of obsession. Clearly there exists a predilection on the part of audiences to make theatrical characters out of their favorite actors, and all celebrities are subject to some extent to such objectification, whether or not they respond with overt exhibitionism. . . . Does this objectification not make "freaks" of all our celebrities?
> —Michael Chemers[38]

Fandom would suggest that religious zeal and libidinal desire are inseparable in the presence of a cultural icon. Michael Chemers points out that fans' objectification of celebrities already renders pop stars like Jackson "freaks." Richardson holds iconic status within the smaller scale of the concert dance community, and his fans alternatingly refer to him as a "god" and sexually attractive. Jackson and Prince have been so obsessed over that fans have most certainly passed out and experienced other extreme responses in their midst.

---

[38] Michael Chemers, *Staging Stigma: A Critical Examination of the American Freak Show* (London: Palgrave Macmillan, 2008), 54.

Figure 6.1 Music video of "Bad" by Michael Jackson (See color plates).

When disbelief, attraction, and the reality of a pop star's existence come together during a siting or concert appearance, fans tend to "freak out," losing all control and composure. The collective effervescence of crying teen girls at a Jackson or Prince concert in the 1980s could have dispelled any speculation of the singers' gender ambiguity. Belief is at the crux of the extreme acceptance of fandom in the face of the erasure of the reality of relations. But perhaps it is less about the kind of belief that is grounded in investigative proof and more about the kind of anthropological belief that upholds systems of magic, religious virtuosos, and even political leaders that is at the root of fans' freakouts. If Jackson and Prince beget fainting spells, Richardson draws gasps. Emulation of Richardson's repertoire occurs in more of a field-specific tunnel, that of professional dance. Richardson's audiences are more likely to admire his artistry than lose hold of their equanimity.

Whether signaling hyperability or the grotesque (or in Jackson's case, both), freakery signals social marginality, even at the top of the social order, from "disabled" to "superhero." Exemplified by both Richardson and Jackson, celebrity often functions such that virtuosity and freakery coalesce, generating a social apartness in which the performer is revered.

Celebrity culture has transposed religious zeal to secular entertainment. The 1980s–1990s represent a time before fame and celebrity born of shallow social media posturings, selfies, and "branding" devoid of skill or thoughtful content. Instead of social media's immediacy, the public's relationship to media was one of physical encounter, as in stumbling across an outrageous *Enquirer* headline in the grocery checkout line or waiting for daily entertainment headlines on TV shows like *Entertainment Tonight*. The uncensored surveillance and paparazzi-driven culture of fan fodder evolved in parallel to Jackson's and Prince's careers. Even though television was the main medium of transfer, there was an accessibility to Jackson's choreography in that fans could, to an extent, mimic and replicate it. An attempt to recreate Richardson's movement style, on the other hand, would take years of training. Thus, an inversion takes place in which Jackson as a person is inaccessible but his movement enjoys a democratic legacy. As Nicole Fleetwood has stated, "Jackson had entered a realm of iconicity that detaches the image from corporeality and lived experience. And yet, his death rendered iconicity unfixed and unstable. His flesh and body had become substantive and organic through death,"[39] as if to suggest that Jackson could only be believed to be real (again) through an awareness of his death. Richardson, relatively free of the burdens of freakery, continues to dance—onstage, onscreen, and in the imaginations of fans, audiences, and dancers alike, who are able to feel the effects of his virtuosity as he labors muscularly and artistically, exceeding expectations of the humanly *possible*.

---

[39] Nicole Fleetwood, "The Icon Is Dead: Mourning Michael Jackson," in *Troubling Vision: Performance, Visuality, and Blackness* (Chicago: University of Chicago Press, 2010), 208.

Conclusion

Desmond Richardson on Tour: Virtuosity's Futures

A book's afterlives may only ever live in the mind. Just as a work of choreography is never really completed, a book's conclusion is almost always an oxymoron. Dancers continue to rewrite a piece as they perform it over time, and readers reinvigorate a book with each individual reading (not to mention the fact that writers, if given the choice, will often want to revise passages ad nauseam). In keeping with this distance from finitude, Desmond Richardson himself is still dancing, performing, teaching, and directing. His career is active and evolving, and he continues to share his unique insight and virtuosity with dancers and audiences across the globe. In the way that virtuosity moves us by pushing at a boundary of form with an incisive degree of excess, imbuing a coda with something slightly beyond resolution, a book's conclusion gives us a glimpse into tomorrow's ambitions while reluctantly humming a lullaby.

As I conclude *Body Impossible*, I will share two examples of Richardson's forays across the Atlantic in order to point to the continued depth and expanse of his influence. These individual sites of transnational exchange could have been chapters unto themselves; alas, this is but a single book. Richardson performed in the 2010 World Festival of Black Arts in Dakar, Senegal, and, shortly after, in performances in Russia and Ukraine. The festival was originally convened in 1966 by poet and politician Léopold Sédar Senghor, the first president of postindependence Senegal, as the *Premier Festival Mondialdes Arts Nègres*, or First World Festival of Negro Arts. African American dance and literary artists featured in the first of three iterations of the World Festival of Black Arts (1966, 1977, 2010) include Alvin Ailey, Katherine Dunham, and James Baldwin, among many others. The festival's history is inseparable from the *Négritude* movement, established in the 1930s by Senghor (influenced by writer Paulette Nardal from

Martinique), poet Aimé Césaire from Martinique, and poet Léon Damas from French Guiana. *Négritude*, along with its antiassimilationist poetics, provided the conceptual framework for the First World Festival of Negro Arts in 1966. *Négritude* was invested in a concept of modernity as progress, and that progress included black intellectualism as well as paying heed to traditional African cultures. In 2010, when virtuoso Richardson performed the solo "Lament" by Dwight Rhoden, his aesthetic was more in line with Afrofuturism than *négritude*. If *négritude* presented the idea of the future as progress, Afrofuturism, by incorporating science fictional and technological aesthetics, imagines possibilities of the future in ways that are less pred—Afrofuturism excites in blurring binaries of genre and gender. In the festival's Senegalese context, Richardson represented the US in a post–civil rights historical moment with an Afrofuturist, post-soul choreographic aesthetic. The shift in the way that blackness is portrayed over time in this festival—from *négritude* to Afrofuturism—is found in the difference between the Ailey concert dance performances documented in William Greaves's 1966 documentary *First World Festival of Negro Arts* and Richardson's 2010 performance. The film, literature, and performance surrounding the World Festival of Black Arts further consolidate Richardson's role as an inheritor of Alvin Ailey's legacy. Working in and through American concert dance's *virtuosic turn*, Richardson reinvigorated the Black Arts festival by more deliberately investigating a black queer masculine aesthetic than his predecessors.

Richardson obscures clear divides between the "classical" and "contemporary," and he is revered in Russia, the epicenter of the most celebrated style of classical ballet, which emerged in the eighteenth century. That Russia is the site of both intense militaristic violence and refined artistic discipline in ballet is beyond the scope of this conclusion, but an important juxtaposition to keep in mind. (As for the confluence of discipline and violence, ballet was never so prominently featured in the news as the 2013 Bolshoi incident in which a disgruntled dancer had acid thrown in director Sergei Filin's eyes.) Diana Vishneva invited Richardson to perform with her at the Mariinsky Theater in 2011. Vishneva is one of the most awarded ballerinas in history and very much a virtuoso in her own right. Like Richardson, Vishneva is known for excellence in classical and contemporary choreography, and any range between. Vishneva danced with the Mariinsky Ballet (formerly known as the Kirov Ballet, as it was named in the Soviet era) and, like Richardson, American Ballet Theatre.

Ballet has always had a gender problem; it can be painfully heteronormative in its representations of characters and roles for dancers, no matter how queer its dancers may be in their offstage lifestyles. Russia is known for racial and gender discrimination, so it's hard to ascertain to what degree the Russian embrace of Complexions Contemporary Ballet and Richardson's dancing is fetishistic. Nevertheless, there is certainly recognition at play in the Russian reception of Complexions and Richardson—a recognition of excellence in classical ballet technique and dedication to virtuosic pursuits. As choreographer Germaine Acogny (who directs Jant-Bi in Senegal) has famously stated, "African" dance has always been contemporary, and vibrant cultural traditions are inherently being updated by current generations. Likewise, classical ballet is continuously modernizing itself. As this book has demonstrated, the elements that transform and maintain contemporaneity in dance—and its virtuosic extremes (even within that which is called "traditional" or "classical" in any given context)—are often dialogic influences from other cultures and practices, from African diasporic street dance to Latinx social dance to South Asian classical dance. While Russian audiences' sense of awe in viewing Richardson or Complexions in performance may stem from a fascination with the Other, the same audiences' embrace of Richardson's and Complexions' dancing is grounded in an admiration for the precarious balance exhibited between technical clarity and virtuosic excess.

Figure C.1 *Desmond Richardson* (See color plates).
© 2022 Mark Andrew Images.

Figure C.2 Desmond Richardson and Diana Vishneva in rehearsal (See color plates).
Photograph by Nikolay Krusser.

At the Mariinsky, Richardson is applauded for his nuanced technique in executing Dwight Rhoden's choreography, which, in turn, is celebrated for its complexity of movement. One troubling angle therein is that Russia also has a recent history of antigay laws and imprisoning feminist punk performance group Pussy Riot and lesbian WNBA player Brittney Griner. Richardson secured his status as a gay icon when he appeared as "king" of the 2013 Life

Figure C.3 Desmond Richardson and Diana Vishneva in rehearsal (See color plates).
Photograph by Nikolay Krusser.

Ball in Vienna; as we also see in the US, contradictions of nation abound, and discrimination lives dangerously close to celebration. Discussed earlier in this book, as Bert Williams's renown grew, his involvement in activism increased, and we find a similar dynamic in Richardson's life. My hope is that those who read this book will come to appreciate virtuosity in dance while reducing its fetishistic reception through a practice of further exploring a dancer's socioculturally derived stylistic influences. Desmond Richardson is an artist unlike any other. He developed his virtuosity through years of immersion in a heterogeneity of styles, from popping and breaking to ballet and modern dance, and he has transformed dance for generations to come.

I consider it a great honor to have had the opportunity to write about Richardson and virtuosity. Writing comes of relationships. I will continue to converse with dancers, artists, choreographers, and performers of all walks of life. Any writing I publish is but a residue of those dialogues. My subsequent body of research, which will result in a book of interviews called *Disavowing Virtuosity, Performing Aspiration: Dance and Performance Interviews* and a monograph titled *Prophylactic Aesthetics: Latex, Spandex, and Sexual Anxieties Performed*, explores corporeal performances of aspiration in cultures of dance, sports and fitness, art, and performance.

Bibliography

Adorno, Theodor. "On the Fetish Character of Music." In *The Culture Industry*, edited by J. M. Bernstein, 29–60. London: Routledge, 1991.
Alexander, Michelle. *The New Jim Crow: Mass Incarceration in the Age of Colorblindness*. New York: New Press, 2010.
Als, Hilton. "I Am Your Consciousness, I Am Love: A Paean 2 Prince." *Harpers Magazine*, December 2012, 60–67.
Bakhtin, Mikhail. *The Dialogic Imagination: Four Essays*. Edited by Michael Holquist. Translated by Caryl Emerson and Michael Holquist. Austin: University of Texas Press, 1982.
Baldwin, James. "Here Be Dragons." In *Price of the Ticket*, 196–210. St. Martin's Press, 1985.
Bel, Jerome. "Jerome Bel and Myself." Interview by Jess Curtis. *Dance March*, 2009a.
Bel, Jerome. Talk in the Department of Theater, Dance, and Performance Studies, University of California, Berkeley, March 4, 2009b.
Bench, Harmony. "Monstrous Belonging: Performing 'Thriller' after 9/11." In *The Oxford Handbook of Dance and the Popular Screen*, edited by M. B. Borelli, 393–409. New York: Oxford University Press, 2014.
Bernstein, Susan. *Virtuosity of the Nineteenth Century: Performing Music and Language in Heine, Liszt, and Baudelaire*. Stanford, CA: Stanford University Press, 1998.
Brand, Dionne. *A Map to the Door of No Return*. Toronto: Vintage Canda (Penguin), 2011.
Brandl-Risi, Bettina. Kulturen des Performativen website. 2010. Accessed December 1, 2010. http://www.sfbperformativ.de/seiten/b12_vorhaben_engl.html.
Brandstetter, Gabriele. "The Virtuoso's Stage." *Theatre Research International* 32, no. 2 (2007): 178–95.
Brandstetter, Gabriele, and Hans-Friedrich Bormann. "Dancers and Artistes: Virtuosic Body Techniques and Media Technologies from the Nineteenth Century until Today." Kulturen des Performativen website. Accessed December 1, 2010. http://www.sfbperformativ.de/seiten/b12_up2_engl.html.
Brooks, Daphne. *Bodies in Dissent: Spectacular Performances of Race and Freedom, 1850–1910*. Durham, NC: Duke University Press, 2006.
Burnett, Allison. *Fame*. Film. Directed by Kevin Tancharoen. Beverly Hills: Lakeshore Entertainment, 2009.
Burrows, Jonathan. "Interview with Dana Caspersen and William Forsythe." 1998. http://www.jonathanburrows.info/#/text/?id=61&t=content.
Burt, Ramsay. *Judson Dance Theater: Performative Traces*. London: Routledge, 2007.
Carpenter, Faedra Chatard. "Whiteness as 'Becoming': The Corporeal Crossovers of Daniel Tisdale and Michael Jackson." In *Coloring Whiteness: Acts of Critique in Black Performance*, 117–60. University of Michigan Press, 2014.
Chemers, Michael. *Staging Stigma: A Critical Examination of the American Freak Show*. London: Palgrave Macmillan, 2008.

Cheng, Anne Anlin. "Skin Deep: Josephine Baker and the Colonial Fetish." *Camera Obscura* 23, no. 3/69 (2008): 35–79.
Chude-Sokei, Louis. *The Last Darky: Bert Williams, Black-on-Black Minstrelsy and the African Diaspora*. Durham, NC: Duke University Press, 2005.
Clover, Carol. "Dancin' in the Rain." *Critical Inquiry* 21, no. 4 (Summer 1995): 722–47.
Defrantz, Thomas. *Dancing Revelations: Alvin Ailey's Embodiment of African American Culture*. New York: Oxford University Press, 2004.
Diepeveen, Leonard. *The Difficulties of Modernism*. London: Routledge, 2002.
Dunning, Jennifer. "Dance: Alvin Ailey at Met, Donald McKayle's 'Rainbow.'" *New York Times*, July 21, 1984.
Dunning, Jennifer. "DANCE REVIEW: The Many Aspects of Complexions." *New York Times*, August 1, 1995. Accessed December 1, 2010. https://www.nytimes.com/1995/08/01/arts/dance-review-the-many-aspects-of-complexions.html.
Dunning, Jennifer. "Reveling in the Artistry Found at the 'Low' End of Art." *New York Times*, January 7, 2002.
Fend, Mechthild. "Bodily and Pictorial Surfaces: Skin in French Art and Medicine, 1790–1860." *Art History* 28 (2005): 311–39.
Ferguson, Roderick A. *Aberrations in Black: Toward a Queer of Color Critique*. Minneapolis: University of Minnesota Press, 2004.
Fiedler, Leslie. *Freaks: Myths and Images of the Secret Self*. New York: Anchor, 1993.
Fleetwood, Nicole. "The Icon Is Dead: Mourning Michael Jackson." In *Troubling Vision: Performance, Visuality, and Blackness*, 207–18. Chicago: University of Chicago Press, 2010.
Foster, Susan Leigh. *Choreography and Narrative: Ballet's Staging of Story and Desire*. Bloomington: University of Indiana Press, 1996.
Franko, Mark. *The Work of Dance: Labor, Movement, and Identity in the 1930s*. Middletown, CT: Wesleyan.
Gilpin, Heidi. "Aberrations of Gravity." In *William Forsythe and the Practice of Choreography*, edited by Steven Spier. London: Routledge University Press, 2002.
Gilroy, Paul. *Black Atlantic: Modernity and Double Consciousness*. Cambridge, MA: Harvard University Press, 1993.
Gomes, Marcelo. "Quotes with Character from American Ballet Theatre." *Movement Magazine*, January 5, 2009. http://www.movmnt.com/abt-quotes-of- character_002767.html.
Gottschild, Brenda Dixon. *The Black Dancing Body: A Geography from Coon to Cool*. New York: Palgrave Macmillan, 2003.
Gottschild, Brenda Dixon. *Digging the Africanist Presence in American Performance: Dance and Other Contexts*. Westport, CT: Praeger Publishers, 1996.
Grosz, Elizabeth. *Volatile Bodies: Toward a Corporeal Feminism*. Bloomington: University of Indiana Press, 1994.
Hamera, Judith. *Unfinished Business: Michael Jackson, Detroit, and the Figural Economy of American Deindustrialization*. New York: Oxford University Press, 2017.
Hartman, Saidiya. *Scenes of Subjection: Terror, Slavery, and Self-Making in Nineteenth-Century America*. Oxford University Press, 1997.
Hodgdon, Barbara. *The Shakespeare Trade: Performances and Appropriations*. Philadelphia: University of Pennsylvania Press, 1998.
Hwang, David Henry, and Prince. "Solo." Track 8 on *Come*, NPG Records, 1994.

Jowitt, Deborah. "The Beauty and Limits of the Dance World's Ongoing Love of Virtuosity." *The Village Voice*, August 11, 2010.
Kisselgoff, Anna. "Ailey Premiere of Sexually Charged 'Episodes.'" *New York Times*, December 14, 1989. Accessed December 1, 2010. http://www.nytimes.com/1989/12/14/arts/review-dance-ailey-premiere-of-sexually-charged-episodes.html.
Kourlas, Gia. "Best (and Worst) Dance." *Time Out New York*, no. 744–45, December 31–January 13, 2009–2010.
Kourlas, Gia. "Supple Limbs in a Sea of Energy." *New York Times*, November 22, 2009. Accessed December 1, 2010. http://www.nytimes.com/2009/11/23/arts/dance/23complexions.html?_r=0&adxnnl=1&adxnnlx=1382498929-JjKubTIXxeuwlHrd0RvwmA.
Kulturen des Performativen. "The Virtuoso's Stage: Performance at the Limit." Kulturen des Performativen website. 2010. Accessed December 1, 2010. http://www.sfbperformativ.de/seiten/b12_vorhaben_engl.html.
La Rocco, Claudia. "Ballet and African Steps, Delivered at Warp Speed." *New York Times*, November 23, 2007. Accessed December 1, 2010. http://www.nytimes.com/2007/11/23/arts/dance/23comp.html.
Lehmann, Hans-Thies. *Postdramatic Theater*. Translated by Karen Jurs-Munby. New York: Routledge, 2006.
Lepecki, André. *Exhausting Dance: Performance and the Politics of Movement*. New York: Routledge, 2006.
Lhammon, W. T. *Raising Cain: Blackface Performance from Jim Crow to Hip Hop*. Cambridge, MA: Harvard University Press, 1998.
Loomba, Ania. *Shakespeare, Race, and Colonialism*. Oxford: Oxford University Press, 2002.
Lott, Eric. *Love and Theft: Blackface Minstrelsy and the American Working Class*. Oxford: Oxford University Press, 1995.
Lubovitch, Lar. "Lar Lubovitch's '*Othello*.'" San Francisco Ballet. DVD. Kultur, 2001.
Lubovitch, Lar, Kevin McKenzie, Wes Chapman. "American Ballet Theatre, a Shakespeare Festival." Videorecording. Works and process at the Guggenheim. January 29, 2007.
Mackey, Nathaniel. *Bedouin Hornbook*. Los Angeles: Sun & Moon Press, 1997.
Manning, Susan. *Modern Dance, Negro Dance: Race in Motion*. Minneapolis: University of Minnesota Press, 2006.
McKayle, Donald. *Transcending Boundaries: My Dancing Life*. New York: Routledge, 2002.
McMains, Juliet. *Glamour Addiction: Inside the American Ballroom Dance Industry*. Middletown, CT: Wesleyan University Press, 2006.
Mendoza, Manuel. "Complexions Contemporary Ballet, Which Opens TITAS' Annual Dance Series, Is Devoted to Multiculturalism." *Dallas Morning News*, October 29. 2009. Accessed December 1, 2010. http://www.dallas-news.com/entertainment/arts/headlines/20110510-complexions-ballet-closes-titas-season-with-spirituals-driven-testament.ece.
Mercer, Kobena. *Welcome to the Jungle: New Positions in Black Cultural Studies*. London: Routledge, 1994.
Moten, Fred. *In the Break: The Aesthetics of the Black Radical Tradition*. Minneapolis: University of Minnesota Press, 2003.
"Much to Admire, Much to Not at ABT's *Othello*." *Arts Place: Life, Theatre, Music, and Dance* (blog). July 15, 2007. http://artsplace.blogspot.com/2007/07/much-to-admire-much-to-not-at-abts.html.

Neal, Larry. *The Black Arts Movement*. ed. Drama Review, Vol. 12 No. 4: 29–39. New York: New York University. School of the Arts, 1968.
Neal, Mark Anthony. *Looking for Leroy: Illegible Black Masculinities*. New York: New York University Press, 2013.
Neill, Michael, ed. *William Shakespeare: Othello, the Moor of Venice*. Oxford: Oxford University Press, 2006.
Ngai, Sianne. *Ugly Feelings*. Cambridge, MA: Harvard University Press, 2007.
Nietzsche, Friedrich. *The Birth of Tragedy and the Case of Wagner*. Toronto: Random House, 1967.
Omi, Michael, and Howard Winant. *Racial Formation in the United States: From the 1960s to the 1980s*. Routledge, 1986.
Paxton, Steve. http://www.youtube.com/watch?v=XrUeYbUmhQA&feature=related.
Pinn, Anthony B. "Sweaty Bodies in a Circle: Thoughts on the Subtle Dimensions of Black Religion as Protest." *Black Theology: An International Journal* 4 (2006): 11–26.
Prashad, Vijay. *Everybody Was Kung-Fu Fighting: Afro-Asian Connections and the Myth of Cultural Purity*. Boston: Beacon Press, 2002.
Prince and Chris Rock. Interview. VH1. 1997. https://www.youtube.com/watch?v=nd97mAsvR0g.
Pugh, Megan. *America Dancing: From the Cakewalk to the Moonwalk*. New Haven, CT: Yale University Press, 2015.
Rainer, Yvonne. 1965. "No Manifesto." In *Feelings Are Facts: A Life*. 263–64. Cambridge, MA: MIT Press, 2006.
Reid-Pharr, Robert. *Black Gay Man: Essays*. New York: New York University Press, 2001.
Roach, Joseph. *It*. Ann Arbor: University of Michigan Press, 2007.
Rogin, Michael. *Blackface, White Noise: Jewish Immigrants and the Hollywood Melting Pot*. Berkeley: University of California Press, 1996.
Roth, Malachi, dir. "Interview with Mel Tomlinson." Unedited footage for *Limon: A Life without Words*. March 19, 1996.
Royce, Anya Peterson. *Anthropology of the Performing Arts: Artistry, Virtuosity, and Interpretation in a Cross-Cultural Perspective*. New York: Altamira Press, 2004.
Royster, Francesca. *Sounding Like a No-No: Queer Sounds and Eccentric Acts in the Post-Soul Era*. Ann Arbor: University of Michigan Press, 2013.
Schumpeter, Joseph. *Capitalism, Socialism, and Democracy*. London: Routledge, 2003.
Shattuck, Kathryn. "After the Breakup, Still Choreographic Partners." *New York Times*, May 3, 2005.
Siegmund, Gerald. "Ballet's Memory, or: William Forsythe's Disappearance Acts." http://www.trete.no/balletsmemory.html.
Sontag, Susan. "Dancer and the Dance." *London Review of Books*, February 5, 1987, 9–10. Accessed February 16, 2013. http://www.lrb.co.uk/v09/n03/susan-sontag/dancer-and-the-dance.
Spillers, Hortense J. "Mama's Baby, Papa's Maybe: An American Grammar Book." *Diacritics*, 17, no. 2 (Summer 1987): 64–81.
Steen, Shannon. *AfroAsian Encounters: Culture, History, Politics*. New York: New York University Press, 2006.
Sulcas, Roslyn. "A Program of Muscular Charm Guaranteed to Energize the Crowd." *New York Times*, November 19, 2008. Accessed December 1, 2010. http://www.nytimes.com/2008/11/20/arts/dance/20comp.html.

Taub, Eric. "David Hallberg: Principal, American Ballet Theatre." *Ballet Magazine*, March 2007. http://www.ballet.co.uk/magazines/yr_07/mar07/interview_david_hallberg.htm.

Thompson, Krista. Guest lecture in "Haunted Visuality." Columbia University seminar taught by Saidiya Hartman (cotaught with Tina Campt at Duke University), November 2009.

Thomson, Rosemarie Garland, ed. *Freakery: Cultural Spectacles of the Extraordinary Body*. New York: New York University Press, 1996.

Ulrich, Allan. "Lubovitch's 'Othello' a Tragedy in More Ways Than One." SFGate.com (*San Francisco Chronicle*), February 28, 2002. http://articles.sfgate.com/2002-02-28/entertainment/17531133_1_iago-othello-and-desdemona-antony-tudor.

Van Eikels, Kai. "The Poetics of the Difficult: Social Virtuosity in Today's Performance-oriented Society." Kulturen des Performativen website. Accessed December 1, 2010. http://www.sfbperformativ.de/seiten/b12_up3_engl.html.

Virno, Paolo. "Virtuosity and Revolution: The Political Theory of Exodus." In *Radical Thought in Italy: A Potential Politics*, edited by Michael Hardt and Paolo Virno, 13–37. Minneapolis: University of Minnesota. 1996.

Vogel, Joseph. "How Michael Jackson Made 'Bad.'" *The Atlantic*, September 10, 2012, 5.

Weber, Max. "Part II: Power." In *From Max Weber: Essays in Sociology*, edited by Karl Manheim, 159–265. New York: Routledge, 1948.

Williams, Linda. *Hard Core: Power, Pleasure, and the "Frenzy of the Visible."* Berkeley: University of California Press, 1989.

Williams, Linda. *Playing the Race Card: Melodramas of Black and White from Uncle Tom to O.J. Simpson*. Princeton, NJ: Princeton University Press, 2001.

Yuan, David. "The Celebrity Freak: Michael Jackson's 'Grotesque Glory.'" In *Freakery: Cultural Spectacles of the Extraordinary Body*, edited by Rosemarie Garland Thomson, 368–84. New York: New York University Press, 1996.

Index

For the benefit of digital users, indexed terms that span two pages (e.g., 52–53) may, on occasion, appear on only one of those pages.

Figures are indicated by *f* following the page number

AAADT. *See* Alvin Ailey American Dance Theater (AAADT)
ABT. *See* American Ballet Theatre (ABT)
Acogny, Germaine, 203
Adorno, Theodor, 17, 78, 85–87, 97, 160n.48
Africanist aesthetics
   AAADT and, 65–66
   appropriation of, 188
   authenticity and, 125
   Ballett Frankfurt and, 113–15, 119–20, 122, 134–35, 137–38
   blackness and, 134–35
   black radical performance's relation to, 5–6
   casting African American dancers and the use of, 119–20
   Complexions Contemporary Ballet and, 17, 92–93, 100
   coolness and, 113–15
   definition of, 5–6
   diasporic dance traditions and, 100–3, 120, 130, 134–35
   hip-hop and funk as channel for, 115
   improvisation and, 115
   motion and speed embraced in, 5–6, 100, 134–35
   ontopolitical critique rendered through, 5–6
   overview of, 5–6
   soul embraced in, 5–6
   virtuosity and, 5–9, 17
AfroAsian politics, 14–15, 55, 56–59, 65–66, 69, 76–77
AIDS crisis, 12–13, 26, 30–31, 36–37, 50–55, 59

Ailey, Alvin, 22, 55, 59, 65–66, 89–90, 188–89, 201–2
Alexander, Michelle, 12–13, 26, 27–28, 33–34, 37
ALIE/NA(C)TION (Ballett Frankfurt, 1992), 134
Allen, Debbie, 28–30
Allen, Sarita, 149
Als, Hilton, 94–95
Alvin Ailey American Dance Theater (AAADT)
   Africanist aesthetics and, 65–66
   AfroAsian politics at, 56–59, 65–66, 69, 76–77
   Ballett Frankfurt contrasted with, 109–13, 130–31, 137, 144
   blackness represented at, 65–66
   bling and, 74–75
   board of directors of, 29n.10
   commodity fetishism and, 66–67, 68, 74–75
   Complexions contrasted with, 79–81, 89–90, 93, 95, 104–5
   diversity ethos of, 56–59
   flesh and, 70–74
   freedom and, 63, 69, 74–76
   hair-whipping workshop at, 69–70
   homosexual imagery rarely used by, 89–90
   hypermasculinity and, 65–66
   inheritor of Ailey's legacy, Richardson as, 22
   labor and, 60–66, 68, 70
   liberalism of the skin and, 66–70
   multiculturalism and, 56–59, 67–68, 70
   "No Sweat" and, 74–77

Alvin Ailey American Dance Theater
(AAADT) (*cont.*)
overview of, 14–15, 56–59
photographic skin and, 14–15, 55, 59,
60, 63–67, 76–77
photographs and posters of, 56–59, 57*f*,
58*f*, 75–76
racial fetishism and, 60–66, 68, 70, 74–75
Richardson on, 75–76
shifting aesthetic of, Richardson as
embodiment of, 56–59
virtuosity and, 56–59, 62–66, 68, 70
American Ballet Theatre (ABT). See also
Othello (ABT/SFB, 1997)
contemporary ballet introduced within,
146–47, 163–64
as rarely hiring black dancers, 19–21,
118, 145
Richardson on, 166
Anti-Drug Abuse Act of 1986, 24–26
Arendt, Hannah, 61–62
Arpino, Gerald, 79–81
Athey, Ron, 137
authenticity, 115, 125, 147–48, 149

"Bad" (1987). See also Jackson, Michael
agency and, 191–98
choreographic falsetto and, 21, 192–95
disability and, 177–91
fandom and, 198–200
freakery and, 21, 177–200
heteronormative machismo in,
Richardson as evoking, 175–
77, 193–94
overview of, 21–22, 175–79
photographs of, 199*f*
Prince's refusal to be in, 193–94
reception of, 182–83
Richardson on, 176
sexuality and, 191–98
virtuosity and, 178–91
white use of black dance moves and, 188
"your butt is mine" line in, 193–94
Baker, Josephine, 67–68, 71–73, 110–11
Bakhtin, Mikhail, 90–92
Balanchine, George, 17–18, 115, 137–38
Baldwin, James, 110–11, 180, 191–
92, 201–2

Ballett Frankfurt. *See also* Forsythe,
William
AAADT contrasted with, 109–13, 130–
31, 137, 144
Africanist aesthetics and, 113–15, 119–
20, 122, 134–35, 137–38
as allowing abandoning of
heteronormative narrativity and, 18
alphabet method of, 18–19
authenticity and, 110–11, 115,
125, 134–35
blackness and, 18, 110–11, 131, 134–35
black radical tradition and, 17–
18, 113–17
by way of fun, 109–17
closure of, 110n.8
creative process at, 126–28, 132–33
deconstruction of dance and, 110–11,
115, 117–22, 129
differences between American and
European dance at, Richardson on, 8,
128, 131
difficulty of dance techniques
and, 136–44
exactitude in technique and, 117–22
experimentalism of, 7, 110–11
fun's relation to dance and, 111–13
illegibility and, 18–19, 129–30
improvisation and, 8, 17–19, 111–
17, 125–36
lack of hierarchy at, 120–21
overview of, 17–19, 109–17
performativity of gender and sexuality
and, 129
Richardson as shifting aesthetics and
expectations of, 118, 131–32, 140
socked foot dance and, 138–44
sonic break and, 122–25
staging of disappearance and, 109, 111–
17, 135, 140–44
structure of, 120–21
typecasting and, 110–11
vernacular dance and, 18–19, 128
virtuosity and, 78–79, 112–13, 125–
26, 138–39
ballet theaters and companies. *See* Alvin
Ailey American Dance Theater
(AAADT); American Ballet

INDEX   215

Theatre (ABT); Ballett Frankfurt;
  Complexions Contemporary Ballet;
  Dance Theater of Harlem (DTH)
Barnes, Clive, 167
Baryshnikov, Mikhail, 78–79, 103–4
Bel, Jerome, 101–3
Bernstein, Susan, 10–12, 17, 85–
  86, 99–100
Black Book (Mapplethorpe), 12–13, 24–26,
  43–44, 50–52
Black Dancing Body, The
  (Gottschild), 98–99
blackface
  authenticity and, 147–48
  blackness and, 19–21, 170, 172
  black-on-black minstrelsy, 172
  brownface and, 170, 171
  corporeal blackface, 146–47, 167–74
  Fame and, 28–30
  freakery and, 181–82
  as masculinist discourse of the
    body, 171
  melodrama and, 146–47
  metaphorical minstrelsy and, 19–
    21, 168–69
  Othello and, 146–48, 153–54, 157–
    58, 167–74
  phallus and, 172
  as reification of whiteness, 170
  Richardson not donning, 19–21, 172
  slavery as specter haunting, 174
blackness
  AAADT and, 65–66
  Africanist aesthetics and, 134–35
  alternative conceptions of, 110–11
  anti-blackness, 43
  appropriation of, 186
  authenticity and, 19–21, 110–11,
    115, 171
  Ballett Frankfurt and, 18, 110–11,
    131, 134–35
  blackface and, 19–21, 170, 172
  black queer masculinities, 13–14, 15,
    16–17, 18, 24–26, 30–31, 34, 36–37,
    44–47, 89–90, 95, 202
  body's relation to, 5, 26–27, 35–36, 39–
    40, 43, 66–67, 73–75, 101–2, 117–18,
    130, 171, 174

classicism and, 43–47, 163–64
Complexions Contemporary Ballet and,
  15, 16–17, 93–95
as defined by improvisation, 116–17
definition of, 8, 17–18, 109, 116–17,
  131, 132, 134–35, 144
Fame and, 28–33, 36–37, 38–39
fetishization of, 39–40
freakery and, 193–94
hypersexuality and, 36–37, 39–40, 44–
  47, 168, 179–80
hypervisibility and, 18, 74–76, 101–
  2, 130
illegibility and, 17–19, 31–33, 144
improvisation and, 116–17, 134–35, 144
motion and speed's relation to, 5, 7, 15–
  16, 17, 82–83, 101–5, 132, 181–82
no "normal" blackness or masculinity,
  17, 105–7
obscenity and, 43–44, 48–50, 51–52
Othello and, 19–21, 163–64, 174
popular music and, 94–95
resistance and, 133
Richardson as exercising praxis of, 131
rich nonfullness of, 8, 113–15, 140
subjectivity and, 17–19, 71, 133, 144
black queer masculinities, 13–14, 15,
  16–17, 18, 24–26, 30–31, 34, 36–37,
  44–47, 89–90, 95, 202
black radical tradition, 17–18, 113–17, 132
black street dance, 4–5, 8, 16, 32–33,
  124, 128–29
bling, 74–75, 101–2
Bonnefous, Jean-Pierre, 153–54
Brand, Dionne, 1, 5–6
Brandl-Risi, Bettina, 10, 15–16, 82–83
Brandstetter, Gabriele, 10, 15–16, 97–
  98, 166
Brooks, Daphne, 17
Brooks, Peter, 146, 156
Buchanan, Patrick, 12–13, 26
Butler, John, 153–54
Butler, Judith, 34

Carpenter, Faedra Chatard, 193–94
Carranza, Richard A., 32–33n.14
Carter, Jimmy, 24–26
Casperson, Dana, 18–19n.27, 132n.76, 134

casting race, 147–51
Chemers, Michael, 198–99
Cheng, Anne Anlin, 14–15, 67–68, 71–73, 90–91n.34
choreographic falsetto, 15–21, 79–81, 88, 104–7, 192–95. *See also* Complexions Contemporary Ballet
choreography's photographic skin, 14–15, 55, 59, 60, 63–67, 76–77
Chude-Sokei, Louis, 19–21, 172–74, 181–82
classicism, 39–52, 117–18, 163–64
Clover, Carol, 186–87
Colter, Jimmy "Cricket," 4
commodity fetishism, 39–40, 66–67, 68, 74–75
Complexions Contemporary Ballet. *See also* Rhoden, Dwight
  AAADT contrasted with, 79–81, 89–90, 93, 95, 104–5
  Africanist aesthetics and, 17, 92–93, 100
  AIDs crisis and, 89–90
  anticapitalist critique and, 17
  author experiences at, 88–89
  blackness and, 15, 16–17, 93–95
  choreographic falsetto and, 15–17, 88, 104–7
  classical technique queered in, 16–17
  conflict between religion and sexuality in, 87–88
  deforming subject and object at, Richardson as, 131–34
  deliberately distorted *penchés* and, 95
  diasporic dance traditions and, 100–3
  excess and, 11
  exhaustion and, 104–5
  founding of, 15, 17–18, 79–81
  hyperkineticism and, 104–5
  hyperperceptions and, 101–2
  improvisation and, 8, 79–81
  influence on dance of, 88–89, 93
  meta-critique of dance and, 104–5
  misfits become prototypes at, 88–89
  motion and speed used by, 82–83, 99–107
  multiplicity of dance styles embraced by, 92
  overview of, 15–19, 78–81
  photographs of, 106f, 107f, 108f
  post-soul and, 93–94, 97
  queer of color analysis of, 90–92, 105–7
  reception of, 82–83, 104–5
  Richardson's role at, 79–81, 82
  sexual and racial difference emphasized by, 89–92
  slower ontology of choreography and, 101–2
  stillness and, 17, 99–107
  strength and vulnerability and, Richardson as embodying, 89–90
  vernacular dance and, 8, 17, 89–92, 93
  versioning and, 92–93
  virtuosity and, 15–19, 78–88, 95–97, 99, 101–7
"Control" (1986), 196–98
Copeland, Misty, 1–3, 78–79
Cross, Derrick, 13–14, 24–26, 30–31, 43–48
culture wars, 12–13, 26, 30–31, 36–37, 43–44, 51–52

d'Amboise, Jacques, 153–54
Dance Theater of Harlem (DTH), 28–30, 41–43, 88–89, 109–10
dance theaters and companies. *See* Alvin Ailey American Dance Theater (AAADT); American Ballet Theatre (ABT); Ballett Frankfurt; Complexions Contemporary Ballet; Dance Theater of Harlem (DTH)
Dancing Revelations (Gottschild), 92
"Dancin' in the Rain" (Clover), 186–87
deconstruction of dance, 110–11, 115, 117–22, 129
DeFrantz, Thomas, 15–16, 62–63, 65–66, 75–76, 92, 93
Derrick Cross (1983), 44–48, 49f
diasporic dance traditions, 100–3, 120, 130
Diepeveen, Leonard, 113n.15, 136–37
disability, 177–91
Doyle, Jennifer, 137
DTH (Dance Theater of Harlem), 28–30, 41–43, 88–89, 109–10
DuBois, W. E. B., 8, 9
Dunham, Katherine, 22, 63, 119–20, 201–2

Eidos: Telos (1994), 138–40, 141f, 142f, 143f
Episodes (1989), 89–90, 93
exactitude in technique, 117–22

INDEX 217

excess, 3–4, 11, 16, 39–40, 81, 84–85, 184
Exhausting Dance (Lepecki), 104–5

Falco, Louis, 30–31
Fame (1980)
   affirmative action and, 39–40
   AIDs crisis and, 30–31, 50–55
   blackface and, 28–30
   blackness and, 28–33, 36–37, 38–39
   black queer masculinities and, 13–14, 24–26, 30–31, 36–37
   charisma and, 39–40
   classicism's ticket and, 39–50
   colonial myth of "discovering" talent, 28–30
   commodity and, 39–40
   criminality and, 33–34
   culture wars and, 26, 30–31, 36–37, 43–44, 51–52
   dance training and, 37
   excess and, 39–40
   fetishization and, 39–40
   "gay" to "queer" and, 50–55
   geography of fame and, 39–50
   "get tough" work ethic and, 37–39
   hypersexuality and, 44–47
   illegibility and, 34, 35–37
   interpellating Leroy and, 32–39
   Jewish players in the arts and, 28–30
   Leroy Johnson compared to Richardson and, 13–14, 24–28, 32–41
   New Jim Crow and, 24–26, 27–32, 33–34, 38–39
   overview of, 12–14
   performativity and, 34
   racial dimensions of dance scene and, 41–43
   Reaganism and, 27–32
   reception of, 24–26
   recognition as a form of policing and, 26–27
   "Red Light" scene from, 45*f*
   release of, 26–27
   revival of, 13–14
   Richardson as passing for straight in, 30–31, 44–47, 51–52
   shame and, 37
   short shorts rather than tights used in dance scene of, 44–47
   social and political context of, 30–31
   talent and, 32–40
   uptown and downtown forms of dance and, 41–43
   violence and, 32–39
   virtuosity and, 31–32, 39–44
Ferguson, Roderick, 15–17, 90–92, 105–7
fetishism, racial, 60–66, 68, 70, 74–75
Figgis, Mike, 111–12
First World Festival of Negro Arts (film), 201–2
flesh, 70–74
Forsythe, William. *See also* Ballett Frankfurt
   Africanist aesthetics and, 109–10, 115, 119–20, 125
   authenticity and, 125
   blackness and, unique relationship to, 18
   body as used by, 140–44
   break and, 134–35
   on creative process, 132–33
   deconstruction of dance by, 109–10, 120–21
   difficulty and, 137–38
   on *Eidos*, 140
   ensemble and, 124
   fun's relation to dance and, 111–13
   genealogies of improvisation and, 125–26
   hip-hop use by, 123–25
   hypervisibility and, 112n.11
   improvisation and, 109, 111–13, 115, 125–36
   influences on, 122–24
   internalizing of space and, 130
   Jewish-Black relations and, 123–24
   leaving the movement and, 136
   on performance of gender and sexuality, 129, 132–33
   resistance of the object and, 133
   on Richardson, 118–19
   Richardson on, 122, 126–28, 129
   staging of disappearance by, 109, 111–13, 140–44
   on survival of ballet, 129
   vernacular dance and, 122
   virtuosity and, 125–26
Fosse (1999), 1–3, 188–89

Fosse, Bob, 21–22, 186, 189–91
Foster, Susan Leigh, 125–26
Foucault, Michel, 37
Frank, Penny, 13–14, 28–30, 123, 152–53
Franko, Mark, 61, 63–65, 137–38, 182–83
freakery
  ability and, 183–84
  agency and, 191–98
  "Bad" and, 21, 177–200
  blackface and, 181–82
  blackness and, 193–94
  categories of, 179
  control freak, 197–98
  disability and, 177–91
  excess and, 184
  fandom and, 198–200
  freak out, 198–200
  freakshows, 180–82, 197–98
  genealogy of, 180–82
  intentional deployment of, 184
  Jackson and, 21, 177–78, 180–86, 193–96
  minstrelsy and, 179
  modernity and, 182–83
  plasticity and stasis and, 184–86
  Richardson as embodying, 182–86, 194–95, 198–200
  sexuality and, 191–98
  super freak, 191–98
  usage of term "freak," 180–82
  virtuosity and, 19–22, 178–91
Freakery (Thomson), 180–81, 183–84
Freaks (film), 182
"Freaks and the American Ideal of Manhood" (Baldwin), 192
from "gay" to "queer," 50–55

Galloway, Stephen. *See also* Ballett Frankfurt
  approach of, 117–18
  Belle Frankfurt experience of, 118
  dance interests and training of, 118
  on Forsythe, 118–19, 123–25, 133–34
  improvisation and, 128
  on Richardson, 140
  tokenism feared by, 118
  upbringing of, 118
"gay" to "queer," 50–55

gender identity. *See* black queer masculinities; heteronormativity
Gilpin, Heidi, 121, 133, 135–36n.84, 138–39
Gilroy, Paul, 8–9
Goldman, Danielle, 128
Gomes, Marcelo, 167–68
Gore, Christopher, 30–31
Gore, Michael, 28–30
Gottschild, Brenda Dixon, 5–6, 15–16, 17, 100, 113–15, 119–20, 134–35
Graham, Martha, 137–38
Greaves, William, 201–2
Green, Al, 90–92
Griner, Brittney, 204–5
Grosz, Elizabeth, 14–15, 71, 73
Guillem, Sylvie, 78–79
Gunn, Moses, 167

Hamera, Judith, 182–83
Harper, Francesca, 109–10
Hefner, Hugh, 192
Helms, Jesse, 26
Hemphill, Essex, 50–51
heteronormativity, 5, 15, 18, 30–31, 34, 35–36, 55, 56–59, 79–81, 96–97, 175, 203
high art, 3–4, 15–16, 41–43, 51–52, 79–81
Hinkson, Mary, 65–66
homoerotics of Iago, 147–48, 158–63
hooks, bell, 50–51
Hwang, David Henry, 96–97
hyperkineticism, 5, 7, 15–16, 17, 82–83, 101–5
hypersexuality, 36–37, 39–40, 44–47, 168, 179–80
hypervisibility, 18, 74–76, 101–2, 130

illegibility
  Ballett Frankfurt and, 18–19, 129–30
  blackness and, 17–19, 31–33, 144
  diasporic dance and, 130
  Fame and, 34, 35–37
improvisation
  Africanist aesthetics and, 115
  Ballett Frankfurt and, 8, 17–19, 111–17, 125–36
  blackness and, 116–17, 134–35, 144

INDEX 219

Complexions Contemporary Ballet and, 8, 79–81
ontological improvisation, 116–17
overview of, 7–8
Richardson embodying black radical improvisatory performance, 116–17
virtuosity and, 79–81
as vital technology of the self, 128
Invisible Film (Forsythe), 129

Jackson, Janet, 177, 196–98
Jackson, Michael. *See also* "Bad" (1987)
admiration for Gene Kelly of, 187
on "Bad," 175–76
as crossover artist, 193–94
death of, 199–200
Elephant Man's remains bought by, 183–84
feminized image of, 177–78
freakery and, 21, 177–78, 180–86, 193–96
heteronormative machismo emphasized by, 175–78
Jehovah's Witnesses, severing ties with, 176, 193–94
odd couples of, 188
plastic surgeries and physical condition of, 183–86
post-soul falsetto of, 192
Richardson on, 176–77, 183–84
sexuality of, 194–96
success coupled with androgyny of, 192
virtuosity and, 21, 181–82
Jacobellis v. Ohio (1964), 9–10
James, Rick, 179, 193–94
Jamison, Judith, 65–66, 188–89
Jarvinen, Hanna, 168–69
Jerome Bel (1995), 101–2
Joffrey, Robert, 79–81
Johnson, Lyndon, 24–26, 39–40
Jones, Bill T., 79–81
Judson Dance Theater, 41–43, 100–1, 102–3
Just Dancing Around (film), 111–12, 124, 140

Kaiser, Michael, 154–55
Kelly, Gene, 186–87
Kisselgoff, Anna, 89–90
Knight, JaQuel, 188

Kochetkova, Maria, 3n.5
Kulturen des Performativen working group, 10, 17, 83–84

Laban, Rudolph, 126–28
labor, 60–66, 68, 70
LaGuardia High School, 1–4, 24–26, 32–33, 35–36, 37, 41–43, 44–47, 50–51, 63
"Lament" (2010), 201–2
La Mobilisation infinie (Sloterdijk), 100–1
La Rocco, Claudia, 82–83
Lepecki, André, 5–6, 15–16, 17, 100–2, 104–5
Limón, José, 153–54
Liszt, Franz, 16, 79–81
Livingston, Jennie, 50–51
Looking for Langston (film), 50–51
Looking for Leroy (Neal), 13–14, 34–35
Lott, Eric, 28–30, 170–72
Lowe, Walter, Jr., 192
Lubovitch, Lar. (ABT/SFB, 1997, See also *Othello*)
authenticity and, 149
blackface and, 167–74
black in white company, white in black company and, 151–53
as borrowing a system of (co)production, 157
casting choices of, 149–50
on choice to pursue choreography, 151
choreographic vision of, 145–48, 149–58
essayistic approach of, 161
family background of, 152–53
formal training of, 151–52
homoerotics of Iago and, 158–63
image as motivation in production of, 156
Jewish background of, 152–53
leitmotifs of choreography used by, 158–63
motion and, 159
on Richardson, 148n.11, 149–50
Richardson on working with, 156
shorter ballets of, 154–55
storyboarding practice of, 19–21, 157

Mackey, Nathaniel, 78, 90–92, 104–5

Madonna, 51n.42, 78–79
Manning, Susan, 19–21, 137–38, 168–69
Mapplethorpe, Robert
   blackness and, 43–44, 48–50, 51–52
   black queer masculinities and, 24–26, 44–47
   classicism and, 43–52
   criticism of, 48–51
   culture wars and, 26, 43–44, 50–51
   death of, 48–50
   obscenity claims against, 12–14, 26, 43–52
   Reaganism and, 43
   reception of, 43, 48–51
   Richardson compared to, 43–47
   trial of, 48–50
   virtuosity and, 43–44
   white identity of, 50–51
Marx, Karl, 39–40, 63, 66–67
masculinities, black queer, 13–14, 15, 16–17, 18, 24–26, 30–31, 34, 36–37, 44–47, 89–90, 95, 202
masculinity, heteronormative, 5, 15, 17, 18, 30–31, 34, 35–36, 55, 56–59, 79–81, 96–97, 105–7, 175
Matz, Robert, 161
McKayle, Donald, 56–59, 60, 69, 75–76, 152–53
McKenzie, Kevin, 148
McMains, Juliet, 168–70
Meier, Tracey-Kair, 138–39n.93
melodrama
   blackface and, 146–47
   definition of, 19–21, 146–47
   Moor's balletic past and, 153–58
   Othello and, 19–21, 146, 153–58, 159–60, 163–67
   racial melodrama, 19–21, 145–47, 163–67, 174
   virtuosity and, 146
Mercer, Kobena, 48, 89–90
Merleau-Ponty, Maurice, 71, 73
minstrelsy. *See* blackface
Mitchell, Arthur, 28–30
Moonlight (Rhoden), 106f
Moten, Fred
   blackness as defined by, 17–18, 109, 116–17, 131, 132, 134–35, 144
   black radical tradition and, 115
   break and, 8, 113–15
   ensemble and, 124
   hypervisibility and, 130
   improvisation and, 17–18, 116–17, 144
   praxis of blackness of, 131
   resistance of the object and, 133
   rich nonfullness of blackness and, 8, 113–15
motion and speed
   Africanist aesthetics and, 5–6, 100, 134–35
   blackness's relation to, 5, 7, 15–16, 17, 82–83, 101–5, 132, 181–82
   capitalism and, 5–6, 100–1
   Complexions Contemporary Ballet and, 82–83, 99–107
   hyperkineticism, 5, 7, 15–16, 17, 82–83, 101–5
   virtuosity and, 11–12, 99–101
multiculturalism, 56–59, 67–68, 70
Muñoz, José, 170

National Endowment for the Arts (NEA), 12–13, 24–26
National Endowment for the Humanities (NEH), 24–26
Neal, Mark Anthony, 26–27, 34, 36–37
Négritude movement, 201–2
Neumeier, John, 153–54
New Jim Crow, 5, 12–13, 24–34, 38–39
Ngai, Sianne, 6–7
Nijinsky, Vaslav, 153–54
"No Manifesto" (Rainer), 100–1

Obama, Barack, 27–28
obscenity, 12–14, 26, 43–52
Ohio, Jacobellis v. (1964), 9–10
Othello (ABT/SFB, 1997)
   authenticity and, 147–48, 149
   ballroom dance and, 169–70
   blackface and, 146–48, 153–54, 157–58, 167–74
   black in white company, white in black company and, 151–53
   blackness and, 19–21, 163–64, 174
   casting race and, 147–51
   choreographing leitmotif and, 146–47, 158–63
   displacements and, 147–51

INDEX 221

Europeanist productions of, 147–48
exclusionary hiring practices in dance and, 148–49
facing the surrogate and, 167–74
handkerchief symbolism in, 162–63
history of productions of, 153–58
homoerotics of Iago in, 147–48, 158–63
hypersexuality and, 168
image as motivation in, 156
melodrama and, 19–21, 146, 153–58, 159–60, 163–67
metaphorical minstrelsy and, 19–21, 169
Moor's balletic past and, 153–58
overview of, 19–21, 145–47
parallels between life of Richardson and, 163–67
photographs of, 173*f*
racially biased criticism of Richardson in, 164–67
racial melodrama and, 163–67, 174
recognition of virtue structure of, 157–58
Richardson's reaction to casting in, 148–49, 150–51
storyboarding and, 157
structuring framework of, 157–58
virtuosity and, 19–21, 146, 157–58, 172

Paris Is Burning (film), 50–51
Pärt, Arvo, 153–54
Paxton, Steve, 116–17
Petrushka (1911), 153–54
photographic skin, 14–15, 55, 59, 60, 63–67, 76–77
Pierre, Cyril, 168
popular art, 3–4, 16, 79–81
post-soul, 16, 21, 79–81, 84–85, 93–95, 97, 98–99, 192
Prashad, Vijay, 14–15, 67
Presidential Scholar in the Arts award of Richardson, 12–13, 24–26, 28–30, 35–36, 39–40, 43
Presley, Elvis, 188
Presley, Lisa Marie, 188
Primus, Pearl, 152–53
Prince
  "Bad," refusal to appear in, 193–94
  Complexions use of, 95
  falsetto music of, 95
  freakery and, 194–96
  heteronormativity and, 30–31
  post-soul music of, 16, 79–81, 94–95
  sexuality and, 194–95
  virtuosity and, 95
Princesse Tam Tam (film), 71–73
Pussy Riot, 204–5

queer masculinities, 13–14, 15, 16–17, 18, 24–26, 30–31, 34, 36–37, 44–47, 89–90, 95, 202
Queer Nation, 53–55
queerness, 34, 35–36, 43–47, 50–55, 78–79, 90–92, 195–96
queer of color analysis, 15–17, 90–92, 96–97, 105–7
"Queers Read This," 52–55
Quintet (Forsythe), 138–39

race and racism. *See* blackface; blackness; New Jim Crow
racial fetishism, 60–66, 68, 70, 74–75
Rainbow 'Round My Shoulder (McKayle, 1959)
  Africanist aesthetics of, 60–62
  artistic context of, 61–62
  chain gang song in, 60
  choreography of, 60
  dance photography and, 60
  formalism and modernist expressionism in, 61–62
  freedom and, 63, 69, 75–76
  labor as driving, 60–63, 69
  photographic skin and, 60
  photographs of, 57*f*, 58*f*
  reception of, 69, 75–76
  staging and circulation context for, 75–76
  virtuosity and, 63–66
Rainer, Yvonne, 100–1
Rathes, Roland, 98n.52
Ray, Gene Anthony, 30–31, 36–37
Reagan, Ronald
  AIDS crisis and, 30–31
  attempt to abolish NEA by, 12–13, 26
  black queer masculinity and, 30–31
  culture wars and, 26, 30–31, 36–37, 43–44, 51–52

Reagan, Ronald (*cont.*)
 defunding of social programs
  by, 12–13, 26
 disenfranchising of black and LGBTQ+
  Americans by, 30–31
 Fame and, 27–32
 mispronouncing Richardson's middle
  name by, 41
 New Jim Crow and, 26, 27–32
 war on drugs and, 24–26
Reid-Pharr, Robert, 47–48, 105–7
Revelations (AAADT), 87–88
Rhoden, Dwight. *See also* Complexions
  Contemporary Ballet
 AAADT work of, 79–81
 aesthetic of, 15, 82, 89–93, 95
 Complexions cofounded by, 1–3, 79–81
 as dancer's choreographer, 102–3
 deliberately distorted *penchés* of, 95
 hyper-visibility of black body and, 101–2
 performance of reflexivity and, 103–4
 on queerness of Complexions'
  choreography, 90–92
 Richardson's influence on, 15, 79–81
Richardson, Desmond
 on AAADT, 75–76
 on ABT, 166
 as Ailey's legacy inheritor, 22
 on "Bad," 176
 blackness, as exercising praxis of, 131
 black radical improvisatory
  performance, as embodying, 116–17
 bodily racial epistemology of, 6–8
 break and, 7–8
 on career trajectory, 189–90
 cultural ideals of masculine
  musculature and virility, as
  embodying, 51–52
 on dance as effort and calling, 70
 as deforming subject and object
  relation, 131–34
 on differences between American and
  European dance, 8, 128, 131
 experimentalism of, 7
 externalization of technique by, 16–17
 first experiences with dance of, 24–26
 flexibility of, 90–91n.34
 on Forsythe, 122, 126–28, 129
 freakery, as embodying, 182–86, 194–
  95, 198–200
 as gay icon, 204–5
 hypervisibility associated with, 18
 on Jackson, 176–77, 183–84
 LaGuardia High School years of, 1–4,
  12–14, 24–26, 28–30, 35–36, 41,
  123, 152–53
 Leroy Johnson compared to, 13–14,
  24–28, 32–41
 on Lubovitch, 156
 as obscuring divide between classical
  and contemporary, 202
 on *Othello* casting, 148–49, 150–51
 Othello's life compared to, 163–67
 overview of, 1–5, 201–5
 as passing for straight, 30–31, 44–47,
  51–52, 175–77, 193–94
 personal style of, 1–5, 7–8, 16–
  17, 78–79
 photographs of, xx*f*, 46*f*, 57*f*, 106*f*, 107*f*,
  173*f*, 199*f*, 203*f*, 204*f*, 205*f*
 Presidential Scholar in the Arts award
  of, 12–13, 24–26, 28–30, 35–36,
  39–40, 43
 quotes on, 118–19, 140,
  148n.11, 149–50
 reception of, 10–11, 43, 78–79, 163–64
 relation to personhood and subjectivity
  of, 144
 Russian reception of, 203–5
 shifting aesthetic, as embodying of
  AAADT's, 56–59
 as shifting aesthetics and expectations,
  118, 131–32, 140
 strength and vulnerability, as
  embodying, 89–90
 support for LGBTQ+ rights and gay
  pride of, 53–55
 Tony Award nomination of, 188–89
 tours of, 201–5
 versatility's role in career of, 4
 virility associated with, 78–79
 virtuosity of, 1–5, 10–12, 16–17, 32–33,
  39–44, 76–77, 78–81, 87–88, 102–3,
  134, 138–39, 147–48, 156
 work ethic of, 39–40
Rize (film), 75n.46

INDEX 223

Roach, Joseph, 21, 87–88, 103–4
Roxas, Elizabeth, 56–59, 65–66, 69
Royce, Anya Peterson, 17, 84–85
Royster, Francesca, 88, 93, 98n.52, 105–7
Rozenblatt, David, 153–54
Ruggieri, Robert, 89–90
Ruprecht, Lucia, 10

Schumpeter, Joseph, 100n.61
Scorsese, Martin, 192–93
Senghor, Léopold Sédar, 201–2
Serrano, Andres, 12–13
sexuality. *See* black queer masculinities; heteronormativity
sexuality, hyper, 36–37, 39–40, 44–47, 168, 179–80
Shaw, George Bernard, 145
Shook, Karel, 28–30
Show Must Go On, The (2001), 101–2
Shvarts, Aliza, 137
Siegmund, Gerald, 129, 130
Singin' in the Rain (film), 186–88
socked foot dance, 138–44
Solo (Rhoden, 1998), 95–97, 99, 102–3
Sontag, Susan, 78, 102–4
soul, post-, 16, 21, 79–81, 84–85, 93–95, 97, 98–99, 192
Sounding Like a No-No (Royster), 93–94
speed. *See* motion and speed
Spillers, Hortense, 14–15, 73–74
staging of disappearance, 109, 111–17, 135, 140–44
Stein, Gertrude, 137–38
Stewart, Potter, 9–10
Stravinsky, Igor, 153–54
street dance, 4–5, 8, 16, 32–33, 124, 128–29
subjectivity, 17–19, 71, 133, 144
Sulcas, Roslyn, 104–5, 140
"Super Freak" (1981), 179, 193–94

talent, 32–40
Thompson, Krista, 14–15, 74–75, 101–2
Thriller, 193–94
Tongues Untied (film), 50–51
Tony Award nomination of Richardson, 188–89

tours of Richardson, 201–5
Tsypin, George, 155

Ulrich, Allan, 163–64
US Presidential Scholar in the Arts award of Richardson, 12–13, 24–26, 28–30, 35–36, 39–40, 43

Vass, Freya, 122n.40
vernacular dance
 Ballett Frankfurt and, 18–19, 128
 Complexions Contemporary Ballet and, 8, 17, 89–92, 93
 virtuosity and, 5, 8–9, 79–81
Vertiginous Thrill of Exactitude, The (Forsythe, 1996)
 Africanist aesthetics and, 119–20, 134–35
 black body in ballet and, 117–18
 classicism deconstructed in, 117–18
 internalizing space and, 130
 pas de deux in, 117–18
 radical significance of, 118–20
 reception of, 117–18
 sensation of fun in, 117–18
 technical difficulty of, 117–19
virility, 5, 36–37, 39–40, 44–47, 51–52, 78–79, 161, 168, 194–95
Virno, Paolo, 98n.53
virtuosity
 AAADT and, 56–59, 62–66, 68, 70
 across the Atlantic, 22–23
 Africanist aesthetics and, 5–9, 17
 anticapitalist critique and, 17
 "Bad" and, 178–91
 Ballett Frankfurt and, 78–79, 112–13, 125–26, 138–39
 black radical performance and, 5–9
 bodily racial epistemology and, 6–7
 border between popular and high art and, 3–4, 16, 79–81
 break and, 7–8
 charisma distinguished from, 39–40, 86–87
 choreographic falsetto and difficult fun and, 15–19
 Complexions Contemporary Ballet and, 15–19, 78–88, 95–97, 99, 101–7

virtuosity (cont.)
    contextual understanding of virtuosity
        and, 10–11
    definition of virtuosity and, 3–4, 9–12,
        83–88, 126n.52
    derogatory connotations of, 85–86,
        98–99
    Eurocentrism in dance and, 3–4
    excess and, 3–4, 16, 81, 84–85, 184
    Fame and, 31–32, 39–44
    freakery and, 19–22, 178–91
    futures of, 201–5
    improvisation and, 79–81
    as a kind of violence, 31–32
    melodrama and, 146
    modern virtuosity contrasted with
        earlier forms of, 86–87
    motion and speed and, 11–12, 99–101
    musical function of, 86–87
    need for investigation of, 3–4
    ontology and, 5–6, 102–4
    Othello and, 19–21, 146, 157–58, 172
    otherness and, 84
    overview of, 1–5, 10–11, 16
    paradox of audience reception and, 3–4
    performance selection and, 4
    religious virtuoso, 21, 86–88, 103–4,
        198–99
    Richardson's virtuosity, 1–5, 10–12,
        16–17, 32–33, 39–44, 76–77, 78–81,
        87–88, 102–3, 134, 138–39,
        147–48, 156
    skepticism toward a form of excellence
        and, 16, 82–83
    skill distinguished from, 39–40
    soloist dancers and, 102–3
    spectatorial virtuosity, 82–83, 101–2
    talent distinguished from, 39–40
    technical virtuosity, 78, 97
    turn toward, 56–59, 78–79
    vernacular dance and, 5, 8–9, 79–81
Vishneva, Diana, 202
Vogel, Joseph, 182–83

Waters, Terk, 108*f*
Weber, Max, 5–6, 17, 85–88, 90–91n.34,
    103–4
Whiturs, Dereque, 89–90
Wiley, Kehinde, 74–75
Willems, Thom, 109–10, 111–12
Williams, Burt, 172
Williams, Linda, 9–10, 19–21, 146,
    156–57, 165
Willi Ninja, 51n.42
Winfrey, Oprah, 27–28
World Festival of Black Arts, 22–23, 201–2

Yuan, David, 175, 184–85

Zane, Arnie, 79–81